HAUNTE

LEAF ACADEMY

By M. L. Bullock

Contents

The October People

Book One

A *Gulf Coast Paranormal Extra*

By M.L. Bullock

Dedication

For Juno.

Prologue—Hugh McCandlish
Leaf Academy, Orange Grove, Alabama, 1937

"Good job, Ollie. Why don't you leave the drawing on my desk? What an artist you have become, young man."

As he placed the picture on my desk, my heart fell to see the subject of his most recent drawing. Did he blame himself for the incident on the playground? He should not blame himself for the bird's death. He never touched the creature. Perhaps this was some sort of tribute to it? Or more probably I was reading too much into the drawing. Perhaps this austere-looking bird was a raven? We recently discussed the poetic works of Edgar Allan Poe, and the American crow and the common raven were very similar. Ravens were notably larger and traveled in pairs; crows were almost always in large groups. It was hard to tell from this image. It was only a single bird, its head perched at an awkward angle, yet the imagery evoked such intense, brooding emotion.

I smiled as I set the paper aside and asked, "I suppose you will be happy to see your father again, Ollie. Are both your parents coming to pick you up tomorrow? I hope to meet them. Are you looking forward to a visit home?"

The boy's long bangs fell over his dark, distrusting eyes. He shook his head, returned his pencils to his desk and left the classroom. He paused at the door as if he wanted to tell me something, but he did not. He did not talk much at all. His mouth was set in a perpetual frown these days, such a far cry from the high-spirited child who had arrived here last month. But the truth was that transitioning to life at boarding school was not easy for some children, even those from good families. It was always easier if you had a friend—I knew that from experience—but this child had none. I could not understand that.

Ollie LeFlore had a constantly solemn appearance, a characteristic that the other boys disliked. They made no secret of it, but they didn't bully him or abuse him, not in front of me. They simply ignored him. I encouraged Ollie to interact with the others, but he never made the effort. And the recent Dead Crow Incident would not help matters. I suppose it wasn't strange after all that he should want to draw the creature in such perfect detail.

The bird had been cawing and crowing as it perched on the metal fence that surrounded the athletic yard. A few of the boys had taken to throwing rocks at it but were cuffed about the ears by the headmaster for their trouble. When we turned our attention back to the animal, it was lying dead at Ollie's feet. The other boys were backing away as if he might kill them too. Nobody saw anything, and as I explained to the headmaster, if Ollie had killed the bird, the boy would have been covered with scratches, claw marks...but there was nothing to see, and I had examined the boy myself. It was as if the bird died of natural causes, falling out of the sky right at the child's feet.

But the odds of that happening were astronomical.

The night of the strange event, I began to work out the numbers. Coming up with the proper formula proved a challenge, and the results were indeed astronomical. One would have a better chance of being struck by lightning—twice—than having a bird fall out of the sky and land at one's feet. But what other explanation could there be? Yes, the bird must have been sickly. It had been Ollie's misfortune that it died that day, at that moment.

Yes, such a rare occurrence.

Mrs. Smith, the school's cook, had her own ideas about the dead crow. And she had no problem sharing those ideas with anyone who would listen...except for the headmaster, of course. "This place, this school is cursed, Mr. McCandlish. It was cursed long before they built this fine building here. The very grounds we walk on are cursed."

I laughed a little and took a green apple from the wooden bowl on the counter. "Yet you work here, dear. What makes you say such a thing, Mrs. Smith?"

"Work here, yes. Live here, no. Never. You couldn't pay me enough copper for that. Everyone knows about the October People. This was their land before it went to the Leaf Academy."

I laughed again, trying to cheer her and myself. Why the mention of the October People should chill me to the bone, I did not understand. Perhaps she was just upset that the school was closed for the fall holiday? I could not think of a reason she would speak so darkly about a local legend.

"The October People? That sounds like a fantastic tale. And what is the difference? If the place were cursed, it would matter little whether you worked here, lived here or only visited. I never knew that curses were so discerning, Mrs. Smith. I think you are having me on; a bit of laughter at the foreigner's expense? I'll have ye know that my own Nanna was a far better storyteller than you, madam. Besides, if you really believed this place cursed, you would na darken the doorway, would you?"

"There *is* a difference, and I would think you would know it. But it being your first semester here, maybe you don't. Tell me, Mr. McCandlish, before you laugh me off, you don't think it is strange, them shutting down the school for the entire month of October? It happens every year, and I can tell you why. We all know why. We leave for the month so The Others can come." She crossed herself before continuing her peeling and cutting of the apples. Her helper, a young lady named Emma, did the same and scurried out with food scraps to take to the pigs. Apparently, Emma did not want to be a part of this conversation. Not in the least.

"Ah yes, the October People."

"Mock me if you like. We all know about the crow, we down here in the kitchen. It is a sign. Mark my words—they are coming. Birds don't just fall out of the sky, sir. No, they don't. Be careful, Mr. McCandlish. Be very careful indeed."

Mrs. Smith was always going on about spooks and haints of one sort or another, but I never put much stock in such ideas. There was nothing she could tell me that would be more frightening than my own grandmother's knotted tales about the McCandlish ghosts that wandered the broken stones of the ancestral castle. I had never seen those venerated stones or any ghosts, and I took my Nanna's and Mrs. Smith's words for what they were, a way of keeping naughty boys in line. But I was no naughty child. I was a grown man and a long way from Scotland.

As nonchalantly as possible, I took a bite of the apple. "Come now, Mrs. Smith. I hope you do not repeat these things to the children. I daresay you may frighten a few of them."

"Not all of them," she said as she waved her shiny knife at the shadow in the doorway. It was Ollie LeFlore. He must have followed me to the kitchen, or he came seeking a treat. I sincerely hoped he had heard none of this conversation. I stole another apple from the bowl and ignored Mrs. Smith's disapproving glance.

"All packed, Ollie?" I handed him the apple as we stepped out into the chilly corridor and left the warm kitchen behind. It was the last day of September, too early in the year for truly cold weather, but I could feel the fingers of fall reaching toward us. I recognized autumn's approach, and the chilliness threatened to permeate my old bones. Unlike the headmaster, Mr. Mitchell, I did not mind the heat of the North American South at all. After nearly a lifetime in chilly northern Scotland, the warm temperatures of Alabama were a boon to my body and my soul. It was always easier to get up in the morning here.

"What's on your mind, then? Out with it. I'll have none of yer sulking."

"No one is coming for me."

I paused mid-bite and squatted down in front of the small boy with the dark eyes and quivering lips. I could see he had been crying, which was very unusual for him. Very unusual indeed. "What do you mean? You mean none of your family are coming today? Ach, na, lad. Surely they will be here tomorrow. They have only been delayed."

"No." He clutched the apple, and a shadow passed over his face. I turned to see the headmaster standing behind me.

"There you are, Mr. McCandlish. I had hoped to find you before I left. We have a bit of a problem, sir. If you will come with me."

I glanced at Ollie, whose expression never changed. I offered him my hand, but he did not take it. The three of us walked into the headmaster's office, and I took a seat on the bench across his desk as he closed the door. Ollie lingered at my shoulder as if I were his protector. Had he been up to something naughty?

"Troubling news, Mr. McCandlish. I hear you plan to stay here at the Leaf Academy instead of taking your holiday off campus. Surely you remember that this is against the rules. There is to be no one here for the month of October." I tossed the apple in the nearby trash can. It made an unusually heavy, dull thump as it landed, like a cannonball dropping to the ground. "This puts me in a very bad position, I am afraid. We have a very strict rule here—everyone, without exception, leaves for the fall holiday, Mr. McCandlish. It is tradition, and more than that, it is a requirement. It says so in your contract."

I glanced over at Ollie standing by the door. It made me sick to see Mr. Mitchell ignore him so, but that was his way. Mr. Mitchell was headmaster, true enough, but he never interacted with the children except to administer discipline or distribute awards at our quarterly events. "But surely the academy can make an exception this time. Ollie has just told me—no, don't sulk, lad. He has just told me that no one is coming to pick him up. He is quite alone, sir." I swallowed at my excuse. Of course,

I'd had no such excuse before a few minutes ago and I had planned to stay here at the Leaf Academy before I knew Ollie was in need, but that was beside the point now.

Mr. Mitchell stroked his slightly over-greased mustache as he thought about my plea. "You say a boy is in need?" The headmaster paled but still did not acknowledge Ollie at all.

"Yes, come, Ollie. Come tell the headmaster what you told me." The boy walked over, his hands by his sides, his head down. "Speak up now. Don't be shy, lad."

"No one is coming for me," Ollie said without looking up. His dark hair hung in his eyes. I would have to see that he got a haircut and soon. The headmaster would certainly complain about the length. *No fops here, boys. No fops at the Leaf Academy.*

Mr. Mitchell shot up like an arrow being released from a bow. He moved so quickly that I jumped up too. What was going on here?

The headmaster was visibly shaken at the news but offered no solace to young LeFlore. "There will be no staff here, Mr. McCandlish. No one to cook, clean or tend to your needs. Or anyone else's, for that matter. I daresay there is room at the Yellow Rose Hotel; that is the closest place. It would be better for you to stay there." Ollie began to cry, and the apple fell from his hand and hit the ground with a plunk. Mitchell's knuckles whitened as he moved behind his chair and clutched the leather back.

"There now, lad. We will figure this out. I am sorry about your family, Ollie. Putting the boy up in a hotel seems a bit risky. He is only a child, Mr. Mitchell. Surely he could spend his holiday with one of us. We could write to his father and ask his permission."

"There is no time for that. Tomorrow is the first of October. Nobody stays here in October. In fact, the staff is leaving tonight after supper. If you stay here, McCandlish, I want you to understand that you will be alone. Quite alone for the entire month."

I was a grown man and could tend to myself, and I welcomed the silence. I had books to read, and there was an interesting star alignment predicted for the middle of the month. I had spent a month's pay on the proper telescope and equipment. I planned to map and record the entire three-day event. But this unexpected turn of events threatened to force my hand. Should I confess to the headmaster what I had planned? No, he did not seem to care now.

"I assure you I will be fine, Mr. Mitchell. I cannot in good conscience leave the Leaf Academy with Ollie's future so uncertain. I will remain until someone comes for him. Surely, you can understand the need here."

"On your own head be it then, Mr. McCandlish." He grimaced as he leaned forward, his pen in hand. "As headmaster of the Leaf Academy, I grudgingly give you permission to remain for the holiday. You are a good man, McCandlish, perhaps too good."

"Thank you, Headmaster. I shall do my best to keep Ollie occupied until his parents arrive."

"And then you will leave. No lingering about, McCandlish."

"I will absolutely not linger about, Mr. Mitchell," I lied quite easily. "Thank you, sir. Come, Ollie."

We left the headmaster behind and walked down the narrow hall that led to the two staircases, one to the teachers' wing and the other to the students' dormitory. The place was already as quiet as a church. There was no laughter, no shuffling of books or scraping of chairs. Hardly any noise at all.

"Ollie, bring your things to my room. You know where it is, don't you? It's the last door on the left, down the hall there.

You can bunk with me. We will be like two friends spending the holiday together."

"We aren't leaving? What will we do when The Others come? They won't like that we are here."

I smiled up at the boy as I squatted down in front of him and he rubbed his red nose with his coat sleeve. "What do you know about the October People? Have you been listening to Mrs. Smith and her stories? It's all rubbish, lad. I don't know exactly what our plans will be, but we will be together. I promise you that. I won't leave you. I will just have to keep you entertained until your parents can retrieve you."

In a surprising gesture, Ollie put his arms around my neck. He hugged me but then released me quickly, running down the hall to fetch his undoubtedly meager things. I felt a shiver at my shoulder. I glanced behind me, but there was no one. Not even a shadow on the wall.

Jumping at shadows now, are we? Too many of Mrs. Smith's stories, McCandlish.

No, it wasn't that. It was something the boy said that gave me the goose-willies.

They won't like that we are here...

Humming quietly to myself, I walked to my room and began rearranging furniture. Surely there was enough room to drag a cot into my quarters. We would make it comfortable and cozy. It would be perfect. I wouldn't be lonely, and Ollie was quiet enough. He might enjoy studying the stars too.

What will we do when The Others come?

And what would Mrs. Smith say when she discovered we stayed the entire month and there were no Others? No October People. No curse. I smiled at that idea. I was one to enjoy disproving such things. *See, Nanna? It was only the wind blowing the curtains. No high spirits here.* And I had been looking for a new subject to study. Why not something like this? I could imagine the headlines now.

Local Teacher Puts Local Legend to Rest

Or better still...

Tenured Professor Debunks Local Legend

Surely they would offer me tenure for such an achievement. Yes, that's exactly what I would do. Ollie and I together. And when it was over, we would have a good laugh together, the lad and I.

A shadow crossed my door. I thought perhaps it was the headmaster or Ollie returned with his suitcase, but there was no one there. No one at all. I stepped out into the hallway and glanced around. No, there was nothing to see.

Just a black feather. Surprised to find it, I picked it up and laid it on my desk. *Better still, I should hide it. No reason to upset the boy.* I opened a drawer and squirreled it away for closer inspection later.

As I closed the drawer, Ollie stepped into the room, a looming shadow behind him. But when I blinked, the shadow vanished and only the smiling boy remained.

"Come inside, Ollie. Close the door. All is well now."

The door closed with a creak.

Chapter One—Jocelyn Graves
Mobile, Alabama, Today

"You know how much I enjoy working with you—the whole Gulf Coast Paranormal team—but I can't commit to another team investigation right now. That last investigation was one I will never forget, but I've got something I have to take care of first, Midas." I pretended I didn't notice his sigh of exasperation echoing through the phone.

Don't feel bad, my friend. I have that effect on people. Just ask anyone who knows me.

Aaron, Gulf Coast Paranormal's newest team member and all-around sexy dude, knew all about how frustrating I could be, and it wasn't that I was playing hard to get. I *liked* Aaron, but I wasn't one to be ruled by my heart—or my hormones. If Aaron really wanted to know more about me, he could just ask Pete. If Pete wasn't still running from the Dogman. I couldn't believe he'd left us in the middle of an investigation, but there was no denying it. If I hadn't seen it with my own eyes, I might not have believed it. Yep, he took the van and left us high and dry. Granted, he came back a few minutes later—I mean, apparently even Peter Broadus had a conscience—but the fact was he'd left us. If I ever had doubts about whether breaking up with him had been the right thing to do, I didn't anymore. Totally the right thing. But I never second-guessed myself, not concerning matters of the heart. There was too much to see, too much to do in this great big world to settle down with someone who was anything less than amazing.

Pete was many things, but he'd never been amazing. He was more like a cluster.

Why was I thinking about him right now?

"You going solo again?"

I was sure Midas didn't mean to sound like my nonexistent father, but he kinda did.

"It won't be the first time. I think I'll do just fine."

I'd just spent a solid week with the entire Gulf Coast Paranormal team, and yes, there were some advantages to having a team on an investigation, but solo gigs had perks too. Less equipment, less drama. I needed some "me" time, and the page that I was holding in my hand was my ticket to that adventure. I read the email again as Midas continued his pitch. The team was short one man since he "fired" Pete. I worked well with the team, everyone liked me. They were heading to Gulfport soon to investigate some abandoned fairgrounds. As much as I liked Midas, he wasn't changing my mind. I was ready to end the phone call so I could get packed and get on the road. Midas was my friend, but my adventure came with an expiration date.

"I promise you that I will think about it. I have to do this other thing first."

He paused for a moment. I knew Midas well enough to know that he was "reading" me, a skill he used when he wanted to protect you from something or just be nosy. That was Midas. He was everyone's Protector. On one hand, I appreciated that about him, but on the other...not so much. "Stop worrying," I said, frowning at myself in the mirror next to me. I put the paper down on the desk and sat in the wonky desk chair. My temporary apartment was a craphole, but at least it wasn't a hotel. Man, I looked a fright. My dreads needed twisting, my eyebrows needed plucking, and I was pale. I typically kept a year-round tan because of all the time I spent outdoors with my photography gig, but my color was fading fast. "I know how you feel about my investigating alone, but it is what it is. I'm not dead yet."

"That's a great motto. Maybe that should be your next tattoo."

I smiled at his sarcasm. "Maybe. I actually like that. I've been meaning to add to my collection."

"Have you forgotten the Sapphire Caves?" he asked me in an attempt at adding some humor to our conversation.

"No, and I haven't forgotten Crenshaw Road either. Dangerous situations happen, Midas, whether there are seven of us or just one or two. It's the nature of the beast."

"For Crenshaw Road, that's a good description for it. Are you sure I can't talk you into bringing someone along? If not me, then Cassidy or Aaron?"

I smiled and shook my head. "Midas Demopolis, stop being an old lady. I'm going by myself. This is a once-in-a-lifetime opportunity. It's only a two-day investigation. I think I can handle it. I'll call you when I'm done."

"At least tell me where you are going. Just to be on the safe side."

I thought about it but decided against it. Although I was certain he didn't mean it this way, telling him would mean I was officially a member of Gulf Coast Paranormal...and I still wasn't sure I wanted to stay in one spot. I mean, I liked this part of the Gulf Coast, I liked the team, but I also liked my freedom.

"Nu-uh. But I will call you when I get done, and I swear I'll have an answer for you."

"Fine, but be safe, Jocelyn. Don't take unnecessary risks. Getting the shot isn't worth breaking your leg. Or your head."

"Got it. No risks and no breakage. I have to go, Midas. Have a good one."

"Bye." He hung up, and I breathed a sigh of relief. I read the email again, aloud this time just to be sure I was reading it correctly.

My client, Mr. Holloway, grants you permission to photograph the property at 1100 Orange Pekoe Avenue for a period of no more than two days. When you've completed your photo shoot, please leave the key in the metal lockbox on the front porch. I will retrieve it later. Also, Mr. Holloway expects that you will send him copies of your photographs for his own study. Please contact us prior to submitting your work to any publications, including local newspapers, books, etc. Good luck.

Sincerely,

Adrian Shanahan

I held the key in my hand. It wasn't one of those cheap keys you could go have made at any big blue store. It was the old-fashioned kind with an interesting handle and was larger than any key I had.

I removed my leather necklace, slid the key on it and tied it around my neck. I couldn't lose it now. I sometimes had a habit of leaving things behind when I started investigating. Like my film case or an audio recorder. Man, this was exciting. The notorious Leaf Academy! Score!

I heard Sherman's toenails clicking on the floor beside me. *Dang it. I forgot all about my dog.* But was he really my dog? The poor guy had turned up on my porch not long after I moved into the apartment complex. I knocked on all the neighbors' doors and inquired with the management, but nobody recognized or claimed the animal. Nobody wanted the hairy, white furball with the soft black eyes and equally black nose. Seemed a shame. He had no collar and no tag, but he had obviously been someone's dog. He was house-trained and sweet, and he didn't bark much. I never planned to keep him, especially since my future was always so uncertain, but he was growing on me and there weren't any other options. I posted his picture on social media but hadn't gotten any responses yet. The local animal shelter informed me that they weren't a no-kill facility. If I left the dog there and he couldn't find a home in a week, he would be put down. I couldn't believe it. I couldn't stomach it. So he got a name, a collar and a place on the couch until I could figure it all out.

"Well, Sherm. I hate to do this, but I have to go away for a few days." I petted his head and rubbed his ears. He rewarded me with lots of licks. "I can't believe nobody has claimed you yet,

Sherman. You are an awesome dog. You deserve a happy home. Sorry about the name, but I have never named a dog before."

He whined once and laid his chin on my thigh. *Shoot. It's like he knows I'm leaving.*

I snuggled with him for a few minutes and then went back to packing my equipment. I wasn't taking everything, just a few cameras and a bunch of audio recorders. I couldn't believe I was being given access to the Leaf Academy. The place had been closed since 1978. They couldn't keep it open after the location had been linked to multiple murders. Total creep-fest, or so I heard.

But what about Sherman?

After a few phone calls, I found a well-recommended kennel that had an opening. "It's only for a few days," I said to him as we pulled into the Happy Paws Boarding Kennel later that afternoon. "And there will be lots of other dogs to play with. You be a good boy, and I'll be back in just a few days. Okay?"

Another whine. With a sigh, I leashed him up and walked him into the kennel. I tried not to look him in the eye. I surveyed the place and mentally gave it a thumbs-up. The people appeared knowledgeable and attentive. I got the impression that they really cared about their guests. Sherman would be in good hands.

Despite all this, I drove away feeling as if I would never see him again. And I was going to miss him.

Don't be so dramatic, Jocelyn. How can you miss a dog you barely know? It's not like he is your childhood pet. You're letting Midas put the chilly bumps on you. You'll be back, and the dog will be fine.

I chose to believe the voice of grown-up Jocelyn and drove away without looking once in the rearview mirror. But for the first time in a long time, I regretted leaving someone behind.

And the tears were real.

Chapter Two—Jocelyn

I could see the place on my phone app, but the directions were leading me in circles. Take Orange Pekoe to Newt Circle. But where was Newt Circle? I couldn't keep driving around. It would be dark in a few hours, and I had cameras and other equipment to set up if I actually found the place. Thankfully, I had a paper map in the glove box for backup. I pulled over to the side of the road and spread the map on the hood. There was no one out here, which seemed kind of strange. Just a few streets over was a residential area with small houses practically built on top of one another. Yes, I could see Kennedy Street and recognized those buildings.

Oh wow. Now I see it.

The Leaf Academy, or the ruins that were once the prominent boys' school, was hidden behind dozens of old trees, mostly oaks with a few pines growing tall and wild. How had I missed this driveway and that building? *It's almost like the place wants to stay hidden, huh?* I hurried back to my car and grabbed my camera from the front seat. I scanned the area to make sure no one was around, since I sure didn't want to get robbed out here in the middle of nowhere, but there wasn't a soul. I locked the car and headed up the narrow driveway. My Nissan could probably manage to navigate it, but I wanted to walk the rest of the way, at least for a first viewing.

I flipped the camera on and removed the lens cap. There wasn't much to see from this distance, but I snapped a few photos anyway. My heart was racing, and I couldn't help but smile at the promise of a new adventure. The road wasn't in total disrepair. Someone had been using it, and recently. Hopefully not criminals. I could see tire tracks and fresh piles of red dirt that had been halfheartedly moved around with a rake. I wasn't quite so alone now. Birds were chirping, and squirrels dashed across the canopy of trees above me. Their playful skittering sent down showers of leaves. I snapped a picture of them but wasn't sure I got anything.

I was feeling anxious about my car. *Maybe I shouldn't have walked up here. I can't afford to lose my equipment—or my vehicle. Yeah, I should go back. If I can't see the school clearly here at this turn of the path, I'll do just that.*

But when I turned the corner and walked into the small clearing, looming in front of me was the abandoned Leaf Academy. A wave of sadness struck me. For sure, this was a sad place. That was my first impression. The front porch was supported by four columns; there were traces of faded paint on the bottom of the columns, but the tops were brown, like the rest of the building. There was an ornate doorway with tall windows beside it and three smaller ones above it. There appeared to be two wings to the academy, and all the windows looked quite firmly boarded up. I wondered what secrets that dark, dirty space held...whether it was haunted or not, it sure as heck looked like it could be.

Snap, snap.

I took a flurry of pictures. First impressions were important when investigating. This was my favorite part. For sure, I couldn't believe my luck. Jocelyn Graves, amateur photographer, freelance writer and part-time paranormal investigator, was about to spend two whole days here at the Leaf Academy. The only price I had to pay was sending copies of my photos to the owner and doing a small write-up about any experiences I had here. Yep, I was one lucky gal. I shifted the camera and held it to my face as I snapped a dozen more photographs. Not too high a price for access to such a time capsule. With any luck, there would be some great artifacts inside. Maybe some classroom equipment or personal items. Those made the best subjects for photos.

I stood in silence for a few minutes as I paced and then walked the front yard as best I could. There was much more to see, but it would have to wait. I had to bring the car up, but I hesitated. I waited for something. My watch beeped, reminding me that I didn't have all day to stand here gawking at this potential paranormal playground. There was work to be done before the actual work could be done, and I was burning daylight. I snapped a few more pictures of the upstairs windows, especially the one on the end there. I didn't *see* anything at all since they were all boarded up, but I could not shake the feeling that there *was* someone inside. Waiting for me.

But there wasn't. Man, I had one heck of an imagination.

It was a fine brick building. Great details too. I hoped tomorrow would be sunnier. I needed all the light I could get for better shots. It was dark back here with so many trees surrounding the place. With a sigh of satisfaction, I began my walk back to the car, looking behind me a few times. Nope. Still nothing in that window. I made the turn that led to the drive and quickly returned with my car. I drove up to the house without incident. It wasn't the smoothest ride, but I'd been down roads that were a lot worse. Recently too.

"Okay, Leaf Academy. It's you and me now," I said as I closed the trunk and walked toward the front door with the two largest cases in my hands. Best to get the heavy lifting done early. I glanced up at the amazing front door again.

The front door that now stood wide open.

And not just a crack. It was all the way open as if someone expected me and wanted me to make myself at home. As I set the camera cases down on the ground, my knees felt a tad bit wobbly. *This isn't right. No way is this right.*

Removing the camera from around my neck, I scanned back through the photos. There! The door was closed. Completely closed! I looked at all the pictures, and it was clearly shut in every one of them.

Okay, Jocelyn. Let's think logically.

If the door wasn't closed good, if the lock was rusty or broken...any of those could explain why the door stood open now. Granted, there should have been some wind or a breeze or something to move that door, but I didn't feel a thing. In fact, it was unseasonably muggy. *Let's take this step by step.*

I walked up the steps and remembered Midas' warning. No broken legs, not this time around. There were a few spongy spots in the flooring, but nothing gave way. With my camera ready, I took shots of the porch, the doorframe, the open door. A fluttering darkness shot past the door but didn't make a sound. Was that some kind of bird in there? No, I would have heard wings, right?

With shaking fingers, I touched the rusty doorknob. It felt cooler than the air around it. Much cooler. *But that's not evidence. Take a look at the lock, Jocelyn.* I examined the doorknob and turned it. It moved, but it hadn't been greased for a while; it was one of those crafty old mechanisms that needed a good oiling every now and then. Each turn came with a subtle squeak. I closed the door and untangled the leather string around my neck. I shoved the key in the door lock and turned the knob, confirming that the lock was working. The door wouldn't swing open by just bumping it. In fact, I had a difficult time reopening the thing with the key. But eventually, it worked. The door opened easily now. I closed it again, stepped back and took a few more pictures. Nice craftsmanship. I didn't know how I missed it before, but above the door were some words carved into a piece of fitted stone. Latin, from the looks of it.

Non timebo mala.

Why did that sound so familiar? I whispered the phrase a few times to help me commit it to memory. Then I walked back to pick up my cases, navigated the steps carefully and approached the door with the key in my hand.

And it was open again.

Okay, Jocelyn Graves. You can write this down. Day one, hour one, paranormal evidence. But at least they want you here. Then that phrase came back to me. I'd seen it before, in a tattoo shop in Fort Lauderdale. I'd almost gotten that one but opted for the wildflower on my ankle. I much preferred icons over phrases as far as tattoos went.

But I knew what this meant. *Non timebo mala.* I will fear no evil.

Chapter Three—Jocelyn

The downstairs was a complete dust bowl despite the fact that every window on the bottom floor was boarded up. Leaving my cases in the front room, I removed the LED flashlight from my pocket and flicked it on. It cast a light blue light around the spacious foyer. There wasn't much to see in here, a built-in bench with hooks for rain gear. But what was that? I could see a door that led to a small office. I poked my head inside but didn't see anything interesting in here either. Basic office furniture, a desk, a broken metal chair and some sagging built-in bookcases. No personal effects at all except a calendar from 1957 and a faded picture in a dirty frame. But I would definitely ransack that desk later.

I walked out of the room and closed the door behind me. Standard procedure when investigating old houses, asylums, hospitals—always close the door behind you. So, now what? I had a few choices, go left, go right or go upstairs. Common sense said clear the bottom floor, make sure there were no vagrants or vandals on the premises, but I wasn't listening to my common sense right this moment. My proverbial sixth sense was tingling. Immediately I began photographing the foyer and then climbed the steps carefully. If I had any hope of sneaking up on anyone, all that was shot. With every step I took in my hiking boots, a floorboard creaked beneath me.

Strange. The window over the landing wasn't boarded up. I was glad for the light, but the glass was so dirty it didn't illuminate much. It cast the stairs in a dingy pale sepia color. No, I think it cast more shadows on the second floor. And that's where I was now.

Non timebo mala. What a strange phrase for a school. I mean, as if going to boarding school wasn't terrifying enough, seeing that would put the fear of God in you. Or the fear of something.

There was no office on the second level, not like the lower level. Clearly this floor was strictly for housing. Right at the top of the stairs, there was an open area with a few worn chairs and some other junk. I had the choice to go left or right and went to the right. There were rooms on either side of the corridor; all the rooms facing the front yard were boarded up. The rooms at the back, however, the ones facing the woods, were not. That was weird. Why board up the front and not the back? More than one window on the back side was broken.

Snap, snap.

But this level felt like it had been abandoned more recently. Odd personal items littered the floor. I could see an old tennis shoe, a rusty toy truck, an old-fashioned chalk slate and a broken wooden toy. I photographed them all as I made my way down the corridor. *Yeah, it's like the folks on this level just left and forgot to take their stuff with them. That is odd.*

I came to my senses after a few minutes of photographing various finds and dug my digital recorder out of my pocket. I clicked the button and began to ask the standard questions. "I'm on the second floor of the Leaf Academy. I felt compelled to check these rooms out first. My name is Jocelyn; what is your name?"

I walked to the window and set the recorder on the windowsill as I took in the view. At least there were no broken windows in this room. But there was also not one stick of furniture and not much of a view. Nothing to see but woods. Gosh, the sun was going down quickly. Too quickly. I'd have to finish setting up, but I had already decided that this would be the room; this would be HQ for the next few days.

"I hope you don't mind, but I am going to hang around for a few days. I brought my own cot and a pillow. Would you mind if I stayed in here?"

I shivered at my own question. I didn't hear a word, but I was convinced that I would hear something once I reviewed the tape. Yeah, I was pretty confident about that. "I am going to take pictures too. Would you like to take a picture? May I take yours?" I snapped a few shots but still nothing. I wasn't alarmed. Not frightened, not apprehensive. Instead, I got the strange sensation that I was expected, that whoever was here wanted me here.

Now that is a worrying thought.

"Non timebo mala...do you know what that means?"

A clicking in the hallway caught me off guard. It was the exact same sound my camera made, only I wasn't taking pictures in the hallway. And there was no possible way that was an echo; that's not how acoustics worked. I took another shot of the empty corner and silently counted off seconds; when I got to ten, I heard it again.

What in the Sam Hill?

I walked into the hallway and looked around. I took another picture just for the heck of it. I counted off again and waited. Nothing. *Hmm...maybe I'm making too much of it.* I stepped back into the room and returned to the previous spot.

"Is that you taking pictures in the hall? Are you taking my picture? I think I hear you. Can you do it again?" I waited another minute, but the phantom photographer did not repeat the sound. "I tell you what. I will leave my camera here on the windowsill. You can use it if you like. See this button? If you touch it, it will make that sound. You can touch it, but don't break it. I will be right back."

I set the camera on the windowsill, pushing it back far enough so it wouldn't fall off, and checked my watch. It was now 4:45 p.m. and time to get this show on the road. If I came back and found photos on the camera after that time, I would know that I made contact with someone. Or something.

Boy, if that's the case, this would be record time, I think.

I hurried down the stairs, retrieved my cases and came back up. Nothing was moved, I heard nothing else, and I didn't bother with the camera or audio recorder yet. I had to make three more trips; by the third, I was winded. I set up my cot and removed my thermal camera and tripod. I was definitely putting these guys in this hallway. I set them up, then grabbed an extra digital camera and slipped off down the stairs to lock the door and check the bottom floor.

I didn't like it down here. How had the atmosphere changed that quickly? It wasn't cozy at all; in fact, it was kind of sickening. Kind of awful. The hallways were cluttered, and there were birds in some of the rooms as well as evidence of rodents. Yeah, I was glad I had decided to stay upstairs. It felt less decrepit on the second floor.

So, what's the plan, Jocelyn? What to do first?

From some of the reports, the auditorium, the big room to my right, was a hot spot for paranormal activity. I supposed the practical thing to do was spend some time in there. And then maybe take some shots in the backyard focusing on the windows. When I walked toward the auditorium, I turned just in time to see a feather falling to the ground.

And it appeared to have fallen out of thin air.

It was a big black feather, maybe from a raven or a crow. I ducked, expecting to see a bird circling me, but saw nothing. I heard birds, but they were tiny finches. Nothing as large as whatever this came from. I took a picture as it landed on the ground. Looking around the room again, I searched for the bird, but there was nothing to see.

Okay, reality check. No way did that float down from nowhere. You probably stirred up the feather when you walked past it, or it fell from a beam above you. There are all kinds of birds in this place. I took a few more pictures of the feather, and then I touched it briefly. It felt kind of crunchy, like it had been here a long while.

And then the hallway went completely silent. All the birds stopped chirping. Even the crickets outside got quiet, like they did whenever there was a predator nearby. When I camped with my grandparents growing up, that was our cue to hunker down. But I didn't see anything, and I sure wasn't a predator. Maybe there was something here I could not see?

That's when I decided it was time to move. The auditorium could wait for a little while. The investigator in me said, "Get in there!" Survivor-Jocelyn voted that down, at least for the time being. Time to go back upstairs and come up with a solid plan.

I put the feather back. I didn't want to touch it anymore.

It didn't belong to me.

Chapter Four—Hugh

The last of the staff left this morning, and I assured the groundskeeper that I too would shortly depart. It was the first of October, an ominous day according to the locals, but I felt no fear. In fact, I felt nothing but relief. I did not realize how much I needed a break from the hectic demands of the Leaf Academy. True, there were a few reports to finish and some light duties to attend to, but I imagined the next month would be restful for both young Ollie and me. First order of business? Write to his parents immediately. The boy was not forthcoming with the details of their delay, but I must have a timeline. I would need to plan for our food and other necessities. But for how long?

"How does walking suit you, young man? I thought we could explore the trail behind the academy. I think that red fox is running around again."

For the first time in a long while, I saw a glimmer of a smile on the boy's face. It was brief, but I was glad to see it. "And I secreted a few more apples. I have them in my pouch. We can take them with us, in case we get hungry. How does that sound?"

"Do red foxes eat apples?"

"No, I do not think they do. I think they prefer mice and rabbits."

"Oh," he said, looking a little sad.

"Come now, don't look so glum. Maybe this fox likes apples. We shall soon find out." We tied on our shoes, and I allowed the boy to carry the bag of apples. I stuffed my sketchpad and pencils in my satchel, along with a canteen of water and a few crackers. I did not think we would be gone too long, but one could never tell. I had a tendency to daydream; it had been so long since I could allow my mind to wander. Still, I had to look out for the boy. He was so fragile and would likely need comfort and companionship. Yes, this had been the right thing. We needed this quiet and solitude, both of us, for different reasons.

We walked out of the room, and by habit I locked it with my key. To my surprise, Ollie put his hand in mine as we headed down the stairs and outdoors. As we were not in school and there was no stern headmaster present to disapprove of such fatherly affection, I gladly accepted the boy's hand. I had never been a father, but I could not imagine a situation where I would not bring my son home for his holiday. How could a good man do such a thing? I quietly pledged to scold his father and remind him of his responsibilities. If it had been me, I would have moved heaven and earth to bring my son home.

But I was no father, nor would I ever be, I imagined. I released the boy's hand as we stepped out into the sunshine and smiled at the sight of the nodding green grass that blew in a pleasant breeze. There were songbirds nearby too, and I thought I could hear the water splashing in the creek. That was certainly just my imagination; I had never heard the water from this distance before. You had to travel through the gate and down the path a little before you could hear the creek. But I could hear it very clearly now. I felt my skin prickle with strange awareness. And just like that, all that was peaceful and wonderful vanished.

A man stood at the far side of the yard just beyond the metal fence. He stood stock-still like some kind of menacing statue. I could not see his face or any of his features, for it appeared to me that he was made entirely of shadow. I heard Ollie's breathing still beside me. He must see him too! I shoved the boy behind me as I watched the shadow darken slightly and then vanish altogether. I realized that I had been holding my breath. Ollie was clutching the back of my jacket.

"It's okay, Ollie. It was a trick of the light. See? There is no one there." I pointed and smiled down at him. Was I trying to convince Ollie or myself? There had certainly been someone there. Yes, indeed. Probably my height, maybe a little taller. He wore no hat and had thick, dark hair.

"Let us go this way. There are many things to see on the front lawn."

"But what about the red fox?"

"Surely we will find him there. Let us hunt for him."

"Okay," he agreed happily. He scampered in front of me while I looked behind us once more. No more shadow. Nothing at all. But he had been there.

All the hopefulness of the day blew away with the fear that overwhelmed me. For Ollie's sake, I continued on with our plan. Otherwise, I might very well have returned to my room to survey the grounds from my window, to look for the shadowy stranger from a safer vantage point.

To my surprise, we did find animal tracks. Many, many animal tracks. Even some that might be attributed to a dog or a red fox, as young Mr. LeFlore wanted to believe. Around lunchtime, we gobbled up the apples and drank our fill from the water canteen, and I decided it was time to return to the academy. For some reason, the thought of returning did not fill me with comfort even though I had many books to read and certainly could find much to entertain myself and my unexpected guest.

However, the idea of remaining outside disturbed me more. True, it was still early in the afternoon, but it was the first of October and the shadows seemed unusually long. When I turned my head slightly, I could see them moving in ways I had never seen before. Once or twice I caught Ollie looking around too, but neither of us admitted there was anything to fear. The boy found track after track, discovering one thing and then another. He even found a black feather and brought me to see it.

"You could add this to your collection," he said as he smiled sweetly.

How could he know that? He had not seen me hide the feather earlier. Or had he? A sick feeling washed over me. Must be all the apples. "We should leave it here, Ollie. Come, let's go inside now. I think it might rain."

The boy was quiet now. "You should take it. Add it to your collection, Mr. McCandlish," he said as he sidled closer and took my hand. Why did he feel so cold?

"No, thank you, Ollie. We should go inside now. We could drown in the rain, lad."

He snatched his hand away and stormed up the path to the school. I could not understand his behavior, but I was ready to be away from this horrible place. No, rain wasn't far away. I could smell it in the air. And what a rain it would be. We raced up the back steps just as the first drops splashed down. I closed the door behind us and locked it in case our unwanted guest attempted to come closer.

Yes, the shadow. I know I saw him.

Certainly, he would not try to come in. But if he did, I would defend myself and my charge. The rain fell harder, and by the time we reached my room it was coming down as if someone were tossing buckets of tears down from heaven, as my Nanna would have described it. Strange that I would think of her now.

"Come on, Ollie. Let us rest a bit and then think about what to cook for dinner." As we hurried down the corridor, I could see that my door was standing wide open. Ollie's hand was in mine again. *Ach, Hugh. He is nothing but a scared lad. Have a care and be kind. Would it have hurt to pick up the blooming feather?* I patted his hand once and went to investigate the open door, but he pulled me back with a surprising strength.

"They are here now, Mr. McCandlish. They have been watching us all day. We have to leave. You have to take me with you."

"We aren't going anywhere, Ollie. Stay put." I eased his small frame against the wall and dug in my satchel for the paring knife I carried for peeling the apples. It felt sticky from the juice, but I clutched it as determinedly as if it were the sword Excalibur. As I stepped closer, I saw the door was only partially open. I pushed it open all the way, but there was no one there. No one at all. No shadows, no interlopers.

Nothing but one black feather.

Chapter Five—Jocelyn

Although I felt unsettled now, my feelings weren't evidence of the paranormal. I wanted this; I'd been writing for months, hoping to get in here. And now here I was at the famed Leaf Academy freaking out over a few feathers. I focused on breathing as I closed my eyes and played back the audio recorders, both the one from the window and the one I carried with me downstairs. I was particularly interested to hear anything from this room or the hallway downstairs. There! I clicked the button and rewound it. Turning up the volume, I shoved my headphones into the plug with shaking fingers.

...me...

Someone was definitely making contact, but the phrase wasn't clear. The voice sounded like a child, maybe a boy? It was hard to tell with child spirits sometimes. I played it again.

...come find me...

And the voice was followed by a series of clicks. Familiar clicks like the ones my camera made. The camera! I'd forgotten to check my camera! I grabbed it and removed the memory card. As I sat on my makeshift bed, I opened my laptop and slid the card into the slot. A folder of pictures appeared, and I knew I would need to study each of them slowly. It was dark now, so dark that I had to pause to flip on my LED lamp. I shut the door while I was up. I had the feeling that at any moment someone would walk into the room. It seemed kind of silly closing the door on a ghost, but hey, it made me feel better. At least for a little while.

Sitting back on the cot, I hit play. The first photo freaked me out. This was a picture of me! I was leaving the room. There were several shots of me and then the closed door. If that wasn't freaky enough, I saw what looked like a face peering back at me from the shadowy corner of this very room. A little boy, if I had to guess, but the way he was turned, I could not see him full on. It was as if he did not want me to take his photo and turned away a little. But I could see the shape of his head, an ear and his profile. I caught my breath and immediately sent a copy of the picture to Midas along with a quick email.

Already seeing results. Wish me luck.

I closed the laptop before I could read what he wrote back. I didn't want to get into a long conversation or be reminded of the downside to investigating alone, but I had to show someone. I was getting evidence, good evidence. The kind I could believe in and rely on. Or maybe I just wanted to prove something to him. Or myself.

I heard a sound in the hallway. "Hello?" I hurried to the doorway and swore I heard footsteps run down the hall. My plan had been to take a nap and then investigate until sunup, but it looked like my plans might be changing. If the ghosties wanted to come out and play, I was game. I leaned against the door with my ear pressed against it. Yeah, footsteps retreating now. The sound was so real I could hear the grit beneath my visitor's shoes. Was this a real person? I mean, a living person? I opened the door and practically launched myself into the hallway.

I caught sight of a pant leg and a black shoe disappearing into another room. That was no child! There was someone here! I raced back to my room and grabbed my flashlight and camera. I wasn't sure what I would do with that combination, maybe blind the guy and then take his picture, but it was all I had. Why would someone in dress pants and dress shoes be hiding up here in the deserted Leaf Academy?

"Hey, I saw you!" I called as I waved my flashlight around. "You may as well come out." I paused in the hallway outside the room that I believed my unwanted guest had disappeared into. A cluster of shadows on the wall beside me fluttered and moved out of my view. Some shadows remained, silhouettes of the tree branches outside, but there had been more shadows before that. It was as if things that imitated shadows had been hiding amongst the real ones. And I saw them move! I had never seen anything like that before. They scurried across the wall and vanished to the opposite side where I couldn't see them. Now what?

I wished I'd thought to bring a K2 meter, but did I really need one? Strange crap was obviously going down at the Leaf Academy, and I was slap-dab in the middle of it. To say I didn't enjoy the adrenaline rush would be a lie, but I was no fool. People who hide out in deserted schools aren't exactly the cream of the social crop. I heard footsteps again and decided to follow the sound, not from the room this time but farther down. I walked down the hall a little slower now, waving my flashlight wildly as if at any moment the man would come running out to challenge me.

Or that pack of wild shadows.

Okay, this felt weird. The door to the next room was standing open, just like the front door had been. Like a crazy invitation from someone who desperately wanted to connect with me. Maybe that's what all this was? An attempt to connect? I had certainly heard that little boy's voice on the recorder. Maybe the guy in the dress pants was a ghost too? Sometimes apparitions could look like regular folks if you weren't paying attention.

"Hello? I thought I saw you come in here. Are you with the little boy? What is your name?" I flipped the camera to video and began to film as I walked into the room. There was no one here and nowhere for anyone to hide. The remnants of an old bed frame were in the corner of the room. There was a closet with no door and a broken window with glass on the floor. Oh yeah, that could be dangerous.

The only interesting thing was a wooden crate. I continued to film as I removed the lid and set it to the side. It was almost too heavy to move with one hand. Inside were lots of old books. I picked one up and scanned the title; it was something in Latin that I would never be able to translate without some help from the internet.

I took pictures of the book, inside and out. Then I reached inside the box and took out the next book. It was dusty with a worn fabric cover. "Journal" was written on the front cover in faded letters. There was handwriting inside, but it was too faded to read without proper lighting. I checked out the other books too. Just some school books, academic studies, nothing helpful at all. But this journal, it might give me some clues about the children and teachers here, many of whom called this place home for a time. I picked up the book and headed back to the hallway.

"If you brought me here to find this book, thank you. I am staying at the end of the hall if you want to visit me. But no touching. I will be waiting."

I walked back to my room anxious to examine the book. There were no more strange shadow formations, no more footsteps. Things had gotten quiet, and this would be a good time to catch forty winks. As I entered the room, I closed the door behind me again. Although I meant what I said about being open to visits, I liked to set boundaries early on. It was the same for the living and the dead with me. You could come this close but not much closer. For some reason, I thought about Sherman. I missed him. Missed hearing his toenails clicking on the floor. Missed hearing him huff as he flopped down beside me.

Huh, I do miss him. Wow, that's a first.

"I'm in here if you want to talk to me, but please knock, okay?" I sat on my cot and took off my shoes but kept them close and left my socks on. It was too grungy in here to have any part of my body exposed to the elements or these surfaces. Before I dug into my newfound journal, I flipped through my own scrapbook. I'd been gathering stories about this place for months. First about the murder in 1937, the poor schoolteacher killed on the bottom floor. Then the second murder a few years later, similar to the first. Another teacher stabbed to death in his room in 1942. They found the body of a maintenance man hanging from a beam in the kitchen in 1950. Someone tried to open this place in the late seventies as a kind of local museum, but that hadn't worked out...no murders had been reported, just a suspicious death, but I couldn't get the man's name.

People believed that this place was cursed because the deaths all happened in October. And there was a fabulous legend about the October People. If you believed the stories, a ghostly swarm invaded this place during the month of October, but I didn't really believe that. What kind of ghost keeps up with the calendar? And why this particular month? Why not December? Yeah, spooky story, but it couldn't be true. Could it? It was October now...

Way to go, Jocelyn. Give yourself the heebie-jeebies before your nap. You'll be dead tired later. I snacked on a protein bar and picked up the old journal. With a flashlight, I scrutinized the name scribbled on the front page.

Oh my goodness! I recognized that name. This journal belonged to Moriah Mitchell, a former headmaster of the Leaf Academy. He was a man who by all accounts ruled with an iron fist and who went on to teach at one of the universities in Florida. He was here for the first murder. I couldn't wait to read what he had to say about this place. But as I strained to see the writing and blinked at the tiny script, I grew tired.

And sleep came far too easily.

Chapter Six—Jocelyn

I must have been dreaming about something crazy because I woke up in a cold sweat and my room was ice cold. The temperature must have dropped twenty degrees since I fell asleep. I slung back the sleeping bag. My watch was vibrating on my wrist; I loved the alarm app on this thing. Yep, it was a quarter past ten. Time to do the work. I sipped on some water, but not too much. There were no working "facilities" in this place, so if I did have to go, it would be in the woods. Yeah, I planned on holding it until the sun came up, so sipping, no downing a whole bottle.

The wood popped a few times, which I chalked up to old boards contracting from the colder temperatures. That happened in old buildings like this one. The façade and columns were brick, but inside this place was wood and more wood from wall panels to floors. Almost every step you took, the floor creaked beneath you. And as I swapped out batteries in the camera in the hallway, I paused to listen. I didn't detect any sounds, but the place had an "opening night" feel to it. Like there were many people outside the building just dying to get in.

Great terminology, girl.

And I knew all about opening night. I had been a drama major before I fell in love with photography. I always got cast in the strangest roles. I played La Sorcière Blanche in some play with a title that escaped my memory now. Later I played the Cowardly Lion in an all-female production of The Oz Story, which I loved. Those were the two most memorable, but I had been on stage at least a dozen times in various roles, and that's what tonight reminded me of. Not because I would be investigating the auditorium either. That couldn't be it. No, it was something else. Opening nights came with a strange kind of excitement, like what I was feeling now.

Yeah, you're a weirdo, Jocelyn.

I swapped out the digital cards in the cameras and replaced them with fresh ones, just in case I needed the digital space. I would hate to miss anything. I'd walked this floor already and planned to do so again, but now it was time to target the auditorium. I would set this rig up in there. It had a handy setting that would snap photos only if something moved. I tapped on the screen and set it for the highest sensitivity setting too. That way, any change in light patterns or shadow patterns would trigger the camera. I had a K2 on my hip, along with an audio recorder in my pocket, and my handheld camera dangled from the strap around my neck. My dreads felt itchy and I needed a shower, but hey, this was the life, right?

I shuffled down the stairs and to my amazement heard a few notes of piano music, but it only lasted a moment. Was there a piano on this floor? It was certainly possible. I hadn't walked through the auditorium yet, and that would be an obvious location for such an instrument. The K2 on my hip began to bleep as I cleared the last step. I stood in the foyer now, near the headmaster's office. To my right was a long corridor and the auditorium; to my left were presumably just classrooms. No time like the present. I set the camera and tripod case down and waved the K2 smoothly at waist height. Point two, point seven...wow! What a jump! It was high to my left and normal to my right. I decided to put off my auditorium visit and follow this surge to see where it would lead me. I reached for my digital recorder and clicked it on.

"Hey, is that you? My name is Jocelyn. What is your name?"

Name...

I gulped at the sound of a deep, gruff voice that I could plainly hear with my own ears. Was it mocking me?

"I said, what is your name?"

Said...

"Is that all you can do? Is that how you get your kicks, mocking people?" I frowned as the K2 went still. Nothing now. I walked a few feet farther down the hall, but it was useless. No spikes now. Dead as a doornail.

"Hey, where did you go? You could at least tell me your name."

Silence met me. With a sigh, I continued my walk down the dark corridor. Man, it was dark, like walking in a tunnel underground. I flicked on my flashlight so I could avoid tripping over random junk. In the foyer, light streamed in from the window over the landing. Here in this corridor, though, there seemed to be an absence of light. Very odd indeed.

Most of the doors were open, so I peeked inside each room but didn't detect a thing on the K2. I headed back to the foyer to gather my things and continue on my mission, but my tripod case was missing.

"What the frick?" I said as I glanced around. Could I have dropped it off somewhere else? No, I knew for a fact I had it with me, along with the camera case. I set them both down here and then followed that spike and...

Oh my God. How in the hell did that happen?

I was looking down the opposite corridor, the one that led to the auditorium, and I could plainly see the tripod. It was out of its case and extended fully, just like I would have set it up if I had not been distracted by some mischievous spirit. I shoved the digital recorder in my pocket and grabbed my camera case. I couldn't turn back now; someone was expecting me. I headed down the hall. Yeah, that was my tripod. Despite my curiosity, seeing my things moved without the help of human hands unsettled me. I remembered to control my breathing and reminded myself that this was why I had come here. I wanted to see this stuff, right?

"Thank you," I said to the air around me. "But let's go in, shall we?" With clumsy hands, I opened the door and dragged my case and tripod inside. Man, the smell. It smelled like rot. Thankfully, not dead animal rot but certainly wood and leaves.

And oh yeah, there was a hole in the wall and the ceiling. How did that happen? Was that a tree branch hanging down? This place sure needed some tender loving care. There were rows upon rows of theater chairs, all light-colored wood that must have been very fine once upon a time. Looking back at the door I just walked through, I was amazed at the sight of the massive doorframe surrounded by wide, dark wood panels. The ceiling was high, really high. I waved my flashlight around and immediately spotted a few small openings up there too. That was weird. The auditorium must extend out some because I was looking up at a starry sky, not the bottom of the top floor.

Interesting.

The walls were covered with moldy once-white plaster panels, and each of those was surrounded by yellowed wood that might have been painted gold. They were like neat boxes, or they would have been if the paint wasn't flaking and the plaster wasn't rotting off the walls. Looking ahead, I couldn't see a clear path to the stage. Some of the chairs were overturned, another oddity since they were connected in clusters of six. Had someone turned over the entire row? No, make it three rows. I guess so. Who would do that? Vandals?

"Hello?" I said more quietly than I'd intended. *Don't be timid, Jocelyn. You'd better show them who's boss.* "My name is Jocelyn Graves," I said a bit more confidently. "I came to see you in the play. Are you performing tonight?" I stepped around the dumped-over chairs and found a space in the center aisle to place the tripod. I took the camera out of the case and set it up, double-checking the settings. Yep, still set to high sensitivity. I hit the wide-angle option to give myself a better shot at capturing anything that crossed that stage.

"I hear you like to perform in the month of October, and I'm excited to see your show. I haven't seen a good play in a while." I waved the K2 around but got only a random blip or two. I kept rolling with the audio recorder. I would have liked to sit down to rest, but none of these chairs looked remotely clean.

Instead, I paced the outer aisles hoping to get some action. I kept my eyes and my flashlight trained on the stage.

"Hello? Why are you hiding? I can see you."

Peeking out from behind a faded crimson curtain, a pale face looked back at me, but only for the briefest of seconds. No! There he was again. It was the face of a boy! Okay, was I talking myself into seeing that, or did I actually see a ghost boy? To be fair, he did look similar to the boy I'd caught in the image upstairs.

"Hello?" I said in a whisper, but he did not reappear. I carefully made my way to the stage.

Chapter Seven—Hugh

I woke up to a horrible sound. Someone was banging on my door. Furiously banging. No, that wasn't it. It was my bed, my very own bed that was banging, shaking about as if some invisible giant had every intention of tossing me out of it. I screamed as I clung to the wobbly headboard and then everything got still.

"Ollie!" I whispered once my heart began to beat at a steady rate again. How could the boy sleep through such an event? "Ollie, are you all right, lad?"

I blindly reached for the lamp on the night table. I found the screw that flipped the light on and twisted it. Nothing. No light at all. Had the electrical service gone down? That would be no surprise; it was still raining from what I could hear, and the electrical often went out during rainstorms. There were no lights on in the hallway, I noted as I scurried to the door to open it. The floor was cold beneath my feet. I searched the boy's cot, but it was empty. Where could he have gone? Had he heard or seen my bed shaking and fled the room in fear? What was happening here? I peered at my bed in the darkness as I rubbed my eyes; clearly, the bed was not resting in the spot it should be in. The footboard was almost a half-foot from the wall. I shoved it into place and slid my feet into my slippers as I pulled on my robe. There was certainly no heat; it was unbearably cold. Where could the boy have gone? To find a warm fireplace? One of Nanna's sayings came to mind, but I did not have the heart to speak it aloud.

Cold as the grave, Hugh. Cold as the grave, dear lad.

Strange goings-on here at the Leaf Academy. Too strange. I checked under the bed briefly, but there was no obvious cause for the violence I had endured. I hurried out into the hallway in search of the boy. He was my responsibility after all. Poor, helpless boy. Imagine leaving him in the care of a stranger?

"Ollie? Ollie LeFlore? Where are you hiding?"

I heard footsteps walking down the staircase. "Ollie? Don't make me chase you in the dark, young man. Ollie?"

Then I heard the sounds of laughter and tinkling glass, as if someone were having a party on the bottom floor. Near the auditorium. No, the sounds were coming from inside the auditorium. And a piano played a lively tune, something sweet and familiar. What was that tune? I knew it but could not recall the name.

As I stepped onto the bottom floor, the power must have been restored, for every light in the place came on. I gripped the newel post and held on while a wave of confusion struck me. I shook my head and rubbed my face with my hand. Yes, I was alive, but was I awake? I rubbed at my skin roughly to wake myself up. I could feel stubble on my face; I needed a shave. I was sweating and in need of a shower to refresh myself. A woman passed me wearing a long red dress and carrying a slender red rose in her hand. She looked so familiar, but I could not place her. Was there a party going on here? Was that why the headmaster had been so insistent that I leave?

Perhaps this was the true reason for the dismissal of the staff for a month. Merrymaking. But who were these people? Yes, there were many people here; they were filing in through the open doors of the academy. And they all knew me, for many of them greeted me. An older woman in a black and gray dress purred my name as she passed me on her way into the auditorium. She too was familiar. A swell of music indicated that the performance was about to begin. Someone said my name again.

Hugh McCandlish! Come sit with me.

The woman in red appeared in the doorway. She wiggled her finger at me as if to summon me to her, but I could not see her face and was not willing to obey her. Emma? The kitchen girl?

"What is all this?" I asked, feeling embarrassed to be walking through the middle of a fine party in my pajamas and robe. What would they think? Why was I here again? Oh, yes. Ollie. The poor lad. I had to find him.

"Leave him to us," a man said. He was about as tall as me but with long, jet-black hair, and he wore strange garb.

Was I going mad? *No, that's not it. I know who I am and where I am. I am not mad. I am Hugh McCandlish. I am a teacher here, and this is the Leaf Academy.* But where was Ollie?

"Leave him with us. He belongs with us," the man said again as he bumped my shoulder with his. He shoved me hard and walked into the auditorium. Was that a threat? Was this stranger threatening me?

Others began to appear in the hallway. I could see them now, yes. I could see them very clearly. A very thin woman, with her hair in two long braids over her shoulders. She looked very much like Mrs. Smith, but certainly that could not be. Was this a costume party? She wore a deerskin dress and leggings. She was whispering words I could not understand; she was speaking a different language! Oh, dear. I was not proficient with languages at all.

"I don't understand you. Speak slower, perhaps." But she walked away and headed to the auditorium. And that's when I heard him scream.

Ollie was screaming my name.

I ran as fast as I could into the auditorium, but my hasty pursuit of Ollie was delayed when the place went black. It was so black I could not see my hand in front of my face. The lights were gone again, but no, that couldn't be right. I could see the many faces around me. They glowed slightly in the darkness; they were not like before, real people with friendly expressions. The absence of light revealed their true nature; they were surely not of this world. *The October People!*

And they all hated me. They wanted me to die!

I ran past them into the auditorium screaming Ollie's name. The stage was empty except for the little boy curled into a ball in the center of it. His hair was mussed, the dark strands covering his face, and he was heaving as if he had been crying for a long while.

"Hush, now. I have you, Ollie." I pulled the boy close and collected him quickly as he shivered in my arms. Poor child. What was going on in this place? I hesitated on the stage wondering whether to go left or right or what to do. From somewhere in the darkness, I heard a man clapping; yes, it had to be a man's hands. They were loud, and then many hands were clapping. The sound was thunderous. And then silence. I raced from the auditorium as lightning filled the hall with a strange blue light. The faces vanished, and I began to cry as I ran with Ollie in my arms, his head on my chest. He was crying too.

We would leave this place come morning, as soon as we could navigate the road. Perhaps the rain would stop by then. We would leave the Leaf Academy and never come back. This place truly was cursed; it was the home of the damned. Mrs. Smith had been right all along, but then again, she was one of them.

This place belonged to the October People—it had always been theirs.

I hurried down the long corridor and raced to my room, holding Ollie as he wept. I lied to him, "It will be all right, lad. It will be all right. We will leave this place when the sun comes up. I promise you. I do so promise. Do you hear me?"

"Yes," he sniffled, but he did not let me go. I did not have the heart to ask him what happened. How did he end up in the auditorium? What devil had led him there and why? Some questions need not be asked or answered. There would be time for that later. Yes, later. At least it had stopped raining.

After a while, I laid him on his cot and pulled the covers around him tightly. I locked the door this time, so he could not walk away in his sleep and so no one could enter. I sat at my desk a good long while. I heard music downstairs and more than once heard feet running past my door, but nobody knocked. I heard no voices. Not like before.

But they were here. They were just waiting for us to step outside into the darkness. But I would not do such a thing. I would not.

I waited for the sun to come up. It was nearly four—it wouldn't be long now, but I felt so tired. So very tired. I decided to lie in my bed, not to sleep but only to rest and wait and watch over Ollie. I shoved my hand under the pillow to plump it up a bit when my fingers brushed against something strange.

I pulled out a long black feather. How had this gotten here? It wasn't here before. It couldn't have been. But it was here now.

I glanced down at Ollie, who was sound asleep now. A brief beam of moonlight passed his face; the light was quickly spirited away by yet another cloud. But during those few seconds I could swear by all the saints above that I saw a smile on the boy's face.

I flung the feather on the floor and stared at Ollie. I was unable to look away now. I stared until the sun rose and the sounds downstairs faded.

And when all was quiet, I fell asleep.

Chapter Eight—Jocelyn

I hung around the auditorium for an hour, but the boy's face never reappeared. I prayed that the camera had captured something. "Please don't tear up my equipment while I'm gone," I said to whoever might be listening. Geesh, how cold was it now? My phone app said 52 degrees Fahrenheit, but I could see my breath.

Wait, that wasn't my breath. It was someone else's, and they were standing beside me. Someone much shorter and invisible. I didn't move but watched the tiny clouds of breath appear and disappear, and they were getting farther away. He was leaving the auditorium! Could this be the boy I saw?

"Hey, wait!" I said, but the tiny puffs of frosty air disappeared and reappeared, each time a little farther away. I ran out into the hall, but there was no trace of anyone or anything remotely like what I saw. He was leading me somewhere, but where?

You know where, Jocelyn Graves. Back to your room. He likes it in there.

I hurried up the stairs, but it was impossible to be quiet. I don't know why I bothered trying. The entity or entities that lived here already knew I was here. Maybe I was afraid to draw more attention to myself. I couldn't say. Then I heard my phone ring. But I turned the ringer off...that's not right. I raced down the hall and dug in my bag to find it. The phone was glowing, and the ringtone brought me some comfort. It was hard to be afraid when your favorite pop singer was singing about being "happy."

"Hello?" I said a little too desperately. What time was it anyway? I glanced at my watch. Was it seven o'clock already? Yeah, sure enough. I could see the sun coming over the forest at the back of the house. How was it I was losing track of time here? I wasn't usually this off-schedule.

"Hi, Miss Graves? This is Melissa with Happy Paws."

"Oh no, is it Sherman? Is he hurt?"

"He's not hurt, but he refuses to eat or drink anything. He doesn't act as if he feels well. I was wondering, is your dog on any kind of medication? Or does he have a condition that we need to be aware of? Maybe something you forgot to list on his paperwork?"

"Condition? Is Sherman okay?"

"Well, I'm not sure. That's why I'm calling. Some dogs don't do well in boarding situations, and Sherman is clearly one of those dogs." She didn't sound upset, but I could hear the genuine concern in her voice.

"He hasn't hurt anyone, has he? He's never been aggressive with me. Never."

She answered in a kind voice, "No, nothing like that. He's moping, not going out, not eating. He might be sick, and if he is, he shouldn't be around our other visitors. I hope you understand. You will have to come get him or send someone."

"Uh, okay. I'm not far away. I will come get him, Melissa. Thanks for the call."

I could hear the sympathy in her voice. "I hate to cut Sherman's stay short since he's such a sweet boy, but we have to be safe."

"All right, I'll be there soon."

"Great, thanks. Sorry again to have to call you."

"No, it's fine. Tell my puppy I'm on the way."

I hung up the phone and paced the room briefly. Okay, change of plans. I'd never worked on a paranormal investigation with a dog before, but it didn't look like I had much of a choice. I only had to stay one more night...surely Sherman and I would be okay. Unless he really was sick. I guess I had to play it by ear. I hated to kill a few precious hours, but Sherman came first.

I grabbed my purse and keys. I'd go pick up Sherman, and then the order of business would be to find food and a public restroom, review some of the evidence and continue the investigation. This would be my last night here at the Leaf Academy. Last night, last chance to see something truly paranormal...although I couldn't imagine how I could top what I had already seen.

Strange, I don't remember laying that feather on my purse. Boy, this bird couldn't keep his feathers, could he? Although I didn't want to, I picked up the feather and set the thing in the windowsill. I'd check it out further when I got back. As I headed out of the room, I stepped into the hall and again caught a glimpse of a pair of legs.

What the heck, man?

I ran to the far end of the corridor and distinctly heard the sound of keys jingling. *Damn it! Nobody is supposed to be here but me!* I opened the door, a door I missed earlier, and ran up a narrow set of metal stairs that led to the roof. Without thinking about the holes I saw earlier, I ran a few feet and then paused.

Yes, there was someone up here, a guy with dark hair, and he was smoking a cigarette. What should I do? Run back down the stairs? Hunker down and hide?

"Hey," he said as he flicked the butt off the side of the building. The sun was up now and cast a golden light on his somewhat handsome face. He looked like a biking enthusiast, the Harley-Davidson kind—from the 1950s. He had on blue jeans with rolled cuffs, a black leather jacket and a white t-shirt. Well, it was sort of white. My sixth sense was screaming at me, "Run, idiot!" but I was fascinated and terrified. Too terrified to do anything like run.

*Weapons, weapons. What kind of weapons do I have? None.
None at all. Just keep your cool, Jocelyn, and stay away from
the edge of the building.*

He walked a little closer to me as he shook another cigarette
out of the pack that he pulled from his jacket pocket. He
offered me one, but I shook my head emphatically.

"No, thanks."

"Not a smoker, huh? Probably smart. Smarter than me."

"I don't think you're supposed to be here, mister. This is
private property."

He grinned and showed brown stained teeth. Gross. "And yet,
here you are, little lady. Here we both are. Probably for very
much the same reasons."

Oh, he must be a paranormal investigator. I breathed a sigh of
relief but didn't let my guard down yet. Not completely.

"You come here often?" I asked stupidly. He laughed, and I
shook my head at my poorly chosen question. "I mean, have
you been here before?"

"Many times." He lit his smoke, and the smell of tobacco
wafted in my direction. "Many times."

"I see." I shifted my position but didn't try to get any closer.
He really needed to go. I couldn't do a proper investigation
with this guy wandering around the building. I was just trying
to figure out how to ask him to get lost, in a polite way, when
he asked me the strangest question.

"Are you human?"

"What?" I clutched my purse tighter as the coldest sensation I
ever experienced crept from my head clear down to my feet. I
was completely encased in cold clamminess. I didn't think it
was a funny question, but for some reason I laughed. "Yeah, I
am human."

He sat down on a broken chair and appeared to be somewhat relieved at my answer. "Thank God. I hate it when they aren't human."

I didn't know what to say to that, so I didn't say anything for a while. But time was not on my side. Sherman was waiting for me, and the clock was ticking on my investigation.

"What if I wasn't?"

His eyes bored into me, and he stood back up. He wasn't menacing exactly, but he didn't look like a happy camper. *Damn it, Jocelyn. You and your big mouth.* "Why do you ask?"

"I just think it's odd, you wondering if I'm human. What if I wasn't? What would you have done about it?"

"I would have to kill you, of course. Kill you and peel your skin off."

With a deep, guttural scream erupting from my lips, I let fear fuel me as I jetted back down the narrow stairs and then the two flights of stairs inside the building. I raced out the front door, fumbling briefly for the key, and then somehow made it to my car.

"Holy crap!" I repeated over and over as I put the key in the ignition and slung the car in reverse. I didn't stop until I got to the end of the driveway and then patted my hands on the steering wheel to steady myself.

What the hell was that? That wasn't a person. No way was that a person. That was something else entirely. No living person had ever scared me so much in my life.

And that was saying something.

Chapter Nine—Jocelyn

By the time I made it back to Happy Paws, I wasn't swearing or gasping for air. Whoever that guy was, his intention was clear—he wanted to scare the hell out of me. Mission accomplished, dude, but I wasn't going to sit around crying. I put in a phone call to the realtor and waited to hear something back from her. Somebody besides me needed to know some weird biker dude threatened to kill me and peel my skin off. I shivered again at the memory of his cigarette glowing and his eyes narrowing evilly. There hadn't been a shadow of a smile on his face. And that was nothing to joke about, anyway.

"I'm here for Sherman. I'm his..."

"Right, you're his Mom. I'll go get him. Sorry it didn't work out." The girl disappeared into the back and returned with my dog and his overnight bag. He immediately began wagging his tail and practically dragged her to me. "Wow! This is the happiest he's been since he got here. Sorry again. If you have to leave again, maybe next time we can try those treats, the kind that help dogs relax. That helps with some of our visitors."

I didn't like that idea at all. I never took meds and sure wouldn't pass them off to my dog. I smiled politely and signed Sherman out. We headed back to the car, ran a few errands and poked around until my phone rang.

"Hey, Adrian, thanks for calling me back so soon."

"No problem. How can I help you?"

I glanced at Sherman in the rearview mirror. He was sitting patiently in the backseat, just happy to be hanging out with his "Mom." He didn't look sick at all to me. Wow, I was a mom. How hilarious was that? And with that realization, all the weirdness I experienced earlier seemed like a dream. "I just want to verify that no one else has been given permission to be at the Leaf Academy. Not at the same time as me, I mean."

"There is only one key, and you have it. Is everything okay? Should I be concerned?"

"No, but I did see someone in there. A man was on the roof, and I think he was inside a few times."

Adrian paused and asked, "What did he look like? Did you call the police?"

"No, I didn't because, well, that would kind of defeat the purpose. I don't want to get the police involved unless I have to. I've seen vagrants in deserted buildings before, but this guy was a bit odd. I just thought someone should know about him." I tried to laugh it off. I felt stupid now calling Adrian over a weirdo. But she didn't seem surprised at all.

She sighed and said, "I should have told you this before, but Mr. Holloway didn't want to influence your investigation. There have been reports over the years, many reports, as you well know, beyond just the rumors about some October curse."

"You mean the October People. I know what they say about the property. I mean, that's kind of why I am there. And I read all about the murders, the one in the thirties and then the two others."

Adrian cleared her throat. "Um, there are more than those. Not necessarily murders but two suicides and several disappearances."

"Oh," I said as I sipped water from my bottle.

"Tell me, Jocelyn, what did this vagrant look like? Did he have black hair? Was he wearing a motorcycle jacket?"

I blinked at hearing her question. "Um, a motorcycle jacket. How did you know? You've had dealings with this guy before? I mean, is he dangerous?"

"He's dead. That's Mr. Holloway's brother. He killed himself there, threw himself off that roof in 1957. That's why Mr. Holloway closed the place. Gary was his older brother; it appears Gary never left. At least that's what Mr. Holloway believes."

"I didn't know. I'm sorry."

"I guess that means you're done with the investigation. Should I come by and get the key? Are you leaving now?" Adrian sounded a bit disappointed but not surprised. I was starting to get the feeling I wasn't the first paranormal investigator to spend time there. What were they hoping for? I was no exorcist, not by a long shot.

"I'm not leaving, Adrian. I just wanted to know about this guy. You know, as far as we know, he could be someone trying to pull a prank."

She blew into the phone as if she didn't believe me. "Who would go to the trouble of doing all that? I mean, just to scare someone? And from 1957 on to today? Even Mr. Holloway doesn't go in there. I think you were kind of his last hope. He wants to sell the place, get rid of the whole shebang, but how can he do that if it's infested with...bad memories? You have to know that's what he's been told. That the Leaf Academy is paranormally and permanently infested with activity. And it's getting worse."

"I think it's time you leveled with me, Adrian. I take it you didn't give me access because you liked my photos or my writing sample. What am I really doing there?"

She paused, and I heard the sound of a squeaking door on the phone. "We know about the ghosts, Jocelyn. It's not that we don't believe it, but we want it on record. And from someone credible, someone who would do their due diligence. I'll be honest, we're not sure what the next step would be, but you come highly recommended to us. Highly. If you want to call it off, we'd understand. I would understand; Mr. Holloway would understand. You couldn't pay me to walk in there, and

I'm trying to sell the place for him. I think he just wants some peace. And I want to help him find it."

I chewed the inside of my lip. "What do you know about a little boy? Have any children died at the Leaf Academy? Maybe a former student?"

Adrian hesitated again. "Not that I know of, but you are not the first person to mention a ghost boy. Sightings have been going on for decades. The first murder victim, Mr. McCandlish—"

Suddenly my phone went dead and Sherman began to whine from the backseat. I pounded on the phone's keyboard, but nothing was happening. I plugged it into the charger, but not even that could breathe life into it.

I turned around in my seat to pet my dog. "Okay, boy. If I'm going to be your Mom and you're going to be my dog—I mean, kid—then you should know this is what life is like with me. I hunt ghosts. In fact, I'm going back now to find one. Possibly a very mean one. Are you in?"

Sherman licked my hand, which I took to mean yes. Not all the dots were connected, but my mission was much clearer than it had been: find out who this "boy" was and what he wanted. And show that creepy rooftop entity that I wasn't one to be pushed around.

I was feeling big and bad until I reached the driveway of the Leaf Academy. For some reason, it looked even weedier, if that was a word. I could see less of the house than before...were the trees trying to block my way?

Okay, October People. Ready or not, here we come.

Chapter Ten—Hugh

I woke up to a tickling sensation on my face. It was Ollie, rubbing that horrible black feather across my forehead. I swatted it away, relieved to see that the sun was still up and the door remained shut.

"Wake up. We have to go now. You promised."

I snatched the feather from his hand a bit more ferociously than I intended. He stepped back and out of my reach. Did the boy think I would hit him?

"Where did you get this feather, Ollie? Did you bring it up from the yard? Did you sneak out while I was sleeping?"

"No, I did not. It was on your pillow."

I swung my feet over the side of the bed. My head felt like I'd been at the tavern all night, an activity I had not participated in for at least ten years but certainly welcomed now. "The things you say, Ollie. We will go, but you and I must talk first." I rubbed my scruffy face with my hand. My stomach rumbled and my mouth was dry, but first things first. "Why were you in the auditorium last night?"

Ollie backed away another step. I noticed that he had dressed already. Suddenly I was overwhelmed with sickness. I could not shake the nausea that threatened to cripple me. After I closed my eyes a minute, I pressed Ollie for information. "Tell me about the auditorium last night. Who were those people? Why did you go there?"

Ollie's dark eyes welled up with tears. "What people? I heard music. I thought someone was here."

The boy was lying to me. He saw those people—the woman in the red dress, the one who looked like Emma, and the strange lady with the braids who looked so much like Mrs. Smith. The menacing shadow that hovered over the place. "If you heard music, you should have told me about it and not gone adventuring by yourself. It's not safe, Ollie." I dressed quickly as I thought about what to do next. If we set off by foot, we would walk about half a day before we came to the first residence. Surely they would help us. Too bad I had no car and no way to call for one...unless I broke into the headmaster's office, which I had every right to do. I was after all the de facto headmaster now, as I was here at the Leaf Academy caring for a student while Mr. Mitchell was on his way to Georgia for his extended vacation. Yes! There was certainly a phone in his office!

"You still haven't explained yourself. Why were you in the auditorium? Why?" I wanted to vomit, but my mouth felt dry, so very dry.

"I heard singing. I thought it was my mother. She likes to sing." He ducked his head and stared at his hands, a gesture that accompanied many a tall tale around the academy. But always from other children, never Ollie. So why was he lying now?

"Your parents are not coming, are they? Tell me the truth. Where are your parents?" He refused to speak to me. I struggled to my feet and put on my clothes. I was sliding my suspenders up over my shoulders when I caught a glimpse of the boy's cot. It was littered with pictures. I recognized the paper, the very expensive paper like the kind the headmaster liked to use. But there was no time to give lectures on thievery and asking permission. I could not take my eyes off the images; they were compelling in a ghastly way. I squatted down and picked them up, examining them one by one. There was a small boy standing on the auditorium stage. A dark figure behind him, with large, slanted eyes. And this was clearly the woman with the braids—and that strange man! Yes! Ollie had seen them too!

But the last picture, the one I now held in my trembling hands, disturbed me the most. Clearly, it was me. I recognized the beard; I usually kept it trimmed neat, but in this illustration I was unkempt. My suspenders were tangled around my arms, and I was dead. I had to be dead; I was lying in the center of the stage with a knife protruding from my chest.

"Ollie?" I asked, unable to formulate a question beyond that.

He put his hand on my shoulder. "We have to go now."

"Why would you draw this? This is a nasty thing to do, Ollie." And then my mind swirled with fear-fueled questions. "Did you kill that bird, lad? Tell me. Tell me the truth. You killed it, didn't you? I believed you were innocent—how could you do such a thing?"

"I did not, Mr. McCandlish! Please, sir. We have to go. They will be coming back soon, and they will be so angry." Ollie's voice shook, but I could not move from the spot. Nor could I stop staring at the illustration of my death.

"Why did you draw this? Don't lie to me, lad! You saw them; I can see by your own expression that you saw them just as I did!"

He took another step away from me, and this time his back was to the door. He fumbled with the button of his coat as he began to cry. "I drew them to show you what will happen if we stay! They're whispering to me, Mr. McCandlish! Whispering so loudly! Make them stop!"

I held the picture up and waved it at him. "What does this mean?"

"Please, we have to go."

And right before my eyes, two black, snakelike hands reached through the closed door and snatched the boy away. One hand was clamped around his mouth so he could not scream, and his eyes were wide with terror. Loud footsteps banged down the hallway, and then there was nothing.

Nothing except the sound of my own shouting.

After some time, I heaved myself off the floor, slid on my shoes and reached for the doorknob. There was nothing for it. I had to search for Ollie. Something had grabbed him, stolen him and spirited him away. But where had they taken him? This must be the work of those horrible creatures—the October People! I glanced down at the foreboding picture.

Did I really have to wonder? I knew where I would find him. I knew where I had to go. If I wanted to save Ollie, that is. Like a coward I paced the floor and considered, if only briefly, how quickly I could run from the place. How long would it take me to put a hundred miles between myself and this repulsive school? But how could I? Ollie trusted me like nobody ever had. If I had ever had a son, he would have been a boy like Ollie. Quiet, thoughtful. And now the lad was caught in this hideous tangle of events the same as me, yet I did not believe him to be the cause of any of it. What should I do?

I heard music. The tinkling of a piano, the sound of a woman's voice, a clear and elegant soprano. Without bothering to lock the door, I trudged into the hallway. I was never coming back, was I? There wasn't a chance I would be able to escape this place. Not with evil creatures lurking in the hallways, snatching children through doors, chasing us, their phantom footsteps always behind us.

As I opened the door and walked into the hall, I wondered how all this had come about. What had I done to deserve this? Was it some cosmic collusion that caused me to be here with Ollie? Was this always to be my fate? My only wish had been to see the star alignment, to enjoy the quiet beauty of the countryside. But that was before a helpless boy needed me.

I took another step and then another. I ignored the many shadowy faces that peered at me from inside the now open doors. And to think, Nanna always told us that spooks only appeared after dark, that they were creatures of the night. But here it was afternoon and they were everywhere. I got the sensation that somehow, the walls were writhing with them. Yes, the spooks were built into the place. They were ground into the bricks, and when the time was right, they sprang to life.

Nanna had been wrong. Golden sunshine filtered through the big window over the landing. I was not surprised to see people huddled together in the chairs; they were whispering to one another, and I was the subject of their conversation. They lined the stairs and waited for me on the lower level. But these weren't living people.

They were dead. And I was about to join them.

Chapter Eleven—Jocelyn

"We're in here, boy. This is where we'll sleep tonight. Or at least where you'll sleep." He made a funny groaning sound, and I laughed at hearing it. Sometimes I felt as if the dog knew what I was saying; more likely, he just understood the tone of my voice. I always knew dogs were smart, but I had no idea they were so expressive until I adopted Sherman.

After my encounter with the dead Gary Holloway, I had to admit that I was happy not to return to the Leaf Academy alone. I still wasn't sure what Adrian and Mr. Holloway expected me to accomplish, but here I was. Yeah, this was why I came, but those kinds of freaky encounters still shook me.

And he threatened to peel my skin off!

No matter how experienced you were, hearing something like that would rock a person. But no way was I skipping out on the Leaf Academy investigation. What I was going to do was take the next few hours to review the research material I brought with me and flip through the journal I found. I looked out the window for a few minutes, just in case Mr. Weirdo showed up again. Could that really have been Gary Holloway? If I had a picture to look at, I was sure I could identify him. I would never forget the clover-shaped mole on his cheek, the definite cowlick at his right temple. If he was really an apparition, he must be a strong one to project himself into our world with such detail.

It was still early in the day, only noon, but my time was running out. I should have asked for one more day; I was pretty sure Adrian would have given me the extra time. No, I better stick with the plan. I opened my soda and sniffed the air. I thought I caught a whiff of stale cigarette smoke, but then it was gone as quickly as I detected it. Sherman didn't move an inch; in fact, he decided my sleeping bag was the perfect place to lie down.

"I thought you were sick. I'm glad you're not, but what are you going to do when I have to really go out of town?" I shook my head at him as I opened the journal. With the combination of daylight and my LED light, I could finally read the name written neatly inside.

This journal belongs to Moriah Mitchell.

The first twenty pages or so were pretty mundane, the usual stuff one might read in a headmaster's journal. Kids behaving, kids misbehaving. Oh, this looked interesting.

I spoke with Mr. McCandlish today. He has seen the boy; the cycle continues. What was thought banished has returned. I fear that the worst will happen for him, but who can prevent it? I cannot. That I know as well as any here. There is no hope for it.

The pages felt dirty beneath my fingers, but I turned them hastily.

McCandlish calls the boy Ollie, and the ghost becomes more visible by the hour. It is God's blessing that many are gone now. McCandlish is fully entwined in the Spider's trap, for it has made itself known to the sad teacher in ways I could not have imagined. I depart this place today, and that is none too soon. I have warned McCandlish that he must not stay here, that he must leave. He will not listen. He will be gone when I return, I am sure of it. May God have mercy on us all!

A sketch of black feathers had been carefully drawn at the bottom of the page. It was actually very fine work from an artistic standpoint, but seeing the familiar image in this old journal gave me the creeps. How was it that I, a visitor to the Leaf Academy more than eighty years later, would see the same feather? But it couldn't be the same. There were probably lots of crows in this area and had been for quite some time. Lots and lots.

The journal stopped abruptly at the end of September 1937, but I kept flipping through the pages. Many pages had been torn out of the book; a few stubs were left, but clearly someone had very sloppily removed some of them. I skimmed the book again. Nope, those pages were gone.

"Come on, Sherman. Let's go down the hall for a second."

I returned to the room where I'd found the box that held the journal and sifted through it hoping to find more of the same. Most of the items were uninteresting, just as I first believed, but then I found an old red paper folder. Inside were the missing pages. These were drawings, a child's drawings by the look of them.

And they were terrible to look at.

A small boy sitting in a chair in the auditorium, a gruesome smile on his face. A dead man lying on the stage with a knife in his chest. A woman floating above him, her mouth open as if she were screaming or singing or saying something. And there were so many eyes, all around the boy and the stage. I took pictures of the horrible images because that was all I could think to do. A shudder shot through me as I slid the papers around and my eyes fell on the last sheet of paper.

This was me.

It had to be me. I was sitting next to the boy, and beside me was the man in the black jacket, the one I believed to be Gary Holloway. This was no Rembrandt painting, but the artist had enough skill for me to identify myself easily enough. My dreadlocks were hanging over my shoulders, a camera dangled from my neck—and my neck! Why was it hanging at such an odd angle?

Why did my neck look like that? Was it broken?

"No!" I said as I let the picture flutter to the ground. I heard the sound of an old-fashioned lighter clicking in the hallway. Sherman heard it too. He got quiet, but his eyes were focused on the open door. He wasn't sitting beside me now, as was his custom whenever I got still. No, the furry canine was poised to pounce, run or snap at the intruder. A shadow passed the door. Sherman began to bark, but like a good dog he didn't abandon me.

Okay, Jocelyn Graves! Get it together! You've got a job to do. Remember?

"Hey!" I yelled as I stepped out into the hallway. I didn't have my camera, but I had my phone. I fumbled with the screen and tapped the camera app. It opened, and I took a panoramic burst of photos. "Who is out here?" No one answered, and my voice echoed back to me. "Are you Moriah Mitchell? Mr. McCandlish? Ollie? Is that you?" Sherman barked once as a small shadow swept across the hall. And then all was still. I petted the dog on his head.

"Well, boy, if we're going to chase shadows, we better do it right. Come on," I said as I hurried back to my room to gather my audio recorder and anything else I could manage to carry. So much for research. The spirits of the Leaf Academy were stirring now, and I was ready to capture the evidence of their existence. *Non timebo mala.* I will fear no evil. I was beginning to understand why they had that engraved over the door. Had the builders of the Leaf Academy always known this place was a spiritual hot spot?

That's when I noticed the picture on my cot, but I'd just dropped it in the other room. I couldn't help but pick it up. Only there were figures missing from the sketch—the man in the leather jacket wasn't sitting beside me now. He was gone, and so was the boy.

I was sitting alone in the auditorium. With my neck twisted at an awkward angle.

What was this supposed to be? Some sort of freaky threat? This had to be a joke, an extremely jacked-up joke. But who would go to the trouble of pulling such a horrible gag on me? Pete Broadus wasn't this smart. And Midas? Never in a million years. Nobody knew where I was except Adrian Shanahan and Mr. Holloway.

Sherman began to growl at the doorway. "I know, I hear it too." I clicked on the digital recorder in hopes of recording the sounds of the footsteps. They weren't heavy ones but small ones, as if a petite lady or a child were pacing up and down the hallway.

"I can hear you out there. Why don't you come in? Don't be afraid. Is that you, Ollie?"

Sherman didn't move, and neither of us could look away as the doorknob began to slowly twist.

Chapter Twelve—Jocelyn

After a few seconds, my investigator's brain kicked in and I stepped back, reached for my camera and hit the video button. Whatever was on the other side of that door seemed to know what I intended. The twisting doorknob ceased, but that was just the calm before the storm.

Tap, tap, tap.

Loud, persistent tapping—no, make that banging—echoed from the wall next to me. I got the feeling that "it" wanted us out of the room. The first bang struck the wall on the left, that was the outer wall, and then it hit the one on the right. And then there was banging on the wall near the windows. I could hear the old windows shaking in the panes, and I prayed that they wouldn't break and shatter all over us. Poor Sherman began barking; he was clearly terrified, but I couldn't offer him any comfort. My dog never barked, never. I didn't blame him one bit. I was shaking in my hiking boots. The tapping became banging, horrible, life-threatening banging that offended not only my ears but also my nervous system. I never wanted to pee so bad in my life. I grabbed Sherman's collar to keep him from launching himself at the wall beside us when finally, unable to stand it anymore, I screamed, "Stop!"

To my surprise, it did. Sherman stopped barking too; he was panting now. I felt the same way, as if I couldn't quite catch my breath. I patted him on the head as I stared at the doorknob. It was all too quiet now.

And then the music started. Swelling orchestra music, like the kind you would hear if you were seated in the auditorium. I shivered as I thought about the horrible drawing with me sitting beside the ghost boy. Was that what this was about? Was the ghost boy trying to lead me to the auditorium? That's where they had found the very dead body of Hugh McCandlish in the fall of 1937. He'd been dead for many weeks, or at least that was what was printed in the newspaper at the time. For the life of me, I hadn't been able to locate a coroner's report or anything like it with Hugh McCandlish's name on it. Was this the Ollie spirit Mr. Mitchell referred to in his journal?

The music got louder. What was that tune? It seemed like I should know it from my college theater days. I walked to the window and with some elbow grease managed to open it a crack. I could hear people applauding, and now a woman was singing. Even though I could barely hear her, I knew this song!

Goodnight, my love, the tired old moon is descending
Goodnight, my love, my moment with you now is ending
It was so heavenly, holding you close to me
It will be heavenly to hold you again in a dream

Immediately I began recording, but from this distance it wasn't going to be hi-def material. I had to get closer. I looked down at Sherman.

"Are you thinking what I'm thinking?" I asked him as I put the device back in my pocket and dug through his overnight bag for his leash. Snapping it on him, I patted his head and gave him a pep talk. He tugged back but didn't fight me too much as the music played on. *It could be an old record player I'm hearing.* The music did sound kind of scratchy, otherworldly.

The stars above have promised to meet us tomorrow
Till then, my love, how dreary the new day will seem
So for the present, dear, we'll have to part
Sleep tight, my love, goodnight, my love

"Okay, boy. This is for all the money. We've got to get close enough to record the sound; that means you can't run off and leave me. And be quiet, okay?" He whined and pushed his cold nose against my hand. "You can do this, Sherman Graves. You're a ghost hunter just like your Mom."

Together we faced the door, and I pressed my ear against it to make sure I couldn't hear anything in the hall. Obviously, there was a ton of activity in the building tonight, but the last thing I wanted to do was walk into Gary Holloway. *Hey, that's kind of trippy. Why is it dark in here?* It wasn't anywhere near sunset. Why did it feel like whatever intelligence was here—and I believed there *was* an intelligence operating here—wanted to keep this place in the dark?

Because you can't see what's hiding in the dark, and it doesn't want you to see it. Not yet.

As I put my hand on the doorknob, the music stopped. Even the sound of applause waned, but there was no turning back now. Clutching Sherman's leash tight, I swung the door open and immediately stepped out into the hallway.

"Hello?" I clicked on the recorder again. I had Sherman in one hand, the recorder in the other and a camera around my neck. I sure hoped I didn't have to take off running again. I wasn't graceful enough to navigate all three and my feet successfully.

I gasped at the sight of the boy standing near the upstairs landing. He had on dark clothing, but I could see quite a bit of detail like the dirty hems of his sleeves and pant legs. Yes, he was very dirty, as if he'd just dug his way out of his own grave. I couldn't see his hands or fingernails from here, but I was pretty sure that if I could I would see that they were filthy. His hair hung in his eyes, obscuring them from view, but I knew he was watching me.

Sherman growled; it was a low, menacing growl. My mouth went dry as I stared into the growing darkness at the face of the boy...or what pretended to be a boy. He didn't move except his head, which rolled slightly as if it weren't quite connected to his neck properly. Or was he reminding me of the picture?

"Ollie? Do you plan to kill me?" I asked without thinking. Why would I ask such a question?

He immediately turned away from me and headed to the top of the staircase without answering my question or offering any further acknowledgement. And there wasn't a sound in the place. No wind, no music, no skittering of rodents across the floor. I gripped the leash and the recorder and walked slowly toward the staircase.

This is why you're here, Jocelyn. Get the evidence. Stay focused. Don't hype yourself up.

Somewhere below me a door slammed, but that was the extent of the noise. Yes, it was quiet in here, too quiet. Sherman didn't make a sound except for his toenails on the grungy floor.

"Down the stairs now. We've got this, boy," I whispered as quietly as I could, an impossible task with the current echo level. With an unsure whimper, Sherman descended with me, and now I had mixed emotions. What was I doing bringing this poor dog here? The Leaf Academy was no place for a pet. Yep, I was a horrible parent. Maybe I should go. I was sure Adrian would understand if I explained the situation to her.

While I reasoned with my cowardly self, I caught a glimpse of something just below us. It was a pile of feathers, black feathers! They were in a triangular formation, deliberately placed where I could find them. As Sherman and I paused on the step, I could hear the song playing. That definitely had a record player feel to it.

Remember that you're mine, sweetheart
Goodnight, my love, your mommy is kneeling beside you
Goodnight, my love, to dreamland the sandman will guide you
Come now, you sleepyhead, close your eyes and go to bed
My precious sleepyhead, you mustn't play peek-a-boo

"I don't know what games you're playing, Ollie, but I'm not yours. And the only person who can call me Mommy is this dog. What do you want? Why are you hanging around here at the Leaf Academy?" I couldn't see him anymore, but I felt a presence—an angry, hateful presence—very near me.

Suddenly I was being shoved to the ground. A pair of small hands hit me in the lower back. Sherman scrambled away from me, and I lost my grip on his leash. I yelled for him as he ran toward the auditorium barking like a madman.

"Sherman!" I shouted as I got up as quickly as I could. I knew without looking that I'd broken my camera. I took it off my neck and set it on the ground while I dusted myself off. And he was there again.

The boy Hugh McCandlish called Ollie. He was a ghost boy, wasn't he? He smiled as if he heard my thoughts, as if he liked my wondering. He vanished as Sherman's desperate barking echoed through the bottom floor.

And then the furry white animal came yelping back to me. "Oh, thank God! What did I tell you, boy? Stay close to me! Are you okay?" I hugged him up as the door at the end of the hall slammed again. I rubbed the debris off my dog and waved at a persistent gnat that buzzed in my ear.

Glancing down both sides of the hall, I couldn't see much. Meager light filtered through a few slits in the boards but beyond that nothing. How in God's name was it this dark in here? I dug out my flashlight and waved it around. With each pass of the beam I saw shadows move, like they were living things eager to remain hidden.

Yeah, you know why, Jocelyn Graves. Non timebo mala.

I dug out my digital recorder. Sure, that Ollie-boy wanted me in that auditorium, but there was something here, an insistent presence I could not ignore. I wasn't running into that auditorium half-cocked. I was doing this investigation my way. If I let fear get the best of me, I would be giving all my power over to Ollie or that weirdo Gary Holloway. Strange that I would have such a thought. Was I sensing Gary near? I wasn't one to have sensitivities like that, not above the normal. And again that gnat buzzed in my ear. Or was that a mosquito? Either way, it was doing its level best to find a home in my ear. I swatted furiously as I kept Sherman close.

"Who is here with me? I know I am not alone. Tell me your name."

Sherman scratched himself as he panted; his full attention was on the end of the hall. All the sounds had stopped except for the horrible bug that was testing my fortitude. I swatted at it again and took a few steps toward the auditorium. Maybe I should go in there now. No sense in waiting until midnight. It was going to get lively tonight, I could tell. I stepped closer, but Sherman wasn't happy about that. I paused to listen.

No sound at all in there. Just the occasional flapping of wings.

Oh, God! What if it was full of crows? I hadn't seen any earlier, but that was before Ollie showed up. Collect the evidence, Jocelyn. Keep a level head.

I scanned back the audio on my digital recorder but didn't hear anything. May as well try again. "I know you're here. Can you tell me your name? Are you related to the boy, the one they call Ollie?" I waited a few seconds before turning it off.

The frantic buzzing stopped as I scanned the file back. I could hear myself, but there was someone else there too! Someone *was* communicating with me. I turned the volume up and scanned it back again. I didn't need audio software to pick that out.

Not a boy.

"Hugh? Hugh McCandlish? Is it you I am speaking to?" I squatted down to pet Sherman as I spun around on the balls of my feet to keep watch over my shoulder. I had the sensation that someone intended to get the drop on me, and I'd already been pushed down that last step. At least it wasn't the top step, but I didn't want to be surprised again. I scanned back the recording, but there was nothing else to hear. Nothing except Sherman's panting and my fear-filled voice.

A lighter clicked behind me, and I sprang to my feet. *Gary Holloway?* Cigarette smoke drifted in my direction, but Gary himself did not appear. I yelled as Sherman wrapped his leash around me. The cigarette smoke hovered in the air like a living thing, fluttered toward me and then dissipated into thin air.

"Gary Holloway? Is that you?"

But it wasn't Gary Holloway that manifested in the hallway. It was someone else, a tall man with a wild red beard and wide, terror-filled eyes. Before I could call out or say another word, he was walking toward me. And then through me! Cold like I'd never felt before covered me—no, it filled me. I felt a bit wobbly, kind of sick as I watched in horror as the tall, spindly man walked down the dark corridor. Although he never acknowledged me or spoke a word, I knew his name.

I was looking at the ghost of Hugh McCandlish!

And there was light coming from the auditorium.

And I was going in.

Chapter Thirteen—Hugh

My feet felt like two blocks of wood. They were so heavy that it took great force to lift them, but I continued on. It was as if my body did not want to go, but my heart would not allow me to turn back. Ollie was a prisoner of whatever darkness called the Leaf Academy home. It was an old darkness, to be sure, one I should have believed in, but it was too late now. Too late to go back and change the direction of my life, to change my plans. The faces around me had all but vanished, yet I heard a great ocean of whispering. With my hands covering my ears, I sobbed like a child as I stepped into the auditorium.

And there was Ollie, standing in the center of the stage, a helpless expression on his face. My feet felt free now, so I ran to the stage ignoring the slithering shadows around me. I hadn't forgotten that snakelike creature, the one with the scaly arms that had grabbed him so cruelly. "Ollie! Come here!"

And then I saw it—the creature! It was tall, taller than me. It was all black with scaly skin, like a dragon's skin, and its yellow eyes were focused on me. I saw Ollie's eyes widen as if he knew it was right behind him but he did not dare look. "Help me," I heard him whisper, but how could that be? His mouth didn't move. And his eyes…they were so dark. Ollie? Was this really Ollie LeFlore or something pretending to be him?

"McCandlish! Please, stop!"

"Headmaster? Thank God! Help me!" I thought I was speaking coherently, but my words came out as so much babbling. I turned back to reach for the boy, and he was gone. The black creature with the scaly skin crawled toward me; it was at the very edge of the stage. It could pounce on me at any moment. No! Those weren't just scales but also feathers! What in the name of God was this thing?

The headmaster raced toward me and gripped me by the shoulders. "What have you done? Have you accepted a gift from it? A feather, perhaps, or a stone? Tell me, Hugh."

I wanted very much to tell him that yes, I had found a feather and that he should help Ollie, but I couldn't make the words come out. Invisible hands were around my throat, choking me.

And then before my eyes the headmaster flew across the room and landed on the stage. The creature had vanished, but Ollie was there. And in his hands was a black feather. He walked to the headmaster, who was crying out in pain, and held it out to him. Clearly Ollie wanted him to take the feather, but the headmaster turned his back to him. His arm must have been broken for it was at a strange angle. The headmaster was crying—no, he was praying. It was in Latin. I knew that phrase. What was it? Oh yes, fear no evil. I will fear no evil. I closed my eyes and repeated the prayer.

But it was too late for me. I had accepted the feather. I had accepted his gift. I watched with great sadness as the headmaster slid off the stage and made his way out of the auditorium. He would not die, although he was badly hurt.

But me? I would certainly die. Unless I gave him what he wanted. He was leaning down over me now. His face changed from Ollie to the black creature. They were one and the same. I understood it now. The hands no longer choked me, but they held me down. What a horrible sight! And then it was the boy again with that familiar sad look on his face.

You promised. You said we would leave here. Take me. Let us go and you will live.

With all my might I wanted to live, to have a life and a family and a son. A good son. But I would have none of those things. I would never be the one to let this thing loose upon the world. Never.

I didn't have to say a word. It knew what I was thinking. With a rage-filled scream, it lighted on me and then I was no more.

Chapter Fourteen—Jocelyn

I pushed the door open easily enough. And unlike the first time I entered the room, it didn't make a sound. *That's weird,* I thought as I stepped inside the massive room. Sherman wasn't eager to join me, but I held the door open and he followed me inside. The auditorium wasn't any more appealing than it was before. There were rows of chairs upended, plaster from the ceiling and walls had fallen on the floor, and the holes in the exterior wall gave me a great view of the overgrown backyard. Yeah, this place was certainly atmospheric. I shook away thoughts of zombies crawling through the breaches.

Sherman barked and paced the aisle; his black nose was to the ground and waving back and forth as if he'd caught a whiff of something. "Sherman, stay close," I whispered as I squatted down to pet him. Immediately my eyes fell on the feather in front of me. This specimen was much shinier and larger than the other ones I'd found on the property. What kind of bird shed that thing? Not a crow. Couldn't be. Could a raven get that big? Maybe an owl? I'd never seen a black owl before. As I reached out to grab it, Sherman intercepted me, snapped up the feather and ran out of the auditorium. I was on my feet thinking to chase him when the door slammed between us. My dog began to bark frantically like he wanted me to know I was in trouble.

As if I didn't already know that. Yeah, I was in trouble. Big trouble. I turned out to face whoever it was that stood behind me.

I had heard no footsteps, yet I knew someone was there. Someone who didn't want me to leave. "Who's there?"

There was a boy, the one I'd captured on my camera earlier. "Ollie?" Fear crept into my bones as I asked the question. I wasn't one to run at the first sign of a spirit or a ghost, but this wasn't anything ordinary. Yeah, this wasn't your run-of-the-mill apparition. His dark eyes bored into mine. He hated me, that's what he wanted me to know. He hated me down to my bones. Why didn't I accept this present? He'd left it for me.

Where did that thought come from?

Sherman stopped barking, and I stepped back and away from the ghost. And as if there were truly a bird flying overhead, another feather floated down in front of me. It hovered in front of my face a few seconds before it fluttered to the ground. The boy stepped closer to me, his eyes not on me now but on the feather.

Take it. It's yours.

The boy's young voice filled my mind even though I did not see his mouth move. His hand was outstretched toward the feather. This was a gift from him, a gift of friendship. He wanted to be my friend, a special friend, but I had to accept his gift first. All his friends accepted gifts from him. I wouldn't be the first or the last, but I would be oh so special.

I couldn't think of anything I wanted less than to accept a gift from this entity. And then it dawned on me—this thing was offering me a gift because it wanted something in return. But what? This was beyond a residual imprint, and no way was this a run-of-the-mill intelligent haunt; I'd never met anything like this before. My investigator's mind raced through the catalog. What was I looking at? This ghost wanted me to enter a covenant with him.

Uh, no thanks. I took a step back. I shook my head no. The boy's face changed completely. Instead of a pale, doe-eyed boy with a shock of dark hair, I was looking at a horrible monster, a wraith with a skeletal face and a hand that reached for me.

Sherman barked furiously now, and I eased back, unsure of my footing. The floor felt weird, kind of spongy. I forgot all about my investigator's mindset and my digital recorder. I glanced down and could see that I was standing in a pile of feathers. *Oh, God! What is this?* I looked back up to see that Ollie wasn't alone now. There were others, including Gary Holloway and a dead lady in a red dress. I was backing away faster now. I didn't dare turn my back on the growing crowd of spirits. Some I couldn't see, but I could certainly feel them. What the hell?

Hell is right, I heard a voice say mockingly inside my head. Was that Gary Holloway?

I reached for the door, but it wouldn't open. I had to turn around and take my eyes off the spirits. I had to put my full attention on getting it to move. "Come on! Come on!" I muttered, trying to stop myself from screaming my head off. I glanced over my shoulder as I banged on the door. Sherman barked up a storm, and I threw my shoulder into the effort to get the door open. Ollie was so close to me that I could almost hear him breathing. How was that possible? Ghosts didn't breathe. With a final bang and a savage kick with my boot, the door opened and Sherman shot through the open door to me.

"No, Sherman!" I yelled at him, praying that he wasn't going to get in a fight with this...whatever it was. "We have to go!" Piano music filled the auditorium, but there was no piano, only a rubble pile of keys and wood where a piano once stood. The music was loud, too loud to be just from a piano. The notes made no sense; it was merely angry noise, frightening, terrifying. I scooped up Sherman and leaped over another feather. *I can't touch it! I can't even touch it!* Sherman barked continuously as I headed toward the front door.

"Oh, God!" I'd locked the door! The key! I reached around my neck and discovered it was gone. *No! Come on, give me a break!* What was I going to do now? There was nothing to do except face the music. I put Sherman down, and together we raced up the stairs. Maybe I took the necklace off up here? The horrible music still echoed from the auditorium, and now there were growls that accompanied it. Oh no! The boy stood at the top of the stairs.

I froze as Sherman whined beside me. The boy held out his hand and offered me a feather. "Take it. It's yours," he said with a sweet smile. I could hear him with my ears now.

"Too late, Ollie. I know what you really are," I said aloud.

"Do you?" he asked as the feather floated toward me.

I couldn't go up the stairs and get past him. I'd have to find another way out. Sherman was thinking ahead of me, apparently. I could hear his toenails clicking on the gritty floor below. I didn't hesitate either. I raced after him, praying that he could find a way out before this creature caught up with me. How many times could I refuse?

Sherman was running full speed down the corridor on the opposite side of the auditorium. There weren't any doors down here, were there? "Sherman!" I yelled, but the dog didn't wait for me.

Thanks a lot, boy.

I tripped once and landed face first on the ground but didn't break anything. My face felt dirty, and my eyes were having difficulty adjusting to the growing darkness. As I got up, I felt metal near my fingers. Oh, God! How did my key get down here? Yes! This was my leather necklace! I grabbed it as I hurried to my feet and tore down the corridor ignoring the feeling that things were following me, that they were piling out of the rooms ready to set upon me like wolves on a scared rabbit. *That's me, a scared rabbit!*

Sherman! You better wait for me, I thought with hot tears on my cheeks. I found him in a dirty room full of antique desks and chairs piled haphazardly atop one another. He hadn't been looking for a way out; he was looking for a place to hide!

"Come on, boy. It's okay. It's me." He whimpered and cowered under a desk. Why would he do that? I glanced over my shoulder as a shadow passed the doorway. Cautiously, I turned my head slightly, not absolutely sure that I wanted to see.

Please don't let this be Ollie.

It wasn't. I caught a quick glimpse of an unhappy face and knew it belonged to Hugh McCandlish! It must have been Hugh who had left the key where I could find it. But then he was gone. "We have to go, Sherman. We can't stay here another minute." I picked him up, and thankfully he didn't fight me.

With my dog in my arms, I ran back down the hall. I was terrified, of course, but I was also angry. Angry at myself that I had brought my dog to a horrible place like this. Angry that I hadn't listened to Midas but instead had come to the Leaf Academy like a high schooler hell-bent on mischief. I had put us both in a bad situation.

"It's okay, Sherman. It's going to be okay," I promised, hoping that I could make that be the truth. There was no sign of Ollie, no sign of the lady in red. Even the music had stopped. Whatever power Hugh had, he was using it. He must be, or else I wouldn't be leaving so freely. Sherman struggled now, but I refused to put him down. I warned him to stay still as I opened the front door and we scrambled out of the house.

It was raining now. I hadn't heard it raining inside, but it was coming down in buckets. Yet the sun was shining! What in the world? It hadn't been raining when I was in the auditorium. I would have seen it; I would have seen rain pouring through the holes in the walls and roof. This was no ordinary rainstorm.

Forget about it, Jocelyn Graves. Just forget about it. You can ponder the meaning of it all later.

I raced to the car, but not before plunging into a mudhole twice. I shoved the key in the ignition and raced down the driveway. I wasn't looking back. Not any time soon.

Chapter Fifteen—Jocelyn

"Hey, Jocelyn. I'm so happy to finally meet you in person. I'm Adrian. You'll have to pardon Mr. Holloway's absence. I'm afraid he's taken a turn for the worse."

"I had no idea he was sick. I am sorry to hear that. And thanks for sending your maintenance guy to help me retrieve all my things. I feel a bit like a chicken, but once I tell you everything, I think you'll understand." Adrian nodded politely. She had a round face, perfect makeup and lovely dark hair that she kept swept back from her face with a barrette. She was dressed professionally, whereas I looked like I just rolled out of bed in my torn jeans and bleached Ireland t-shirt. "And I really am sorry to hear about Mr. Holloway."

"He is such a nice man. Really active until he turned eighty; then it was just downhill from there. I know he hates that. He's always been such a force of nature, at least in our family."

"Oh," I said with surprise in my voice. I unzipped my laptop bag and pulled out my computer carefully. "I didn't know you two were related."

"He's my grandfather."

"I'm sorry I didn't put that together. Does that mean you'll be handling the Leaf Academy property someday? I know you said you didn't enjoy going there."

"Yes, I think so. My children and I are the only Holloways left, and I most certainly don't want to pass the property down to them if it's as bad as I suspect."

I turned on the laptop but paused before digging out the jump drive. This lady was very afraid of the spirits of the Leaf Academy. She had reason to be, I could not lie about that, but I couldn't leave her feeling helpless. I decided I would do my best to give her some hope and offer her something she could use to battle the forces that believed the deserted building was their home.

"I wish I could tell you how to put an end to the goings-on there. I really do. Unfortunately, that's not in my wheelhouse; however, I know someone who may be able to help you. His name is Midas Demopolis. He's a friend of mine and the leader of Gulf Coast Paranormal. I saw a lot at the Leaf Academy, but it will take a team to really dig into the place's activities. I'm going to consult with him, if you don't mind. I don't want to dump this information on you and leave you to deal with it on your own."

"Really? You would do that?" She dabbed at her eyes with a tissue. I sure didn't mean to make her cry.

"Of course I will. I think you should know that bringing peace to that property is going to be a process. It is not going to be a one-smudge-and-done job. You'll have to call on whatever faith you have if you want to rid the place of the current residents."

"So it is haunted? For sure? No doubt in your mind? My grandfather always believed that. He believed that the Leaf Academy killed his brother. Is that possible?"

"The Leaf Academy is haunted and in a deeply malevolent way. There's something old there, maybe even ancient." She was taken aback by my comment. *Rein it in, Jocelyn. Show the evidence.* "I found this journal while I was exploring the place. I'm surprised no one else spotted it." I dug the dusty book, along with the drawings I'd tucked in it, out of my backpack and slid it toward her.

She flipped it open as she slid on her glasses. "What's all this?"

"I found this journal in one of the rooms on the second floor. It belonged to Moriah Mitchell, the headmaster of the Leaf Academy when Hugh McCandlish was murdered."

"Really? I hired someone to remove all those boxes, all the personal stuff. Apparently they didn't get everything." She began skimming through the pages. "What's this?" she asked as she removed one of the drawings. The expression on her face said it all. She thought it was disgusting too. "Wait...is this you?" She looked at me closely and then at the drawing.

"Yes, I think so. So much happened; I hardly know where to start, Adrian."

"Did you draw these? Because they look really old."

"I think they are really old. Probably at least eighty years old. If I had to guess, I would say that the boy, the one that Hugh McCandlish called Ollie and the same one that Mitchell refers to in his journal, was the artist. Here's where it gets weird; I don't believe he's actually a boy at all. He may never have been a boy."

"Really? Why do you say that?"

"Well, I have a theory, but I'd like to show you the rest of the evidence I have for you first."

She let out a deep breath and said, "Okay, I'm ready."

"This was the first day. I caught the image of the boy like right off the bat." I plugged my jump drive into the laptop and pulled up the folder of images I planned to show her. There he was, the 'boy' Ollie. "You can see the hair, the profile of his face. This is his arm." I pointed at the screen.

"Oh my God. I can see him!" Her hands flew to her mouth. "My grandfather was telling the truth all along. He saw him too, when he was a teenager, before his brother died. And here in this photo, this...spirit looks so lifelike. And you saw this with your own two eyes?"

"Wait. Mr. Holloway saw him?"

"Yes, but he doesn't like to talk about the encounter much. His father owned the place before him, and he and his brother spent many summers there trying to repair it. Old Mr. Holloway wanted to make the place an office complex, but it never worked out. After Gary died, my great-grandfather was so devastated that he never wanted to do anything else there. All the work stopped."

"I can understand that." I showed the shaken brunette a few more pictures and then clicked on the audio file. "Listen to this, Adrian."

I played the friendly "come find me" first and then the growls I'd captured in the auditorium. Suddenly, Adrian began to wipe at her eyes. She was clearly horrified.

"And this horrible thing is connected to my family. It killed my great-uncle. God forbid my grandfather passes and I have to handle this. I want to sell the place, but how can I? Who's going to buy it? I never liked going in there, and now I know why."

I had more to show her; I hadn't even reviewed the hours and hours of audio and video. But this was enough. I closed the laptop. "Are you okay? Can I get you a glass of water?"

She smiled politely and dried her eyes one more time. "Yes, I will be fine. It's just I half-hoped it was just a story, just a family legend, but it can't be. And how did you get those pictures? I don't understand. Something in that journal has you disturbed too."

In for a penny, in for a pound.

"There are several different kinds of hauntings, residual, intelligent..."

"I've seen some of the ghost hunting shows. I think I understand that part, Jocelyn. Clearly, this thing is intelligent. Right?"

"Yes, but it's more than that. I think what's at the Leaf Academy is extremely rare. There are ghosts, many of them, as you may have already guessed. But I don't think they want to be there. I think that the negative entity—this thing that pretends to be a little boy named Ollie—is actually what's known as a maelstrom. Have you ever heard of that?"

She shook her head, her eyes locked on me. "No, what is it?"

"Like I said, it's a rarity. Maelstroms create pandemonium wherever they appear. From what we know—the paranormal community, I mean—these maelstroms draw unhappy spirits to them and capture them, like a spiritual whirlwind. They don't willingly let the trapped spirits go, nor do they move on once they've established themselves in a location. Not easily. Maelstroms gain strength from the captured spirits, and it is this entity's goal to continue to add to its unhappy community."

"How did it get there? Is it human?"

"I don't believe it is human, but it might have been a very long time ago. How it got there? I can't tell you that either, but it has been lurking there for ages, at least as long as the academy was open. Moriah Mitchell knew about 'Ollie,' and he had to have heard about him from someone. He tried to help Hugh McCandlish, but he wasn't strong enough or prepared enough to take it on. Maelstroms like to play mind games with their targets. Like this picture. It was playing with me, threatening to kill me. Luckily for me, my dog was with me. He saved my life."

"Really?"

"Yeah." I shuddered at the thought. "I am really sorry about prematurely ending the investigation, but the truth is I wasn't prepared for it either. It is strong, and it wants out of there. Right now it can't get out, but who's to say it won't try again?"

"What are my options? Burn it to the ground?" Adrian eyed me seriously.

"Would that help? I couldn't say, but I promise you this isn't over. Gulf Coast Paranormal, that's Midas' team, they can help you and they won't charge you a thing. Please, let me call him before you do anything. It's worth a shot, right?"

"Yes, it is. If it brings peace to my family or to the spirits trapped there, I am willing to wait. I just hope we can figure it all out before my grandfather leaves this world."

I squeezed her hand. "We'll try, Adrian."

"And you'll call this Midas person for me?"

"I'll do it tonight."

Half an hour later, I left Adrian's realty office and headed home. No, it wasn't mission accomplished, but Sherman and I had made it out alive. And that was all that mattered. My heart went out to Adrian. It really did. I hoped that Midas could and would help her.

We'd have to see about that. In the meantime, I had to go home.

My best friend was waiting for me.

Epilogue—Jocelyn

A good hot shower for me and a nice soapy bath for Sherman helped set my mind at ease, but there was one last thing to do. Did I really want to do it? Gosh, why was this so hard? I was pretty sure he wasn't going to say no.

Screw it. I'm doing it.

I tapped the number on the screen and waited for him to pick up. I cleared my throat awkwardly as I heard his voice on the phone. "Hey, Aaron? It's me, Jocelyn. I was wondering if you liked pizza. I mean, did you have plans for dinner? Because I was thinking about grabbing a slice or two. I thought it might be nice to have someone to talk with, besides my dog."

His warm laugh filled my ears, and I instantly felt better. "No plans, and pizza sounds perfect. Nothing exotic, though. No pineapple for me."

"No pineapple for me either. I'm a pepperoni girl. See you at the Golden Mushroom? Around six?"

We agreed on the details and I hung up the phone. I was so glad Aaron didn't say anything skeezy or flirty. Pete used to do that all the time, and it drove me crazy. I didn't like my relationships filled with a lot of innuendo or flirtatious banter. Okay, once in a while, but not every conversation.

So, I was doing this, right?

I had one more call to make. The phone rang a few times, and just when I was ready to hang up I heard Midas' voice on the line. "Hey, Jocelyn. Glad to hear from you. Are you back home?"

"Yeah, I got home yesterday."

"I take it you found what you were looking for?"

"And more. Listen, I'm calling to let you know that I wear a medium and I will need at least two shirts. I don't do laundry as faithfully as I should."

"I've got those. Does this mean you'll be going to Gulfport with us?"

"I'd like to, if there's room still. I don't want to bump anyone if the van is full."

"Not full, and we're taking the SUV too. There's plenty of room."

I tossed Sherman his yellow squeaky ball, which he immediately brought back. "I went to the Leaf Academy, Midas. I hate to admit this, but I'm totally out of my league. Gathering evidence? No problem. Telling the client she has a maelstrom on her property? The pits."

The line went so quiet I could have heard a pin drop. At least he didn't say I told you so. "You're okay, though?"

"Yes, thanks to my dog and a ghost named Hugh McCandlish. I was hoping you could talk to Adrian, maybe connect her with a local ministry that has experience with evicting maelstroms. Someone that would be committed for the long haul 'cause it's not going to be an easy task."

"Of course I will. You'll have to fill me in."

I breathed a sigh of relief. "Thanks, Midas. I appreciate that." I smiled and threw Sherman his toy again. "One more thing...I called Aaron, and we're going to have pizza tonight. I just thought you should know."

"Great. I'm sitting here with Cassidy. We're headed to the Causeway for seafood and beers. And for the record, I don't have to know all the details of your personal life. I know you, Jocelyn. You always behave like a professional."

Images of me running from the Leaf Academy with my dog in my arms and falling in the mud not once but twice filled my mind. Nobody had to know about that, did they? Everyone loses their nerve once in a while. *Right, big professional here.* I glanced at the load of camera equipment still piled up by the front door. I was in no hurry to review the remainder of the evidence, but I would—in the next day or seven. I'd been very selective about what I'd shown Adrian, and I had a sneaking suspicion there was so much more.

"Thanks for the vote of confidence. Y'all have a good night."

"You too, Jocelyn." He hung up the phone, and I wrestled with Sherman for a while. He was so happy to be home with me, he didn't even try to follow me when I walked to the door in my little black dress and dress sandals a few hours later.

"I'll be back, Sherm. Don't wait up."

As I closed the door and locked it behind me, I heard the flicking of a lighter. The old-fashioned kind. I froze momentarily but didn't look back. No, I wouldn't look back. I just wasn't that kind of person. I didn't run exactly, but I hurried to the car and headed to the pizza joint.

Time to leave the dead behind. At least for a little while.

The Maelstrom of the Leaf Academy

Academy

Gulf Coast Paranormal Series
Book Eleven
By M.L. Bullock

Chapter One—Shanafila
1703

The hot liquid snaked through my body almost as quickly as I gagged it down. It immediately numbed my tongue and throat. As I choked, an immense buzzing noise like many crickets screeching at once filled my brain. My knees buckled beneath me, and I fell to the ground like a dead man. The taste of blood and dirt filled my open mouth as I landed face first in the grassless soil. I struggled to spit out the dirt.

I could no longer see. I could not speak. Could not move. Could do nothing but listen and wait. I could hear everything. Soon the blackness would clear.

Remember what he told you. This is how it is when you spin the Sacred Wheel, when you walk the Invisible Path. Remember why you are here.

Fula Hatak tapped softly on the sacred drum. I listened and waited. Soon, my sight returned to me. First, I could only see the outline of the shaman, but as I waited and watched, I saw more. Yes, I could see him. His shaggy black hair shook as he worked at his magic. He looked very much as his name described, "Crow Man."

The sound and sight of the drum gave me comfort, for by hearing it I knew that a part of me remained tethered to the physical world, my world. And when my task was complete, I would return home to the arms of Yukpa, my Other Half. *This is only a brief journey,* I reminded myself. A journey that I must make if I hoped to take my place as a leader in my tribe. This momentary sacrifice, this seeing, would make me the leader that I must become.

Oh, but the pain in my body took my breath away. *Oh, dear wife. I die for you!*

I heard Yukpa's soft voice in my ear. It was all I needed. *Remember why you are here, Shanafila. See what you must see. Learn what you must learn. What does the Sun Father say about the Waliki? Will we live or die?*

I watched and waited. I could see nothing and no one except Fula Hatak and his drum. As I lay immovable in the dirt, I recalled my last happy moment. The day we left the village for this deserted dry patch of land. The Medicine Hill was a holy place, no doubt, yet it was also forbidding, or so I perceived it to be. But it should not be so. I should see life! I should see a new day for the Waliki.

Go, Shanafila, my brave husband. Go and see what you can see. I will pray that the Sun Father sends you a strong vision for our people.

I blinked at the memory of Yukpa's arms, the soft warmth of her breath on my cheek as she kissed me farewell. That had been many days ago. Six of us had hiked to the holy hill, but only three of us remained. The others, two young brothers named Talako and Chufwa, had broken the ritual by speaking to one another. Despite Grandfather Imafo's warning, they had broken the silence surrounding the customary fasting from food and words. They would return home in shame if they chose to, or they could make their way through the wilderness as outcasts forever. That would not be my fate. I had held my tongue and would journey onward. I had to!

Only Haloka and I were left to catch any glimpse of vision that the Sun Father might bestow upon our tribe. We had been pushed to the edges of our territory. If we ventured to the east or south, the Alibamu would kill us. But what was beyond the river, we did not know. Our numbers had dwindled in recent years; there had been frequent fighting with the growing ranks of the Alibamu, and a strange sweating sickness had killed many of our old people.

Grandfather Imafo chanted softly now, as if he and the drum were two voices, two voices but the same. He sang of soft black skies and shining lights above. He sang of the first Father and Mother and of their love that birthed the first rainbow. I got lost in the music and closed my eyes. Eventually, the pain diminished and I felt still. Very still. Like a watchful bird. I knew I would see something before I saw the first thing.

Yes, I knew I would see a vision.

Footsteps. Small footsteps. I could hear them racing around me. I could not turn my head, but I saw a child's bare legs and heard him laughing playfully.

Come back, little one. I am a friend.

But no matter how much I pleaded, the boy remained just out of my direct line of sight. I could see him with only my peripheral vision and only one eye as I remained prostrate on the ground, helpless to move an inch or chase after him. I focused all my efforts on working my fingers, but I had little success until I saw my pinky fingers move slightly.
Then I could hear the sound of a great tearing as if someone had sliced through fabric with a knife.

And I was standing beside myself, yet I had no worries. Only peace. I felt only peace. *Find the boy! He must be the deliverer of the message! Go find him, Shanafila!* As I searched for him, I could see him disappearing into the woods just beyond the holy hill. He was a young boy, only a few summers old. Five, maybe six. His laughter drew me to him. Yes, I should follow.

No! Do not leave this sacred place! My mind warned me, but my feet would not obey. I had to see this boy's face, for he seemed so familiar to me. But surely he was not. I had never seen a boy like that. Although he wore a short tunic, he was not Waliki. He was not even Alibamu. His skin was too pale, his body too frail-looking to be of Waliki blood.

I paused at the edge of the hill but did not tarry there. I would follow wherever he led me. Maybe he needed my help. Pushing the branches away, I pursued him as I walked deeper into the forest. Soon I could not see the sandy hill or hear the drum of Fula Hatak.

I had gone too far. Yes, too far. But I must follow even though I was not in my body. I left my body on the sandy hill. What if I could not get back?

The child's whispers drew me on. He called my name.
Shanafila! I have what you want!
I knew it! I had to pursue him. He would have the token, the evidence that I had indeed journeyed to the Spirit World and seen with my own eyes the future of our tribe. For I had no doubt that we would have a future. I practically laughed aloud as I imagined the Waliki growing, becoming stronger. A tribe large enough to defeat the Alibamu, if peace could not be found. Our people always followed the Way of Peace.

Yes, and look where that has gotten us. We need to fight if we must! Fula Hatak did not agree with me, and so we were here. Here in this strange place looking for a sign, a token. An offering of hope given to us by the hand of our ancestors.

This boy was not my ancestor, not of my tribe, but I had seen no one else and nothing else. Nothing but all these trees. Pines, scrubby oaks, sticker bushes aplenty. How very cruel to see that the Spirit World was no different from the forlorn wilderness where our tribe had been banished. I always believed, for the old ones always told us, that the Spirit World was a much nicer place with lakes full of fish, forests full of deer. Where were all the living things? I saw no deer, heard no squirrels scampering across the leaf-covered forest floor. Nothing except my own empty footsteps. The sand and leaves felt cool beneath my toes. My buckskin trousers were cool too. As I traveled deeper and deeper into these unknown woods, I felt unsettled. The boy whispered my name again and again.

"Here I am! Come out, please. I am a friend."

I continued seeking as five minutes passed, then thirty. Then at least an hour. It was hard to track the time in this place with the sunlight obscured by the canopy. The wilderness felt hostile now. Not friendly, not welcoming. The boy continued to elude me, and hopelessness welled up inside me. Thorns tore into my flesh as I journeyed on, then the sickness that baptized my journey returned. I felt discouraged by all of it and also terrified.

Shanafila, Shanafila! I have what you want.

Then it occurred to me that this may not be a messenger of the Sun Father. This could be Chufki, the Trickster, or one of the Bopholi, little people who hid in the woods. The Bopholi loved nothing more than to steal the souls of anyone fool enough to pursue them.

I should go back. I must go back, but which way?

As I began to panic, I realized I was standing in the center of a tight ring of young saplings. I could see no way forward, no way out, and I could not recall how I got here. I would have remembered entering this ring.
Right before my eyes, the ring got denser. Vines crawled up from the ground and wrapped themselves around the saplings. I barely had enough room to twist my body around, and when I did I was shocked to see that the vines were everywhere. Wrapping, twisting, covering. I reached for my blade, which I always carried on my hip, but it was not there. It was forbidden to bring weapons to the Medicine Hill.

But I had broken that rule. Nobody knew I had the small blade hidden in my sack. I had been careful and had shown it to no one. I thought about it now and wished for it, wished I had it in my hands. I had to get out of here! I had to flee or else I would be twisted into this strange hut that was forming around me. I saw only one opening, a slender one that I might be able to shove myself through, but I could not wait. I could not dally.

As I forced my way through, a few vines tried to wrap around my ankles, but I escaped. Somehow, I escaped. Again I found myself face first in the dirt, but I wasn't alone. The child's bare legs were beside me. My journey was ending; I could feel Fula Hatak's magic fading.

How would I ever get back? What would my people do without me? Without a token from the Sun Father?

Finally, I was at the place of tears. The place no warrior should go. Tears slid down my face. Tears for my wife, my tribe and myself. A shadow passed over my face. It was the boy. I could see him plainly now. Dark hair, even darker eyes. He was holding out his hand to me. And in his hand was a black feather.

At last, a token. The thing I needed more than anything.

For you, Shanafila. For your journey, Brave Warrior of the Waliki.

I felt no joy when I accepted the offering. No peace. No happiness. The boy placed the large, rough feather in my hand, and I closed my fingers around it. Suddenly, I wasn't in the woods. I was on the Medicine Hill and the drum had ceased.

Fula Hatak stood over me, his weathered face so close to mine. His brown eyes searched my own. He smiled in relief, but his joy was short-lived. I raised my hand to show him the feather, to prove to him that I had received the token. The promise that the Sun Father had a plan for the Waliki.

I watched in horror as Fula Hatak let out an agonizing scream.

Chapter Two—Midas

"Once upon a time, this was a grand place. Or so I've been told. I guess I can see that. She has good bones," Adrian Shanahan mused, staring up at the staircase as if she expected to see someone standing there. "You just don't see woodwork like this anymore. It's all prefab stuff now. Believe me, people would pay top dollar for beautiful workmanship like this, but the Leaf Academy has such a horrible reputation. There's no way I can sell this place or keep it."

I nodded and looked up and down the long hallway. This place was massive with more than ten thousand square feet. A paranormal investigator's dream. Or nightmare, depending on which department you worked in. Joshua, my tech guy, was not going to like this square footage, but I didn't plan on covering the entire property. That would be impossible. There were three floors, an auditorium and various other small buildings. Like most abandoned buildings, this one had its share of rodents, broken glass and empty rooms. But then again, maybe not that empty.

I completely believed Jocelyn. This place scared the hell out of her. Yes, there was more here than met the eye. I couldn't imagine investigating this place by myself like she did. She was fearless, no doubt about it, but she was also a bit of a rogue. And that could get you in hot water if you weren't careful.

"Shall we?" Adrian asked as she walked through the door on the left. Shoot, this place had a creepy vibe. Who would leave a chair in the hallway? "Honestly, Midas, I don't know why I am doing this. I really do have every intention of tearing it all down. Board by board, brick by brick. Jocelyn's report convinced me that there's no saving this place. What else can I do with it? It would take a fortune—a fortune I don't have, by the way—to restore it. And even if I did, there would be no guarantee that the repairs would expel the...current residents. I think the best thing I could do is demolish it."

If she wanted me to convince her otherwise, I wasn't going to try. I was just grateful to be given a chance to look inside the place and do our investigation before she gave the bulldozers the go-ahead. Maybe it should be torn down. That wasn't my call, but to hear her make such a threat inside the facility gave me the chills.

Adrian trailed behind me as I went from room to room. I flashed a light in the last empty room. The boarded windows did not allow in a beam of light. Strange that one side of the building would be boarded up and not the other. Hmm...this looked like it could have been office space. There were two large desks and a dilapidated file cabinet jammed together in the corner.

"Thank you for inviting us to check it out first. I don't know what's in your best interest, but I can promise you that my team and I will do our very best to get to the bottom of the activity. I guess it would be a difficult call to make, either way. So many rooms. Do you happen to know how many?"

"Thirty-three. That's what is in the property description, but I haven't been in every one of them. I don't want to either. When I was a kid, my grandfather did not want me to come here. But like most teenagers, I didn't listen. I snuck inside with my girlfriends in high school. Just to have a look around."

Her confession shocked me; I didn't peg Adrian Shanahan for a risk taker. Cautious, reasonable, professional, yes.

Frightened teenager? I couldn't imagine that. "Really? Did you experience anything while you were here?" I asked as we walked back to the foyer and then on to the other wing. We still had two other floors to walk.

"Yes, I did. Come to think of it, I am not sure you will see anything at all since it's January. The activity usually occurs in October. That's been the tradition. Just ask Jocelyn. She must have told you all about it."

"She did. Is that when you had your experience, Adrian? Was it October?"

She bit her lip and nodded. "Yes. I confess I didn't tell Jocelyn about it. I didn't want to influence her findings, but I guess I should be honest about it. I mean, I can't go around pretending it didn't happen. It did happen. I know it did, and I wasn't the only one who saw them."

Just mentioning the details of her experience seemed to be enough to make Adrian nervous. I wanted to put her at ease, so I said, "I believe you. I have seen things too. Long before I started the group."

"It wasn't my idea to come, but my friends wanted to see the place. It was a stupid dare. My girlfriends didn't even put it together—they didn't know that this place belonged to my grandfather. Just that the Leaf Academy has had a reputation as being...occupied for a long time. We came in this way. I'll show you."

We walked in silence together until we reached the end of the hall. Her arms were folded, and she rubbed them as if she were cold. It was damp and chilly inside even though it was quite a warm day for January. *Don't make too much of that, Midas Demopolis. Cold chills aren't evidence.* There was a door here, but it had been boarded up some time ago. I tugged at the wood. It seemed sturdy enough.

"I had this closed up after they chased us out of here. I didn't want anyone else to see what I saw."
I clicked on the flashlight and waited for Adrian to continue. When she didn't pick the conversation up, I decided to nudge her a little. Ever so slightly. "If you had to describe what you saw in one word..."

"Hellish. That would be the word. Listen, I'll tell you all about it, but I want to finish this tour first. Is that okay? I hate talking about this place when I'm in here. It's like someone is listening."

I agreed to her request, but my interest was certainly piqued. Hearing other people's stories was almost as interesting as conducting an investigation.

"Here's the auditorium. It's pretty cluttered, though, and some of the ceiling is coming down. As you can see, it extends out from the rest of the building. Once it had a lovely skylight. That must have seemed magical when it was new and intact. They could watch the stars while they listened to the orchestra. The town held many a concert here, and this was the location for all the school events. The graduation ceremonies were long, but the Leaf Academy attracted many a notable speaker."

"I can believe that. Do you mind if I walk up to the stage area?"

Adrian shook her head. "Go ahead, but I'll stay right here if you don't mind. This is where it happened."

I hesitated because I didn't want her to feel uncomfortable and then decided to make it a quick trip. I just had to check it out. I'd heard so much about it. I stepped over broken chairs and chunks of the fallen ceiling. Along the perimeter of the fallen room were piles of plaster, evidence that the walls had once been something to see. In my mind, I replayed Jocelyn's account. I carefully went up the stairs and stood on the stage. The floor didn't feel spongy, but that wasn't always a reliable measure of stability. I stepped carefully and used the additional light to make my way to the center of the stage. Jocelyn had been standing here, and the boy...Ollie. He would have been there. I waved my flashlight around at the row of dusty, moldy chairs. It would be easy to see things in here, especially in the dead of night, but Jocelyn wasn't one to make up stuff.

I left the stage and joined Adrian in the hallway. She shuddered and said, "I hate this room. Let's go upstairs. It's not great up there either."

The rest of the building was as I expected. Some of the rooms were bare-bones empty, while others were stacked with junk including some antique furniture. Most of the furniture was broken but certainly interesting.

"The teachers' rooms are to the right, and the students' are to the left. The kids were bunked together, two and sometimes four to a room. The teachers got the better deal, only one per room, but their rooms weren't very large. If you follow me, I'll show you one room in particular that might be worth your attention. It's at the end of the hall. Nobody likes that room. No one alive, anyway." Even though Adrian suggested that I follow her, she fell behind. She clearly didn't want to be here, but she had been kind enough to show me the hotspots and I didn't want her to leave in tears.

"I'll go, Adrian."

"You aren't leaving me in this hallway. It's just as bad as that room. Lots of people see shadows and black mists on this floor." She had her arms folded again, a clear sign that subconsciously she wanted to protect herself from whatever might be lurking in the halls at the Leaf Academy.
As soon as I hit the doorway, I saw a stack of papers fluttering to the ground. Old papers. Drawings, sketches. I didn't need a flashlight in this room; the windows weren't boarded up. And in fact, there was a filthy view of the overgrown forest. But the papers...they had been moving. Luckily, Adrian had been far enough behind me that she hadn't seen anything. Still, I could feel the creep factor ratcheting up by the second.

"Stay right there, please," I whispered as I entered the room and checked behind the door. There was no one here. No evidence of rodents and no open windows. All six of the panes were intact, and the wooden frames were so old they were probably swollen and stuck in place. I halfheartedly tried to lift the thing, but it didn't budge.

There was a bed frame and a cot in here. Not much else. Except for a pile of drawings—all of black feathers. I squatted beside them but remembered Jocelyn's warning.

Don't pick up a damn thing, Midas. Nothing. The entity wants you to accept his gifts.

"What is it, Midas?"

"It's just some drawings. I think we've seen all there is to see. Are you ready to go?"

"Yes, been ready." She glanced at the pile of papers but didn't ask about them. I was glad for that. I wasn't exactly sure what to tell her. But those papers had been shuffling around. I heard them and saw them.

I glanced over my shoulder as Adrian and I walked down the first set of stairs and then the next. I couldn't shake the feeling that someone was not only watching us but following us. Making sure we left the Leaf Academy.
I wouldn't admit this to anyone, but I was happy to be leaving. Unlike Jocelyn, I wasn't a fan of solo investigations, especially not a place this size. But I would be back. As soon as Adrian would let us.

Chapter Three—Midas

"I need coffee and some distance from this place. There's a coffee shop in town," Adrian suggested as she backed the car around and spun out of the driveway. She must have forgotten about taking me for a tour of the grounds. I didn't think I should remind her.

I buckled up my seat belt. Seemed like an especially good idea. "Sounds great. If you think my vehicle will be okay," I replied as my mind replayed seeing those sketches floating to the ground. My opening the door could have caused a draft—that was a possibility. Although I believed Jocelyn, I had to go into this investigation the way I normally did: take the scientific approach first and whatever you have left, what can't be explained, study that. Yep. Debunking what I saw would be the first order of business when we got the equipment unloaded and set up.

"Your van will be fine. Trust me on that. Nobody comes out here. I'll bring you back in a few minutes, but I need some fresh air. Fresh, faraway air."

"That's fine, Adrian. I could use some coffee."

She smiled weakly as she turned off the soft jazz playing on her radio. "Thanks for understanding. Tell me the truth, Midas. What do you think about the place? Tell me I'm not crazy. It's haunted, isn't it? I mean, I know it is, but I'm not a professional."

"It's not short on spooky ambiance, that's for certain. And I do believe that there is activity, yes. You and Jocelyn are both credible witnesses. I'm not going to sugar-coat anything—

Jocelyn is convinced that you have a unique and troubling entity in residence. It's so strong that it has created a kind of vortex, all on its own. How much has she told you about her experience there?"

Adrian shifted gears and shook her head. "She didn't tell me much, but she does believe it is haunted. It's stupid that I should doubt my own eyes and ears, my own experience. What happened to me was like something out of a horror movie. Here's the thing, Midas. I know the Leaf Academy is haunted. I mean, I know it deep in my soul. There are malicious spirits there. And although their presence is felt strongest in October, they are at the academy all year round. That night in high school, my friends and I broke in. What's crazy was I could have stolen the key from my grandfather and then put it back; he would have never known. But I didn't want anyone to know I was related to the owners, and it seemed more exciting to break into the place. Big mistake."

"Go on," I prompted her. I had the feeling Adrian was on the verge of telling me something.
"We were smoking in that upstairs room, the one at the end of the hall that we checked out last. Really, my friends wanted to do it. I wasn't much of one to smoke, but you know how it is when you're in high school. You do stupid things to please your friends."

"We have all done crazy things as teenagers. Smoking isn't so surprising. Were you guys doing anything else? Maybe a séance or using tarot cards or a Ouija board? I'm not judging you, but it would help to know."

"Nothing that scandalous. Just cigarettes, Midas." She shifted down and eased the car into the parking lot of the Dipping

Donut, then put it in park and turned it off. "Karen and Betsy were my best friends. Funny to think we aren't friends anymore. Karen is gone now, and Betsy and I never speak. Karen was kind of the alpha of our small group of friends. She was always pushing the envelope, and until that night I was happy to follow her. Everything had been so harmless until that point. She wasn't happy just breaking in to smoke a cigarette—we had to do it in that room. Lots of stories about that room; other kids had gone there. People say they see a boy in that window." Adrian fidgeted with her keys and grabbed her purse.

"Let's get that coffee," I suggested as I got out of her stylish BMW. She agreed, and a few minutes later we were hunkered together at a small rickety table in the corner of the Dipping Donut. I suddenly wished Cassidy were with me. She would have been scribbling up a storm, I was convinced of that. There was no one else in the place except the owner, who was busy prepping the dough.

"You guys went up to the room. Did you see anything on the way up there?"

"No, but you can imagine how we all acted. Like giggling idiots. All except Karen. It was like she had some sort of...I don't know. It's like she was on a mission. She had to do it, and we had to go with her. You know, back in the nineties, nobody talked about any of this stuff. Not out in the open. And we thought of ourselves as brave. I mean, we were hoping to get scared but not nearly killed."

A loud machine in the kitchen kicked on, and Adrian jumped at the sound. No way was this lady making any of this up. Her experience at the Leaf Academy had left a lingering effect on her. Another reason to investigate, especially if she was planning to tear it down. Maelstroms were so rare; I'd only learned about these commanding, powerful spirits recently. And I'd never actually encountered one.

"I'm sorry that you had such a terrifying experience, Adrian."

She reached for a napkin from the antique silver napkin holder on the table and dabbed at her eyes. "Thanks. To be honest, I was nervous about my grandfather bringing in Jocelyn Graves, but seeing how professionally she conducted herself and how highly she recommended you...calling you just seemed like the right thing to do. This is the next step."

My phone vibrated in my pocket, but I didn't reach for it. Whoever it was would have to wait. "I am grateful for your trust, and I know it took a lot to make that phone call."

"Why do you do it? I can't imagine investigating ghosts and whatever else you might encounter for a living. Why?" Adrian twisted the napkin in her hands.

"I hear that question a lot. Mostly from my family," I said with a smile. "My cousin Dominic went missing when I was a kid. We were close in age, and he was my best friend. Later, I understood what happened. Dom had been kidnapped and murdered, but while everyone was searching for him, I saw him. Actually, he visited me a few more times, came to my bed at night.

He was talking to me, but I couldn't hear him. I couldn't make it out. I can't tell you how frustrating that was. I loved Dom so much and wanted to help him. I saw him a few other places too. I think he wanted me to find him, but I couldn't. I was just a kid. They found his body not long after his last visit to me."

"I'm so sorry. What a horrible thing to happen. I guess there are different types of spirits; I confess I don't know much about them, and what I do know..."

I agreed with her. "Sometimes the dead need help. If I can help them, I will. Other times, it's not so nice, but we have to take the good with the bad."

Adrian put the napkin down and shook her head. "What about the evil dead? What if they don't want your help, Midas? What if the ghost isn't human?"

"I've encountered non-human entities before. It's scary at times, but we usually find a way of bringing the client information that is useful in expelling these entities."

"Like an exorcism?"

I shook my head. "We don't do those. But one of our team members, Sierra McBride, is a sensitive. She helps the dead move on if they will listen. We do have contacts for exorcisms if it comes to that, but we can't jump to that conclusion. Tell me what happened to you. You felt threatened?"

"Yes. Karen had some cigarettes—those long skinny ones. I never bought any myself, but I'd smoked once or twice with them. Just to fit in and be cool. Anyway, we agreed with Karen that we were going to do it, all three of us. She wanted to smoke in that room because she'd heard that it aggravated the ghost there. He was supposed to be some kind of teacher or a principal, I'm not sure which. Karen liked the idea of aggravating a teacher—anyone in authority. She was kind of a wild child. I liked that she didn't want or need anyone's approval. I liked that about her until that night. She was not the best influence, I know that now. As I mentioned, Karen died a few years ago."

Adrian's hedging around the actual events of that night did not surprise me. After all these years, she couldn't come to terms with what happened to her, didn't want to believe it. I waited for her to share her story, but I couldn't wait much longer. The donut clock on the far wall ticked loudly, reminding me that I promised to have dinner with Cassidy. We'd been missing each other recently. If she wasn't busy training or working on a client's artwork, I was off helping Papa Angelos in his diner. The old man couldn't get around too well anymore.

"Betsy had the matches. She struck one and put the flame to the cigarette tip, but it went out. Like someone blew it out. We laughed about it and blamed it on the wind. But then she lit another one and it happened again. That pissed Karen off. She thought I was doing it—she even called me a few names. I was so freaked out, but I didn't get it. Not yet. My hair was standing up all over my body, but I didn't want to believe what was really happening. Karen took the cigarette from Betsy and made us both back up a few feet, far enough away that we couldn't blow out the flame. Her fingers were shaking, but she popped another match and tried to light the cigarette. I'll never forget it. It wouldn't work. She tried several times, examined the box and then remembered she had a lighter in her purse."

Adrian closed her eyes and bit her lip as she recounted her experience. "She flicked the lighter, and the flame leaped up. Really high, too. It turned completely blue like it was burning really hot. But she wasn't going to stop. I could see the tip of the cigarette catch and heard her take a deep draw off of it, but then she dropped it. Her head flung back, and her feet were dancing in the air. Before I could speak or think or anything at all, I felt a hand around my throat too. A monstrous hand. It had to have belonged to a really big person because it went all the way around my neck."

She rubbed her neck at the memory. "I think the two of us hung in the air for at least five seconds, maybe more. I thought it was going to kill me—choke me to death. It didn't attack Betsy, but it got me and Karen."

"How did it end? Do you remember?"

She sighed and kind of collapsed in her seat. "Of course I do. I will never forget any of it. Betsy made it stop. She was screaming and praying the Lord's Prayer, and I think that's why it quit. I'm glad she did because I'm pretty sure I would be dead if she'd decided to run off and leave us. As soon as my feet hit the ground, I was gone. All of us were. The three of us ran out of there like bats out of hell."

"It sounds like a terrifying encounter with something that meant to do you harm."

Her eyes were wide as she nodded in agreement. "It was the scariest damn thing I ever experienced. I will never forget it. Never."

After a few moments of silence, I asked, "Anything else you can remember?"

"Yes. I heard a voice. A man's voice. It was like he was right at my ear, almost inside my head."

Now the hair was creeping up on my neck, but I didn't let on that anything she was telling me was disturbing. It wouldn't do her any good to tell her how strong that entity had to be if it spoke and manhandled them. "What did he say? Could you make it out?"

"He said, 'No smoking!' His voice was really angry and really loud. I don't know if my friends heard it. I can tell you what, though, I never smoked again."

"I bet. Adrian, we're going to do all we can to see what is haunting your property. Thank you for sharing your experience with me. I know how tough that can be. Are you ready to go back? I've got to pick up my van and meet one of our team members."

"I think so. As long as I don't have to get out. I feel kind of icky now."

"You don't have to get out, but I would like to walk the grounds before I go. If that's okay?"

She dug in her purse and handed me a set of keys. "Sure. Here are the keys to the school and the outside buildings. Please, Midas, you all be careful. I hope you guys can figure it all out. And I really hope this investigation doesn't piss anything off."

"We will be more than cautious, I promise you. I think we already have all the evidence we need to establish there is an active haunting at the Leaf Academy. But I would like to bring you some peace, if possible, and dig deeper. And maybe help whoever is there."

"Oh, wait. You'd better have this too. I started reading it and had to quit. Maybe it will help you. It's Moriah Mitchell's diary. He was the headmaster in the 1930s. He knew more about what was going on than people believed he did."

"Thank you, Adrian. This kind of artifact does help."

She tugged the purse up on her shoulder. "You're an optimistic kind of guy, aren't you?"

"Yes, but I'm not a fool. And I'm sure as heck not going to light up a cigarette while I'm there."
"Good thinking, Midas. Well, let's go. No time like the present."

We left the donut shop and headed back to the Leaf Academy. Adrian wasn't joking around. She didn't get out of the car. All the front windows were boarded up, but I couldn't quite shake the sensation that I was being watched from somewhere on high. Hm...maybe I'd pass on the outbuildings. There was so much going on inside the school that there was really no need to go poking around in the various sheds, the dilapidated greenhouse or the boarded-up annex building. Everything we needed, paranormal-wise, was in the school. I put the journal on the passenger seat and tossed the keys in the console, then I got out and stared at the building.

A maelstrom, huh? How are you going to deal with this, Midas? What's the game plan?

My emotions were all over the place. I experienced a heady mix of excitement, fear and curiosity. This was what I lived for.

Okay, Demopolis. Get your head in the game. Time to think like a professional.

And then I heard the voice. A familiar voice. One I hadn't heard in a long time.

Midas...help me. Midas.

And in a flash, I saw the image of a pale-faced boy standing on the porch near the main entrance. His mouth hadn't moved, and he said nothing else, but his presence infuriated me. "Cut it out!" I shouted back without thinking. Nobody answered. No one said a thing. I got in the car and slammed the door, then put the keys in the ignition and drove away. Now that ticked me off!

Whatever this spirit was, I knew one thing for sure. It was a trickster. There was no way that was Dom's voice, although it wanted me to believe that it was. Dominic was dead and gone. He'd passed over long ago, and I didn't believe for a minute that he was hanging around me hoping to resolve any unsettled business he might have. What would that be? No, it wasn't my dead cousin, but that had been his voice I heard.

And this entity knew it. And it knew we were coming.

Chapter Four—Cassidy

"Poor baby. I know, I know. I'm a terrible Mom." Domino meowed one more time before snuggling back up in his bed. This latest trip to the vet would be one he never forgot, but at least he wouldn't be populating the neighborhood if he managed to slip out of the house again. And that was totally possible because he was a sneaky rascal. I think my cat believed that whenever anyone rang that doorbell, especially the pizza guy on Friday nights, that was his cue to race out the door. I'd been training again and was pretty fast but not quite as fast as Domino.

The thing was, once Domino got outside, he had no real destination. He'd stand in the middle of the yard and look around, so he was easy to catch. It was like a game for him. At this point, he probably believed it was a horrible game that ended with a preventative trip to the veterinarian.
I heard the familiar tap on the back door. *Midas!* I thought with a smile. "Hey!" I said as I swung the door open and welcomed him inside. He didn't look well, and there wasn't a hint of his usual "happy to see me" expression on his face. In fact, if I had to pick one word to describe him at that moment, it would be ashen. And with his light olive skin and swarthy looks, he almost always looked the picture of health.

"What is it? Midas?"

He immediately began pacing my kitchen, his soft gray t-shirt clinging to his well-toned arms. His hand was over his mouth, and his dark eyes were troubled. I closed the door and glanced in the driveway. No, he was alone. This wasn't typical Midas Demopolis behavior. My fiancé wasn't usually this unsettled about anything. That was my job. He had a peaceful persona and was middle of the road, easygoing and steady as a rock in all things.

What the heck? I could only imagine the worst. Had sómething happened with Papa Angelos? No, that couldn't be it. But Midas mentioned earlier that he was going to the Leaf Academy. I got the shivers just thinking that whatever he was experiencing now might have something to do with his visit. That didn't bode well for our upcoming investigation. Jocelyn had told us the place was a total creep fest, but the blonde was skimpy on the details...at Midas' request, I gathered. As usual, he wanted the team to go into the investigation with our right brains ready to roll. Or was it the left? Whichever side preferred logical thinking. I couldn't remember. After some of the creepy encounters I'd had, it was hard to be nonchalant about any kind of paranormal work.

"Midas? Talk to me."

He pulled out a chair, sat at the table and finally looked me in the eye. "I heard Dominic's voice at the Leaf Academy. I know it wasn't him, but it shook me. And I saw that boy, the one Jocelyn was talking about, the one that haunted McCandlish."
"Hey, don't jump to any conclusions, remember? What did he look like? Could it have been a kid checking the place out? Maybe someone who saw you there and wanted to have a peek inside?"

He sighed as he leaned back in the chair. "That's possible, I guess, but it doesn't explain hearing my cousin's voice."

"What did he say?" I asked as I touched his warm hand and squeezed it.

"He asked me to help him. What's funny is I was just telling Adrian about him. You know I never talk about him, but I felt like I needed to."

I went to the refrigerator and grabbed him a bottle of water. He looked like he needed one. I twisted my lips thoughtfully as he cracked open the bottle and took a long drink.

"It's not usual for spirits to listen in on what we have to say. Obviously, this is not a residual haunting but an intelligent one. It heard you guys talking about your cousin, and it wanted to connect with you." I gave Midas the hopeful version of what I believed. This ghost or whatever it was could have been mocking him, trying to trick him. It was highly doubtful that it was merely parroting back what it heard.

"I would think so too, but I didn't tell her about Dominic until we left the Leaf Academy. She was really upset, and I was trying to comfort her. She wanted to get away from the property, so we went to a donut shop down the road. I told her there. We must have been at least a mile away from the Leaf Academy. Is it following her?"

I tapped my fingers on the table as he spoke. That last bit gave me pause. "That's possible. Is she haunted, do you think?"

"She says the last thing she saw was at the school. She and two girlfriends broke in there in the '90s. They went there hoping to provoke the spirits by smoking on the premises, more specifically in the upstairs room. The one Jocelyn was telling us about."

"Hugh McCandlish's room? The one he shared with Ollie?"

"Yes, that's the one. They got choked, and a male's voice told them to stop smoking."

"Wow, that's a first for me." After a minute of thinking, I offered my thoughts on the matter, "It must be pretty powerful to have overheard your conversation from that distance. Maybe it just picked it out of your brain when you got back? That doesn't comfort me to know something could hear our thoughts, but I think I would rather believe that than believe it can follow you around and eavesdrop."

He finished off his water and tossed the bottle into the garbage can. "You're probably right. How about we stay in tonight?"

"That means, 'how about we work tonight,' doesn't it?" I asked with a grin.

"Would you be okay with that?" I could sense his excitement. Midas was an adrenaline junkie when it came to the paranormal.

"Yes, but let me check on the kitten first. And then put on some jeans. Are we working at the office? Never mind, that's a dumb question. Be right back. And you're buying dinner."

"Agreed," he purred as he kissed me. "I'm going to call Sierra and Josh and see what they're up to."

"Midas, let them have a night off. They have a baby, remember? Joshua has been working a lot of hours lately," I said as I recalled a conversation I had earlier with Sierra. "You'll just have to deal with being stuck with me for a research assistant." Midas sat on the couch as I hung out in the hallway door. Of course, I was joking around, but the look on his face let me know he didn't find it amusing. In fact, he looked even more shook up than when he arrived. "Give me five minutes to change and grab my supplies."

"That sounds great. I'll call Papa Angelos. I promised I would check in with him to see how his day went."

"Give him my love," I called as I hurried down the hall to change my clothes. I put my hand on the doorknob and tried to open the door, but it wouldn't open. That made no sense; there was no lock on the door. I stepped back and stared at it. What the heck? Glancing down the hall to the living room, I could see Midas on his phone. I bit my lip and tried again. Still nothing. I put my shoulder into it as I turned the knob, but the door still wouldn't budge. In fact, it kind of felt like someone was on the other side. I could see shadows under the door when I peeked down at my feet.

"Hey! Who's in there?" I yelled as I tapped on the door with one hand and kept twisting the knob. Midas was coming up the hall when it finally came open. "Midas?" I waved him over furiously as the door swung open.

There was no one there. Not a shadow. Not a living person. Nothing at all. "The door was stuck, and I swear...hey, what's that?"
In the center of my bed was one black feather. It hadn't been there before. I was a stickler for making my bed every morning. I had no feathers lying around, and it couldn't have been Domino bringing me a present. He could barely make it to the litter box, much less jump on my bed.

"Close the door, Cassidy."

I stepped out of the room and did as he asked. We tried the door again, and it opened just fine now. Whoever had been blocking me, whatever it was, had left the room. And left this gift behind. I'd heard enough of Jocelyn's story to know what this could mean.

Midas and I were being invited to the Leaf Academy.

Chapter Five—Cassidy

"Sorry, sweet boy, but I can't let you wander around the house while I'm gone. It's not safe." Kissing my cat's head, I put his basket in the laundry room along with his food and water dish and closed the door behind me. He complained immediately, but he wasn't going to talk me out of this. He couldn't understand how shook up I was, nor did he understand the possible danger we faced. But then again, maybe he did know.

Uncle Derek's ghost used to pop in occasionally, and Domino hated him. He didn't come around anymore, or at least not where I was aware of him, but I kind of hoped he would come by. I believed that in a strange, disconnected way, Uncle Derek loved me and would protect me if he could. But maybe he couldn't. If the feather arrived by the hand of whatever entity waited for us at the Leaf Academy, I could only imagine how this investigation would go. But that couldn't be right. There had to be another explanation.

Get a grip, Cassidy. You know what's going on here.

I grabbed my backpack and keys and walked out of the house behind Midas. I glanced around once more as I stepped outside, but there wasn't anything to see. Nothing at all. What about that feather? I couldn't very well leave it on my bed, but I didn't want to touch the thing either. Midas promised to help me figure it out when he dropped me off tonight. I wasn't sure what he could possibly propose. How could we safely remove the item without putting one or both of us in further danger? And Midas...he wasn't himself. Seeing his cousin, or the thing pretending to be his cousin, clearly had a horrible effect on him. Not that I could blame him. I would die if I saw my late sister hanging out anywhere.

"Jocelyn is on her way to the office. She's going to go over the case with us—I told her about the feather. I have to ask, just to say I did. Do you think there is any possible way that you brought the feather inside and just forgot about it? Maybe the cat?"

"One hundred percent no. Did you see that thing? It had to be at least twelve inches long. That's not something that gets picked up by accident, and my poor cat can barely get in and out of his box, much less jump up on the bed. And where would he pick up a feather? I don't let him outside."

Midas fiddled with his rearview mirror, and an awkward silence passed between us. Finally, he said, "Adrian Shanahan gave me the journal, the one that Jocelyn found. It's right there in the back seat."

I glanced over my shoulder to look for the item. "Journal? Whose journal?"
"A former headmaster, Moriah Mitchell. He describes the haunting in detail, she says. They knew about the October People but chose to pretend nothing was going on."

I reached for the journal and mused, "That sounds familiar. Nothing much has changed in the world, has it?" I rubbed my fingers over the faded cover.

Midas said in a stern voice, "I still can't believe Jocelyn went by herself to that place. It's huge, and every corner feels...occupied. She's probably the most reckless person I know."

I didn't argue with him. I didn't know Jocelyn as well as he did, but I wouldn't necessarily call her reckless. Fearless? Yes, she was that for sure. I skimmed through the pages carefully. This was an old book, and I didn't want to damage it. Midas swore softly under his breath as a rogue motorcyclist jetted around him. "Now that's reckless," I declared as I clutched the door and waited for him to regain his composure.

"He's got a death wish," he answered as the SUV rolled down the narrow Mobile streets. "Do you see anything interesting in there?"

Confident that we wouldn't die in a fiery car and motorcycle crash, I opened the book again. I glanced at page after page of faded writing but stopped when I came to a section of riveting sketches. I blurted out, "These drawings don't match." I didn't know how I knew that, but I did. I flipped through at least ten pages, each more detailed and disturbing than the last. I flinched at the images of a raven's eye and beak, and a pile of feathers. Lots and lots of those. But the last sketches were spellbinding. Many, many faces—an old woman with a twisted mouth and a bun of dirty gray hair, a woman with an oddly long face and an open screaming mouth. The most haunting of the drawings was not as frightening as the others, but it was no less intense. This was a drawing of a young man, of Native American descent if I had to guess from his clothing and his lovely, long dark hair.

"What makes you say that?" Midas asked as his turn signal ticked. He stared at me even though the light had changed.

"It's green," I told him as I flipped on the map light. The SUV crept forward and onto the road that would take us to the Gulf Coast Paranormal office. "They're different in ways that are hard to explain, but I'll try it. Maybe it's more of a feeling. Look at this. No, wait. On second thought, please don't look. Keep your eyes on the road, Midas. I can see that Mitchell's handwriting is carefully slanted. There's not one extraneous dot or loop. This guy isn't an artist. That and the pressure is different."

"Come again?"

"Some people write with a light touch, and others press down very firmly on the paper. Moriah Mitchell wrote with a light touch. These drawings are different. They're really good but also kind of childish and drawn with a heavy hand." I couldn't stop staring at the young man. He was beautiful, with fierce dark eyes and full lips. I shook my head and closed the book. I had to get my head in the game.

Before I knew it, we were pulling into the parking spot in front of the office. Midas turned off the vehicle and leaned closer. I thought he wanted to get a better look at the drawing, but he kissed me instead. It was a lovely kiss, all warm and inviting. The tension between us took a back seat as he stroked my cheek with his fingers and pressed his forehead to mine.

"What's that for?" I asked as he hovered close.

"Just because. Thanks for indulging me. I'm sure this is not what you had in mind for our date night. I never want to put you in danger, Cassidy. Never."

"I know, Midas. I know that. And I had no plans, and I love what we do as much as you do." He breathed a sigh of relief at hearing my promise that I held no ill will about our movie night being postponed. "Explain to me where that feather came from? Other than by the hand of Casper the Unfriendly

Ghost. Do you think it's from the Leaf Academy spirit? Seems like kind of a coincidence that it would show up now. Especially after all the feather drawings in this journal."

"I have no theories yet, but I can promise you I will remove it if it's not gone when we get back."

I shuddered at the thought. If it had been left by this spirit, that was bad enough, but to think about it returning to retrieve it...the idea made me sick to my stomach. "I don't want you to touch it, but I don't want to touch it either. Let's go check out this journal. Maybe Moriah Mitchell left us some clues. Hey, there's Jocelyn. I don't see Aaron with her. Do you think he'll ever come back?"

Midas shrugged as he unlocked the office. "I'm not sure. He hasn't said, and I don't want to push him."

I stared at the approaching figure. I could tell by her signature lope that it was Jocelyn but with one marked difference. She'd cut off all her dreadlocks. Instead of long blond twisted strands of hair cascading down her back and shoulders, she was sporting a super-short hairstyle. Kind of a pixie cut but a bit edgier. I liked it, but I liked her dreadlocks too.

"Hey! Wow! You look great!" I greeted her as she got closer.

"Yeah, well, I hate it. I got a wild hair, pardon the pun, and this is the result." She shrugged as she stuffed her hands into the pockets of her ripped jeans, sighed and followed us into the building.

"How have you been?" I hadn't seen Jocelyn in weeks. Mostly because she stayed on the road with her photography work.

That and paranormal cases had been hard to come by lately. The rumor was there was a new group of investigators in town who were digging into the action. Midas acted like he didn't care, but I had a feeling he was a little let down that the phones weren't ringing off the hook. He disappeared into his office, and I flipped on the lights.

"I'm doing great. Still avoiding taking that trip to California. I told Midas I was going to go after we wrapped the Gulfport investigation, but I bailed. Just couldn't face it. Mom's really eager for me to go home, but I'm...not. I went and took photos of some interesting Pensacola lighthouses instead. Nothing in the way of the paranormal, but with old places like that, you can't help but get the feeling that you're in the presence of history. How is your cat? Sierra told me you took him to get snipped."

Jocelyn was like that...she offered you some information but not too much. I remembered that her mother lived in California and that she was sick. And I gathered that they didn't get along very well, but beyond that, I couldn't say why she didn't want to return to her home state.

"Yeah, Domino's not real happy with me. How's Sherman?"

"Good. It's funny, I can't imagine life without my dog now, and I'd never owned a pet before. Not beyond the occasional fair fish. You know the kind, the ones you win at the fair that never live past the weekend? I've had Sherman for almost three months, and he's my family. He's a good traveler too. That helps." She smiled her lopsided grin.

Midas greeted her, and while I could tell he noticed her hair too, he was much less likely to make comments about anyone's personal appearance. "Are you ready to go back to the Leaf Academy?" he asked as he sat at the table and invited us to join him.

"Ready or not, here we come, right?" She rubbed at her short hair and crossed her legs under her as she sat in the chair, as was her custom.

He shook his head. "You have a choice, Jocelyn. I'm not going to make you go back. I can't do that. I won't."

She visibly breathed a sigh of relief. "I am grateful to hear you say that because I'm not sure I want to go back. Crazy, huh? I mean, it's not your typical haunt—this is what we live for, right? Whatever resides at the Leaf Academy is calculating and intelligent. And I think it is a killer."
Midas paused as he flipped open his laptop.

Jocelyn stood up and paced as she continued, "I've been doing this for five years. That's not as long as you, for sure, but I'm convinced it is a maelstrom, Midas. This entity knows your weaknesses. It exploits your fears, and it is relentless. It plays for keeps. I can't say it enough, I can't stress it enough, don't take anything from that place. Not a rock, not a button and not a damn feather. I feel bad enough that I removed Moriah Mitchell's journal. I see you have it there. And then you find a feather at your house?"

Midas and I locked eyes at the mention of the feather. Jocelyn didn't have to guess; she knew what we were thinking. "I couldn't believe it when you called and told me that. See what I mean? It knows you are coming."

"You think it wants us to stay away?" I had to ask. I wasn't sure what to think about all this.

"Oh no. Quite the opposite. It wants you to come. It wants you to accept the gift, but it wants something in return." A loud noise startled me, and I smothered a yelp of surprise.

"It's a truck backfiring. That's all," Midas said in a comforting voice.

Man, I was on edge. I had to get it together if I was going to make it through this investigation.

"How is Adrian?" Jocelyn asked with some concern.

"Scared and ready to tear the school down. I'm glad we get to go inside before she takes such drastic measures. It is a gorgeous building."

She sat back down, leaned back in her chair and fiddled with her shoelaces. "Did you see the stone over the door? Do you know what it means?"

"I didn't pay any attention to it. What does it say?"

"It's a carving that reads, '*Non timebo mala.*'" She fidgeted nervously and continued, "It means, 'I will fear no evil.'"

I shook my head in disbelief. I'd never heard of such a thing. "Wow, that is frightening. Why in the world would they put something like that up there? Unless they knew about the history of the place? Unless the builders wanted to protect themselves or the people inside."

Midas opened the journal and turned to the first page. "From what I gather, from what you are telling me, that stone is not working. Would you mind telling us about your investigation? You've shared a little with me, but I want Cassidy to hear too."

"Sure," she said as she tapped her fingers on the table. Clearly, this subject made her nervous. As she began sharing her story, I reached for my small sketchpad. I hoped I would receive some impressions while she spoke. For some reason, my mind went back to the handsome young man in Moriah Mitchell's journal.

"The auditorium is one of the worst, most haunted places on that property. It's always cold in there, even though part of the roof has caved in. It got so cold once that I could see my breath in front of my face. I know that is typical of paranormal experiences, but this was extremely cold. We've seen drops in temperature that have preceded paranormal activity, but nothing this drastic."

As she spoke, I began to absently sketch on my pad. I wasn't getting anything yet, but I could feel the spiritual "warm-up" happening. "Besides the cold spot is the boy. But he's not really a boy, Midas. According to Moriah Mitchell, the boy is a face for a very old, very murderous spirit. One that's been on that land for a long time. Long before the school was there. Hugh McCandlish knew him as Ollie."

"Fascinating. McCandlish appeared to you, right? Was he a translucent apparition, or did he appear more physical?" Midas took notes on his laptop.

"Yes, he did. He was more solid...I could see the color of his hair and stuff. You know he was murdered there, right? In

1937. He rescued me, Midas. Sounds crazy, huh? At least he's there. I get the feeling that Ollie can't control him although he very much wants to. He wants all the souls." She bit her lip as her thoughts turned inward. Then she remembered where she was in the conversation. "The key...I lost the key. I couldn't get out without it. The damn thing went missing, but McCandlish brought it back. I'm sure he did. Yeah, he was the only good spirit there. The only one that wasn't completely enslaved to Ollie."

I shivered at her description and sketched her face. She squinted at my drawing and flashed her white teeth in a contagious smile. "Hey, that's me."

"Tell us about Gary Holloway. You saw him too. Cassidy, he was the previous owner's brother. He supposedly committed suicide on the property."

"He jumped off the roof. Can you imagine? He was terrifying."

In a quiet voice, I asked, "What did he look like, Jocelyn?" "Gary liked to smoke, and his teeth were stained. He was smoking during our interaction. He wears blue jeans with rolled cuffs, but strangely enough, I don't remember his shoes. He asked me if I was human and threatened to peel my skin off."

"Crap," I said as my stomach lurched.

"I can't tell you how terrifying that was, how shook that encounter left me. Ollie, the maelstrom of the Leaf Academy, is operating on such a level of manipulation. He is a serious threat to anyone who is weak-minded. That evil—it took my breath away. If you were a non-believer and went inside, you'd leave a believer. It's truly a horrible place. Amityville has nothing on the Leaf Academy."

Jocelyn's voice trailed off, and we all got quiet. "I know I have said this once, but I can't stress this enough. It is vitally important that you don't pick up anything. Nothing. Tell Joshua and Sierra, too. Don't let them go in without tattooing it on their brains. Don't pick up a rock, not a piece of wood. Nothing at all. For whatever reason, this maelstrom thinks that your acceptance of his gifts is an open door. If you accept anything, if you pick anything up, you are making an exchange."

I swallowed at her description as I thought about the big black feather on my bed. "What kind of exchange?"

"I don't understand it all, but I got the feeling that if I accepted that feather, any of them, I would lose my soul. Sounds like something from a horror movie, right? Nevertheless, it's all happening at the Leaf Academy. You know what? I have to go with you guys. If for nothing else but to make sure you remember that. I can't let you guys go without me. You need me to keep an eye out for you. I'm going, Midas. You can count on me." She wiped at her eyes with the back of her hand.

"If we go on that premise, then Cassidy was offered a gift earlier. A big, black feather. We've got to get rid of it without this spirit believing we've accepted his gift."

"Tricky to say the least, but it's been my experience with this maelstrom that it won't be there when you get back. I can't remember seeing those feathers again after I refused them."
I felt sick to my stomach. The idea of Ollie coming to my house not once but twice was making me physically ill. "Midas, I

have to go home. My cat…my house…" I stuffed my sketchbook in my book bag and slung it over my shoulder.

"We'll all go together, Cassidy." Grim-faced, Midas closed his laptop and immediately began turning off the lights. He locked the door behind us as the three of us filed out. I was sure this was not how he wanted the night to end. He wanted to do some preliminary research, but my heart was heavy. If anything happened to Domino while I was gone, I would never forgive myself. We all rode in Midas' SUV in silence. When we got to my house, every light in the house was on. It was lit up like a Christmas tree. A horrible, haunted Christmas tree.

As soon as the car came to a stop, I shot out and raced to the front door.

Chapter Six—Shanafila

After days of fasting from words, it seemed strange to hear them spoken loudly now. Fula Hatak's voice conveyed anger and fear, and both seemed directed at me. I could not understand him at first. I was caught between worlds as the remnants of the medicine lingered in my brain and dulled my senses. I heard the fear in the shaman's voice, and the sound did not bring me peace. As Fula Hatak's screams faded, I realized that I was not dreaming, and the sensation that I had left the Spirit World jarred me. The sensation reminded me of my first memory.

My father and I spinning, the canoe twirling about in the whirlpool, my stomach rolling and churning.

I was glad to be in my own world again, away from that black-eyed spirit that posed as a child. I was glad to be back inside my own body. Relief washed over me as I felt the mortal shell tighten around me. I wiggled my fingers and toes. Yes, I could move, and I had to get up and tell Fula Hatak what I saw. I tried to pick myself up off the ground, but Fula Hatak would not allow me to move. I felt his heavy foot on my back; he was pinning me to the ground as he screamed again. And then the screaming ended and he began to mutter.

"You doomed us all! We will pass into the Land of Darkness, Shanafila. By your hands. By your hands!" With one last shove, he lifted his foot and began waving his arms about like a madman. And then he began his song. This was not a song I recognized, and its words chilled me to the bone. I had failed in my mission. That was clear enough.

"No, Fula Hatak!" I yelled as fear gripped me, but I could say nothing else. The medicine drink still held the power to make me sick. I gagged on vomit and turned my head to retch. It was a relief to get the sickening fluid out of my body, but it left me feeling as weak as an abandoned baby squirrel. Thankfully, Fula Hatak stepped away from me as his song faded. I leaned on my side and struggled to regain my composure.

The old man screamed loudly again and pointed his finger at me. "Nalusa Falaya! You saw him—this is his gift, Shanafila! You have taken his gift, and now we will all die. Young and old, guilty and innocent. Even our dead are cursed because of you!"

I could hardly believe my ears. Was I dreaming still? Where was Haloka? Grandfather Imafo? Was this all a dream? My eyes rolled around, and I struggled to control their movements. I shut them tight and waited for Fula Hatak's declaration to end. Was I the last man to survive the journey to the Medicine Hill? I could not say, but I had never felt lonelier.

Fula Hatak sang my Death Song as I imagined my wife, my sweet Yukpa, waiting for me with open arms. Would I die now? Would he slice my throat and leave me to bleed in the sand?

Oh, Yukpa. I have failed you, wife.

I imagined the feel of her soft, strong arms. How I wanted to be in her arms again. To hear her whisper my name...*Shanafila!* I longed to feel the cool breeze on my bare skin as we lay in the green fields near our village with the moon high above us, Yukpa's welcoming body beneath me. Truly I had lived and loved. These memories were more than I deserved. And now I would never rub her growing belly again or teach my son the ways of our people.

Yes, I knew we would have a son. A Waliki boy, a strong brave who would lead our people back to their homelands. We had lost our way after the Time of Wars. Before his untimely death, my father had led us to seek the Way of Peace. But you could have no peace with neighbors who wanted to kill you. We were a defeated people. We had lost our lands. We were too far from the sea, too far from the orchards that nourished us. There had been too many wars with the Alibamu and the Chickasaw.

I had come to the Medicine Hill believing that I would see the way forward. I thought I would see a future for the Waliki, but I had seen nothing. Nothing except the boy.

But he was no boy. Even though I had not thought so before, I believed Fula Hatak.

I had encountered the Nalusa Falaya, the Soul Eater. I had forgotten the story, like so many of the stories of my fathers. There were no fathers to tell them anymore, except for Fula Hatak and Grandfather Imafo. I should have known the truth, but in my condition, I could not recall the moment when I accepted the feather. I knew deep in my soul that I had not accepted it...but now I wasn't so sure. No! Yukpa! I wanted to think of her, not the feather or the Soul Eater. The sweet images faded, but I could still see; I saw my home. And I could see a sea of blood. Bodies were everywhere, Waliki bodies. My people—tall and thin, their long dark hair muddied and bloodied. There was no life in any of them.

"No!" I screamed against the vision. This was not what I wanted to see. Not at all. I began to cry out to the old man.

"Why, Fula Hatak? I did nothing!" But I remembered the boy with the mesmerizing eyes, eyes like two dark caves. He had given me no choice. I had to accept the feather or die.

This is what you came for, Waliki man. Take it!

"This is the end of us! You have brought death to our people, Shanafila. You will not return with me. You cannot return!" Suddenly, with the strength of the bear, I rose up and threw myself at the old man. He could not stop me from returning home to my Yukpa. I was Waliki! I had done nothing wrong except walk the Sacred Path as I had been asked. I had come to the Medicine Hill at Fula Hatak's request. Before I knew it, the shaman and I were wrestling in the sandy soil. With as much anger as I could muster in my woozy state, I threw him on the ground and put my knee in his chest. When had I ever been so angry? Never. And I wanted to kill Fula Hatak, kill him with my bare hands.

"Stop, Shanafila! The blood of our people is already on your hands. Will you take my life too?"
I shuddered at his words. Nausea hit me again, and I closed my eyes to steady myself. That was a mistake. At that moment, Fula Hatak struck me with his strong fist. He hit me hard on the side of the head, and the world went black. I did not dream or feel or see anything.

Not until the boy appeared.

My eyes would not open, but I felt the toe of his moccasin poking me in the side. I felt my skin try to climb off my body.

Waliki!

Suddenly, a sharp kick struck my rib cage. I wheezed as I sat up and pushed at the invisible boy. He responded only with an evil laugh; it was not a sound that comforted me or conveyed joy.

The boy's mocking laughter terrified me, and finally, I could see. The sun had set, the air felt warm, and mosquitoes buzzed around my face. I could not see the boy, just the black of night, the sandy hill and a line of trees a few feet away. Yes, this was the line of trees that encircled the Medicine Hill. This was a place for dreams and visions, or so Fula Hatak told us before we came to the sacred spot. I had no reason to disbelieve him.

I spun around and called into the blackness, "Fula Hatak! Forgive me. I was not myself!"

Nobody answered. Clearly, Fula Hatak and the other Waliki had departed from the hill and left me behind. He had forbidden me to return home. How could he do that? I had seen the spirit of this place, and hadn't I been sent to retrieve a vision for our tribe? That's when my eyes fell on the feather again. It was at my feet, just waiting for me to pick it up.

To claim it. Again.

This is what you came for.

I stepped away. Just as I was making my way into the forest, I heard the boy's mocking laughter in my ears. It hung in the air and continued. It seemed a horrible, endless thing.
I have to get back to the village! Yukpa needs me!

I ran, awkwardly at first, as if my legs were two blocks of wet sand. But then I picked up speed and began to run as quickly as ever. Slender tree limbs slapped me as I hurried through one thicket and then another. I could feel the blood in my mouth as a branch popped my lip, but I did not let it stop me. Finally, I recognized where I was—I could see the path stretching out before me now.

Feeling even more anxious, I raced faster. My lungs were burning, and my sides hurt. My mouth was sticky and dry. And I was not alone. I could hear them running with me.

Black shadows of men! The Dark Ones!

They raced with me, ran with me. Was I one of them? No! Never!

I had to stop for a moment, to breathe and regain my bearings. It was easy to get lost in the dense part of the forest. This had not been my home. These were strange lands to my people. My shaking hands hugged the tree trunk as my eyes searched for a way forward. But the Dark Ones knew the way, and they did not wait for me but raced on ahead of me. I heard a strange screeching noise, many voices screeching, cackling with delight. I could see the trees moving ahead of me. The branches shook as the Dark Ones vanished deeper into the woods and raced toward my home. I gulped and then screamed at them.

"Stop! No!"

I ran, but I could not make up the distance between us. That's when I heard the first of the screams.

The screams of children, and women and men. The cries mingling together were like a horrible song, rising in the sticky night air and lifting to the heavens. In a moment that seemed to last forever, the chorus of shrieks grew louder and louder, and I felt sicker and sicker.

The Dark Ones were murdering my people, and there was nothing I could do to save them.

Nothing at all.

And I had led them here.

Chapter Seven—Jocelyn

My arrival at the Leaf Academy was as gut-wrenching as I expected it to be. Who was I kidding? I had never been more scared in my life, and here I was back in the haunted school. Like a complete idiot. I would never forget encountering the spirits of this place—the many entities that called the Leaf Academy home. Those experiences were etched into my brain. It wasn't likely that I would ever forget the terror I felt during my short stay here.

From Gary Holloway to the little boy—Ollie, as some people called him—to the random spirits I saw in the hallway outside and inside the auditorium. Yes, I would never forget their faces, their dead, decomposing faces. And all those feathers. It had all started when I walked up the steps of the school. I'd turned away for one second, then turned back to see the door standing wide open.
Like someone had been waiting for me and wanted me to come inside.

Was the Gulf Coast Paranormal team ready to come up against such an intelligent predator?
Ollie definitely knew we were coming. But why did he show up at Cassidy's place and not mine? Hmm...I thought about that for a second or two.

Clearly, Cassidy's gift was the difference. She was some sort of medium. I mean, how else could you describe her? She saw the dead and sketched their pictures. I on the other hand occasionally got lucky and captured them with my camera. Fortunately, as I predicted, the feather wasn't there when we got to her house. Not a trace of the thing. Cassidy packed a bag and grabbed her cat and spent the night with Midas.

I wasn't backing down on my theory that this entity was nothing less than a maelstrom. An ancient maelstrom whose sole goal was to possess, kill and control as many souls as possible.

But to what end? I could not say. How could someone think like a maelstrom?

I shivered as I reached for the camera cases. What good was all this going to do? I had tons of pictures of this place and a few ghosts. Did we need anything else? Oh well, this was my job. Kind of. Best to put a good face on for the rest of the team. It was all hands on deck. Midas was determined to get the proof he wanted—cold, hard evidence that there were such beings known as the October People hanging out here in the crumbling Leaf Academy.

Poor Midas. If he thought he could reason with this thing, he was in for a rude awakening, but I took comfort in the knowledge that I wasn't here by myself. And these people were the best at what they did. Sierra and her abilities as a sensitive, Cassidy and her drawing, Josh and his...what exactly did Josh bring to the table? I wasn't sure I liked the guy, most days, but like most jobs, you didn't always like the people you worked with. Not in the *let's be friends* kind of way. Once again, Helen and Bruce were supposed to be with us, but they'd essentially dropped off the map and didn't really do too many investigations anymore.

And Pete?

Well, there was no coming back for Pete. He wasn't welcome, and I couldn't say I blamed Midas. My ex had always been a bit of a coward. Midas had already given him multiple chances. I can't say I would have forgiven Pete after discovering his secret hookups with Midas' ex Sara. Yeah, Midas was a nice guy. Too nice sometimes.

For some reason, the memory of Midas' confession came back to me. It had been years ago, during one of those rare occasions when he actually got drunk. It was in Panama City after our investigation in the Sapphire Caves. That was long before Cassidy joined the crew, back when Midas was still with Sara and I was with Pete. We had been the four amigos, the Delta Force of the paranormal before everything went mainstream.

Yikes. Just thinking about Pete Broadus made me experience deep regret. So why again was I thinking about him?

Get your head in the game, Jocelyn.

I glanced at our leader. His jaw was clenched, that familiar expression of determination on his face. I wondered if anyone else knew that Midas Demopolis was a tormented soul. Somewhere in that handsome head of his, that nagging question rolled around: *What could I have done differently? How could I have let Dominic down?*

He grieved for his cousin to this day. That was how Midas worked. He always took the blame for everything; he took the blame for every bad situation. And it wasn't like he was one of those guys who just thought the worst about the world and all the people in it. No. Midas took an optimistic view of every situation. And everyone. He was an old soul. He was the guy that you went to because you knew he would get things done. Or at least comfort you. A prime example was me calling him after bolting out of the Leaf Academy. Yep, I ran out of the building with Sherman in my arms. I ran through the mud and the rain and forgot all about my commitment to the truth. And some of my equipment, which I was later able to retrieve. In the full light of day, of course.

Yes, I too found comfort in knowing that Midas was just a phone call away, that he would be there when I needed him. I both loved and admired that about him, but I could see where it might not be a good thing for him. It wasn't healthy for anyone to shoulder everyone's loads, everyone's problems. I looked at Cassidy as I carried the two cases and followed behind Joshua into the open door of the building. I wondered if she knew that about Midas. Or was she too focused on those big muscular arms? Too wrapped up in those dark, soulful eyes?

"Watch your step, Jocelyn," Joshua warned me as I tripped into the school. He reached a hand out to steady me, and I murmured my thanks. I carried the cases to the table that Cassidy and Sierra were setting up. I didn't think putting our headquarters right here in the foyer was a good idea, but I kept my mouth shut. I suggested that we keep our monitoring station in the van, but I was overruled. I did emphatically warn the group during our meeting: *Don't pick up anything. Don't touch anything. And if you see a feather—run!*

Joshua had laughed at my warning, but Sierra cut him off with a sharp look. He wasn't that bright, I decided. He would be the first one the maelstrom went after. Intelligent spirits such as this one enjoyed making believers out of non-believers. Everyone in the paranormal community here on the Gulf Coast had heard about the goings-on at the Leaf Academy, and some had heard about the October People. This was as serious as it got.

After a few more trips to the van, we had everything unloaded and the front room was full of our equipment. Midas raised his hands slightly as if we were a group of schoolchildren and he a principal.

That's an apt comparison since we're in an old, deserted school.

"Well, we're here. We've got three days. Three days to catch all the evidence we possibly can. Three days to find answers for Ms. Shanahan and maybe get to the bottom of these legends."

"Why just three days? What's the hurry?" Sierra asked. I liked her, but we didn't have very much in common. I wasn't married with children, and I didn't dress nearly as sharply as the sassy blonde. Yeah, I felt like a fifth wheel tonight. The odd man out. Funny, I never used to feel that way. I liked being alone, being the free spirit. But suddenly I realized I wanted something more. I blamed it on Sherman. My dog slowed me down enough for me to realize that I needed to love someone. I could keep a living thing alive.

Not for the first time this evening, I missed Aaron. I was certain that I had almost talked him into coming with me tonight, but he backed off at the last minute with some lame excuse that his brother needed help rebuilding a carburetor. Like I believed that. Aaron was about as handy as Sherman. But I didn't argue about it and didn't push him. Aaron's accident at that amusement park in Gulfport had shaken him to the core. And his grandmother. Not that Aaron was a mama's boy, or in this case a grandma's boy, but he listened to his Nina in all things. I wasn't sure she exactly liked me, but that was okay. It was probably just as well.

As a matter of fact, I had been weighing my options. Did I really want to put roots down here in Mobile, Alabama? I wasn't really sure.

"Because Adrian Shanahan wants to demo this place. And soon. I guess I could plead for longer if we needed it, but I think that with the level of activity that Jocelyn experienced here, we should have no problem getting some real evidence of these spirits. Anyway, one of the hotspots is going to be in this lower hallway. So if I'm facing the door, it's the hallway to the right, and down that hallway is the auditorium. The other location that's on this list is on the second floor—it is the bedroom of Hugh McCandlish, the man who was murdered in the auditorium. I think we covered much of this at our meeting, but I want you to be aware that no place is really off-limits for investigation. It is a lot of ground to cover, but to begin with, let's focus on the targeted areas. I think tonight after we finish setting everything up, we should pair off and hit these hotspots just to kind of get a feel for the place."

"I hope the headmaster's office is on your list. There were some weird happenings in there the last time," I said as I raised my hand like a kid at school. I suddenly felt nervous and reached out to fiddle with my dreadlocks when I remembered I no longer had them. Why had I cut my hair off again?

"Let's take it slow, guys. I think our normal procedure of working in pairs will keep everyone safe. But this evening, I want us to take turns investigating the same room back to back. So instead of having Cassidy and Sierra upstairs in the bedroom and Jocelyn and Joshua down here in the auditorium, let's not separate our focus. Let's investigate one room at a time for now. I want to be close to you guys if anything does happen. I want you to be safe; these spirits can get very interactive, very physical. Don't forget a guy fell or jumped off the roof. There are also reports that another man threw himself out of a window and a third guy was stabbed on the stage at the auditorium. This is a dangerous place for living people."

Everyone agreed and got busy working with the equipment. We placed a thermal camera on the second floor, a laser grid at the end of that hallway and a proximity meter in McCandlish's room. Next, we put cameras in the auditorium and in the hallway outside it, and then set up the computers for monitoring. When we finished checking connections, Cassidy unfolded a chair and slid it under the table. "I am ready to hit that auditorium. What do you think, Sierra? Are you up to it?"

I grabbed my camera bag and said, "Can we break some protocol here? How about letting me tag along too? I'll hang back and take pictures." It was kind of my way of saying, "I'm not taking no for an answer." Midas liked that idea, and we gathered up our equipment and headed toward the auditorium. Nobody spoke as we made the long walk down the hall. The floors felt just as gritty as before beneath my sneakers. The boarded-up windows at the front of the school put half of the building in perpetual shadow. It was surreal being back here. I realized that time meant nothing at the Leaf Academy. It didn't matter what month it was: October, April or January—this place was a home for the dead. They were here. I could smell their staleness, and that strange taste of electricity filled my mouth. Like putting a battery on my tongue. Yes, whether it was rainy or sunny, winter or spring, the Leaf Academy belonged to the dead. I was afraid my teammates were about to have their worlds rocked, and I wasn't sure they were ready for that.

Ready or not, here we come, I thought as I walked behind tiny Sierra and athletic, toned Cassidy. Yeah, I was the third wheel for sure, but I knew something they didn't. I knew the power of this place. I knew that tricksters lived here who wanted nothing more than to bring Sierra and Cassidy into their ranks. And me. Like Midas, I decided then and there that it was my mission to keep everyone safe. They were walking into unchartered territory.

"By the way, y'all. If anyone asks if you're human, just say yes," I whispered as the two of them paused outside the yawning cavern that used to be the auditorium doors. I pushed ahead of them and stepped into the room with my camera at the ready.

And it was a good thing too.

There was a performance of sorts going on. Yes, we were just in time.

Chapter Eight—Cassidy

In the center of the stage were three crows. Not massive paranormal-looking creatures, just plain old everyday crows. None of the three were large enough to sport the gigantic black feather I found in my house yesterday. They were waddling around, absently pecking the grimy floor as if they owned the place. They spotted us immediately, their black eyes pinned to our every move. As if we could read one another's minds, we all froze. Jocelyn lifted up her digital camera slowly and snapped a photo, but the soft whirring of the flash set them to squawking.

"Jocelyn, I don't think that's such a great idea. Back up...slowly."

I reached for her, but she did not move. Not a muscle. Sierra was clearly spooked. I said, "Shoo! Go away, birds." The crows tilted their heads in strange ways, and one bird hopped to the edge of the stage as if to challenge us. Not knowing what else to do, I ever so slowly reached for the walkie-talkie and tapped on the speaker button. "Midas? Are you getting this?"

"Yes, proceed with caution. They'll probably leave in a minute."

Proceed with caution? That's the best advice he could come up with? Wow, way to help out, Midas.

Jocelyn glanced back, her camera still in front of her face. "He's right. Let's leave them alone and just wait it out." I nodded in agreement, but I wasn't sure how to proceed. I didn't know much about birds; I was just getting the hang of cats.

Suddenly, the crow at the edge of the stage made an ear-ringing noise, a kind of cackle and caw all at the same time. That's when the smell hit me. I don't know how I could have missed it before—I smelled decay. But that wasn't hard to imagine, not in a place like this. The whole place was rotten, and this room was no exception. The auditorium itself was large for a school, especially a school for boys. But as Midas mentioned earlier, the local orchestra used to have their performances here too, and the headmasters were always open to hosting community events. I could very well imagine the place full of excited music lovers. I could almost see the finely dressed orchestra raising their arms, obedient to every flick of the conductor's baton.

But as hard as I tried, nothing in here stirred me to sketch or draw or paint. The image burned in my mind was of the handsome young man I'd started to work on the other night. And as far as I knew, he wasn't a part of the October People legend.

After staring at the birds for a full two minutes, Jocelyn suggested that we move ahead. "I think they'll leave if we get closer, but we should do it together. There's only three of them."

"There's three of us too," Sierra complained as she shook her head. "But you're right. We can't do any investigative work with these birds around."

"Then it's settled. On the count of three, we go to the stage. They can fly out through that hole up there. I'm pretty sure that's how they got in. You ready, Cassidy? Sierra?"

I shrugged. "Sure, but what exactly are we going to do?"

With a confidence I hadn't expected, Jocelyn answered, "We're going to make a lot of noise and wave our hands around. That should scare them."

Sierra's expression said it all. She wasn't too keen on this idea, but if we were going to do a proper investigation in here, we had to get rid of the crows. On a quiet count of three, Jocelyn, Sierra and I rushed the stage waving our arms and screaming like wild banshees. What we weren't prepared for was the dozen or so crows on the ground in front of the stage. We hadn't seen them from our earlier vantage point.

"Holy crap!" I shouted as the birds flew up and around us. One bird tugged at my shirt; I didn't think it was intentional, but it scared the heck out of me. Sierra's blond hair was being pulled, and she had a scratch on her arm. Multiple scratches.

"Sierra! Get down and cover your head!" I covered my eyes with my hands to protect them, and through my splayed fingers, I could see Sierra squatting down. Jocelyn was nowhere to be found, and Midas was screaming into the walkie-talkie. The birds lifted and circled above us, blocking out the little bit of light that streamed into the decrepit auditorium. I heard Jocelyn swearing, so I knew she was close by. I wanted to call out to her, to reach her or Sierra, but I was frozen with fear. Then I heard the sounds of running footsteps, and without looking I knew that Midas had arrived on the scene.

"Get out of here! Get out now!" Joshua and Midas yelled in concert at the swirling birds that quickly evacuated the auditorium.

"Sierra? Little Sister, are you bleeding? What about you, Jocelyn?"

"Yeah, I think so. My arm is stinging. One of those birds bit me or scratched me or something. Cassidy? Are you okay?" Sierra moved her hair out of her face while Josh examined her wound.
I nodded and said, "I'm still alive. I had no idea all those other birds were down there. Did you see them before we came closer?"

"No. But at least they're gone now. Ouch, Joshua! It hurts." Sierra withdrew her arm from her husband's probing fingers. Joshua looked at Midas and said, "I think I need to do a little doctoring here. Does anyone else need first aid? Anyone else have scratches or claw marks or anything? It's really important that we take care of your wounds because there's no telling what kind of infection you can get from a place like this."

Still clutching Midas' arm, I shook my head. "No, I'm okay. A little shook up, but I'm okay. What about you, Jocelyn?"

"Yeah. I'm good. Like you, just a little shook up. Well, we got rid of them. Sorry I put us in danger. Like you, I didn't see the rest of that flock. I just assumed it was a couple of birds...I'm really sorry." Jocelyn was getting upset, but it wasn't really her fault. We knew what we were up against coming to a place like this. There were always animals, birds—things lingering in closets and in dark places. It was part of our job description. Luckily, Sierra put Jocelyn's mind at ease, and she and her husband left the auditorium to get the first-aid kit from the van. We didn't normally bring it inside if we were going to set up a monitoring station in any building. But we always had it close by. Just in case.

"If you two are up to it, let's continue and I will monitor from the front room. I guess the element of surprise has been eliminated, but we have to try, right?" Midas' steely expression reminded me that I was here to do a job. Adrian Shanahan depended on us, the Gulf Coast Paranormal team, to determine whether there was an actual maelstrom spirit at the Leaf Academy. What she would do with that information, I wasn't sure, but I was going to do my part. I rubbed the dust and dirt off my sleeves and tidied my hair as best I could. I slid the walkie-talkie back onto my belt loop and reached for my digital recorder. It was still in my pocket and still in good working order.

"We're ready when you are, Midas. Just give us a minute to get our bearings." Jocelyn checked the camera and grinned at me. I just knew she was having the time of her life. *Yes, fearless. Be more like Jocelyn*, I instructed myself. Midas left us alone in the auditorium, and thankfully there were no more birds or other animals in sight, so we set about doing our first EVP session together at the Leaf Academy.

"This chair was where I was sitting in the picture. The one that I found. Yeah, right there. I think if we start there and then move to the stage, we might get some kind of response. Strange to think that students used to call this place home, right? Can you imagine being away from home and having to live in a place like this? I mean, it's not even Hogwarts cool. It's more like a prison for kids."

I held a recording device in my hands, unsure what to say. If Jocelyn thought she could connect with the ghosts of any kids lingering around here by saying negative things, then maybe we would get a response...but I wasn't sure what kind. I clicked the audio recorder and put it on the back of the chair that Jocelyn identified.

"Cassidy Wright in the auditorium with Jocelyn Graves at the Leaf Academy. Night one investigation." I paused for a second or two and then continued, "My name is Cassidy, and this is Jocelyn. But if you have been listening, you know that. Are you here? What is your name? Are you a student at the Leaf Academy?" Jocelyn took pictures of the chair, the front, the back and the sides. She reviewed them quickly but shook her head. She hadn't captured anything. And I didn't feel anything. That was so odd because I could smell decaying wood and something else, something I could only identify as death. The aroma surrounded me; it was closing in on me, but it was also elusive. They didn't want us to see them or feel them or hear them. Yet I had to try. Jocelyn and I asked a few more questions. The EVP session lasted for at least thirty minutes. We scanned each recording session and listened after every round, but there was nothing to hear.

Nothing at all.

"I guess this place wants to make a liar out of me, but I know what I saw. I know what happened. And you didn't imagine that feather. We are being toyed with, stalked, and I don't like it." Jocelyn stomped out of the auditorium, and I followed behind her. I couldn't be sure, but judging by her sloped shoulders and quiet mannerism, it looked like she was crying. I caught up to her and could see tears in her eyes. And as I tried to comfort her, to listen to whatever it was she needed to express, I finally heard something.

Something I didn't expect.

I heard Kylie call my name...

Chapter Nine—Cassidy

"Jocelyn! Wait! I believe you. I swear I do. You won't believe what I just heard."

Jocelyn spun around, her eyes wide. "What? What did you hear? Did you see something?"
I frowned and sighed deeply. Midas was walking toward us; clearly, he was concerned about Jocelyn and me. "Don't tell him, but I heard Kylie's voice. My sister. Don't say anything to Midas."

Jocelyn gave me an inquisitive look, but there was no time to explain anything. She did not know that Midas had heard Dominic's voice when he came to check the place out with Adrian. I felt as if I needed to protect him from knowing that there was something here that could mimic the ones we loved, the ones who had passed. She agreed in a quiet whisper, and then Midas was with us, his face flushed with excitement.

"I think it's time to switch out. Let me and Josh go in and give it a shot. You know how these spirits are; sometimes, they have favorites. Clearly, it is not ladies' night at the Leaf Academy, but that's probably to be expected. You know, there were no women here back in those days except for the few who worked in the kitchen."

I handed him my walkie and the digital recorder. "I'm okay with that, and I'm all for getting out of that room for a few minutes. So what are you thinking, another 30 minutes? I'm eager to check out the other rooms." I faked a smile as Josh walked toward us. Sierra was taking her seat in front of the monitors in the front room. She looked fine, especially for someone who had been mauled by a flock of crows a few minutes ago, but I could see the bandage on her arm when she pulled her hair back into a ponytail. She waved good-naturedly at us as Jocelyn handed Joshua her camera. He was also carrying a proximity detector in his hand, and I could practically guarantee that there were a few other gadgets in his backpack.

"We are going back to the front room and will watch it from there. Look out for birds!" I said in an attempt at humor. None of us were feeling it. Midas nodded his head, and Joshua scowled at me as if I would bring him bad luck just by mentioning the birds. Jocelyn and I walked toward Sierra, and Jocelyn immediately began to quiz me.

"Why are we keeping secrets from him? I don't like that."

"Neither do I, but what choice do we have? I don't in any way believe that my sister is here. She and I have made peace with one another, and I know where she's at—and it's not the Leaf Academy. Whatever is here, I don't even like saying this, but I believe it can read our minds. It knows our deepest fears and preys upon them. It uses those fears, those heartaches...it uses them against us. Midas is not in a good place right now. I don't understand why, but Dominic's death..."

Sierra called, "Hey, Cassidy. Come here a second. Take a look at the upstairs monitor. The laser grid. Is that just my eyes playing tricks on me?" Jocelyn and I scurried over to the collection of monitors on the table in front of Sierra. She positioned herself in front of the one that monitored the auditorium, but the image of the upstairs rooms, the second-floor hallway and Hugh McCandlish's bedroom, were flickering off and on.

As if someone were tinkering with the equipment, messing around with the electrical outlets. Those two cameras were not connected in any way. Everything we had was portable, wireless. Why in the world would two separate cameras be glitching out? And then it stopped.

"That was funky. If it does it again, someone will have to check that out."

"We will keep an eye on it. But for now, let's watch those guys."

I sat beside Sierra, and Jocelyn sat in the chair on the other side of her. Jocelyn asked, "How is your arm? Is it cut deep?"

"No. Not at all. But my husband likes to pretend to be a medic. It really was just a surface scratch."

"I am no doctor, Sierra, but you sure were bleeding." I frowned at her before I turned my attention back to the screen. "I'm glad it was nothing serious."

"What do you think about this place? Are you receiving any information?" Sierra asked me.

"Nothing at all. Not really. Our EVP sessions were quiet, but I know there's more than that."

"I know what you mean. When I tap the air around me, I can't explain it any better than that, whoever or whatever is here retreats. And that's not good. I have a nagging feeling...well, I'm not going to jump to any conclusions. It's not only that there's nothing interacting with us. It is as if there is a lack of anything. A strange nothingness. I'm sure I'm not making any sense to you guys. I don't like it. I would've thought there would be a lot of residual activity here, you know? Whenever you have a bunch of kids around, there's going to be residual activity. But that's not the case here. It's like someone came through with a big old spiritual vacuum cleaner and just sucked everything up. And in its wake...nothing."

Cassidy...
I froze at hearing my name being called yet again by that familiar voice, my dead sister's voice. I tried not to make any sudden moves and hoped that one of my friends would acknowledge it. But neither one of them indicated they heard anything, so I kept it to myself.

This was a cruel trick. I agreed with Jocelyn one hundred percent; whatever lived here at the Leaf Academy was certainly a trickster. And you know what? From what Sierra was describing, Jocelyn might also be right about labeling this thing a maelstrom.

Apparently, maelstroms could create vortexes or portals, I couldn't remember which. They were so powerful that they pulled things toward them, and they used their energy on it until the spirit they captured had nothing left. Kind of like an energy vampire but in a ghostly inhuman way. Which made me think that whatever was here wasn't human at all. For the next half-hour, we watched the guys walking around the auditorium doing their EVP sessions and testing out their equipment. But like us, they didn't hear or see anything. At least we got to witness a swarm of crows. The whole thing seemed so surreal just thinking about it.

"Earth to Cassidy. Are you listening? These cameras are glitching out again. Someone's got to go up and check the connectors. You know, those particular connectors are pretty loose to begin with. It wouldn't take much for something to bump them or do a number on them. Would you mind going up?"

"No, Sierra. I don't mind. I've got this, Jocelyn. You guys keep your eyes on the screen. I'm getting some sort of weird feeling. I know we don't run the show on feelings, but I can't ignore it either."

Jocelyn shot up from her chair immediately. "You heard Midas. We have to stick together. No going around this place by yourself. That's the rule, remember?"

"But if you come with me, Sierra will be by herself, and she's already been attacked. I don't want to put her in further jeopardy." Lying to my teammates was easier than I could've imagined, which made me feel horrible. But at the same time, I wanted to see this place for myself. If for no other reason than to give whatever it was that was stalking me and pretending to be Kylie a chance to manifest. Of course, that's never fun, but I felt like I could connect if I was by myself.

"Never mind. Midas and Josh are on their way. Midas doesn't look very happy." Jocelyn pointed at the screen, and then the three of us looked down the hall expecting them to appear, but they didn't. When I looked back at the screen, I didn't see either of them. Where could they have gone? "What the heck?" Sierra said, "That's not humanly possible. I've been watching the screen, and those guys were there one minute and gone the next. Come on, ladies. Let's go see what's going on in the auditorium. I am not ashamed to admit that I already don't like this place."

I agreed with Sierra, but I held up my finger and reached for the walkie-talkie on the makeshift table. "Cassidy to Midas. Where are you?"

A scratchy sound came over the walkie-talkie. I banged it on the palm of my hand, which didn't help. It sounded as if the batteries were dying, but that couldn't be right. Joshua was always so careful to load fresh batteries into all of our equipment. As a matter of fact, that was the most expensive part of keeping Gulf Coast Paranormal running other than the overhead for the office. We bought batteries like some people bought printer paper or other office supplies. "I can't hear you. If you can hear me, we are heading your way."

Before we could make our way toward the auditorium, I noticed that the monitor screens connected to the upstairs cameras were flashing. It's kind of like they were switching off and on, but we didn't have any strobe lights up there. Nothing that would make two cameras that were not connected go off and on like that. Before anyone could stop her, Jocelyn was grabbing equipment and making her way up the stairs.

"I will be back here in five minutes."

I called to her, "Jocelyn! We've got to go get Midas and Joshua. We don't know how long that's going to take. What about staying together?"

Jocelyn shrugged absently as she stepped on the bottom stair of the long staircase. I wasn't going to be able to talk her out of it, I could see that. But who was I to judge her? I'd been wanting to go up there by myself just a few minutes ago. I wondered why that was. I wasn't one to wander off by myself unless I had to draw something. Reflecting on it, the feeling was like some sort of compulsion. I was compelled to go up the stairs. Something wanted us to go up the stairs.

And it wanted us to go up one by one.

Chapter Ten—Midas

Joshua had picked the wrong day to start acting squirrelly. We'd barely gotten through the first fifteen minutes when he was ready to chase shadows outside the auditorium. Not that I hadn't seen them too; in fact, one particular shadow looked very humanlike, but that didn't mean there was anything out there. This was an old building that had been sitting abandoned for quite some time. The chances of us crossing the path of some derelict or homeless person were pretty good. It wasn't like we hadn't encountered people looking for a place to sleep or get warm in the past. But Joshua saw that shadow and was gone like a bullet out of a gun.

"Hold up, Joshua! Wait for me!" To his credit, he did pause momentarily, but it wasn't enough time for me to be comfortably close to him. After Little Sister's crow attack, it was hard to relax and just enjoy the investigation. My walkie-talkie was making clicking sounds. I reached for it and tried to call Cassidy but wasn't successful. Joshua and I were standing outside the auditorium by a bit of broken wall looking down the side of the building. Although the sun had gone down, there was just enough light to cast awkward purple shadows against the wall. It added to the spooky effect, and I could swear I saw a small shadow bounce and then vanish around the side of the building. I could tell by the look in Joshua's eyes and the expression on his face that he was more than willing to chase that shadow down.

I reached for his arm and tugged at it. "It's never a good idea to go running after shadows, Joshua. I saw it too, but he's not going anywhere. I kind of get the idea that he wants to draw us out. Let's go back and check in with the rest of the team. So far, we've seen crows and a possible shadow person, but that's the most activity I've seen here."

Joshua's sigh let me know that he wasn't happy with that plan, but I was still the boss. Luckily for me, he followed me back inside and didn't give me any lip. Cassidy and Sierra were barreling into the auditorium as if their shoes were on fire.

"Where did you go?" Sierra yelled at Josh breathlessly. "You were there one minute and gone the next. You didn't hear us calling you?" The sound of panic in her voice surprised me.

"I saw a shadow. We went outside to follow it, but it disappeared around the corner."

"Did you see it?" Cassidy asked me. "What did you see? What did it look like?"

"It looked like a shadow. It was kind of tall, almost as tall as me to begin with, but then it shrank. It was more child-sized. By the time we got to see it leave, it had shrunk down pretty significantly."
Cassidy continued her questioning as any good investigator would. "Could it have been a bird flying over? We know there are crows here." She tilted her head toward Sierra, who agreed with her. "Could it have been an actual person? Maybe someone looking to steal equipment or just find a place to get high?"

"All great questions, but no. It wasn't the shadow of a bird, and it wasn't a person, not a living person. We would've heard something. Footsteps or something. And we haven't seen anyone, but maybe..." I searched the room and noticed that Jocelyn was missing. "Jocelyn at the monitoring station?"

Cassidy's face flushed, and she shook her head. "She wouldn't listen to us. She wouldn't wait. A couple of the cameras on the second floor are cutting in and out, and she went up to check it out. I told her it was a bad idea, but then you guys were gone, and so..."

I swore under my breath as we hurried out of the auditorium. I had given those guys specific instructions. *Nobody separates. We investigate with a partner.* Leave it to Jocelyn to go rogue within the first hour of being here. So typical of her. "Let's go, you guys. All of us are going together. Grab some gear. We'll check out the second floor while we are up there. But please, no more splitting up."

Nobody said a word as we gathered the equipment and headed up the squeaking staircase. The entire floor was shrouded in darkness. It was darker than I expected. I could see the laser grid shimmering on the wall next to Hugh McCandlish's bedroom. Everything looked fine. The blue lights were lined up, each one of them shining perfectly. The camera pointing down the opposite end of the hall was on. Just as a precaution, Joshua checked the connections and confirmed that everything was working properly. The smart thing to do would have been to call out for Jocelyn, but it didn't feel like the *right* thing. I had the feeling that we weren't alone on the second floor of the Leaf Academy.

And then I heard footsteps, heavy footfalls. They were a little unusual because each step was accompanied by a kind of tinkling. No. Not tinkling, jingling. Like a cowboy wearing spurs. There were no cowboys here. Never had been.

And then Jocelyn stepped out of the room beside us with her finger to her lips. Nobody said a word. We all froze and listened to the stomping feet and the strange jingling that accompanied them. Footsteps were leading away from us to the opposite end of the hall. If I wasn't mistaken, that far doorway led to the roof. We heard a bang, and then everything went quiet. We all looked at one another, and if there ever was a collective sigh of relief, it was in that moment. But then we remembered why we were there at the Leaf Academy. We had come to find proof that a maelstrom, or at least a ghost or two, was calling the place home. Well, that was either a homeless person or something else. We gathered close and began to talk about what we had heard.

Josh said in an excited whisper, "We caught that on camera. I'm sure of that. Those were footsteps, right?"

Cassidy rubbed her lip with her finger; it was a kind of tic that presented itself when she was thinking. Nervously thinking. "Yeah, but didn't it seem like an odd kind of sound? Like a bicycle bell—something metallic."

"Jackboots," Jocelyn answered in a whisper. "You know, biker boots. The kind that guys used to wear in the 1950s. I've heard them before, when I encountered Gary Holloway." She visibly shivered and rubbed her arms at the memory of the threatening ghost.

"Well, you know what they say. Strike while the iron is hot. I think we should go see what Mr. Gary Holloway has to say for himself. But remember the rules, everyone. We stay together on this investigation. No more wandering around by yourself." I tried not to stare down Jocelyn, but everyone knew who I was talking about...including her.

She didn't argue with me but pointed at the cameras. "I just wanted to help out. The cameras were glitching, but I got distracted by a swishing sound coming from that room." She fiddled with her camera and stepped in behind us as we made our way to the roof.

"Hey, Jocelyn. Why don't you lead the way? I haven't been to the roof yet. We didn't make it that far during our walk-through. Show us where you first saw Mr. Holloway." This was my way of trying to mend fences, but it would also be useful to know where she interacted with the ghost. And to be honest, besides the brief glimpse of the shadow that disappeared outside and the strange assembly of crows, this was the closest we'd gotten to encountering anything paranormal. I couldn't figure out why that was, but sometimes things were slow to get started. I had no doubt that we would eventually see what it was we came here to see.

Midas... Midas, come find me... I'm here.

"What is it?" Cassidy was squatting beside me, and I was doubled over in the hallway with my team gathered around me. The pain in my stomach was so real, it felt as if somebody kicked me.

Someone with a small foot. A small, savage foot.

"I'm not sure. I just gotta catch my breath."
But that was Dominic. I knew his voice. Even after all these years, I knew his voice just as sure as I knew my own. What if I had been wrong? What if Dominic really was here and wanted me to come find him?

That's when everything got blurry.

Chapter Eleven—Shanafila

My feet carried me closer to the makeshift village that my tribe and I had most recently called home. This wild place had never truly been our home, for we had been driven out of our ancestral lands. We had valued peace too much, sought too many compromises. And because of that, we were no more. Peace had been my father's wish, and when he passed from this world, I took up his cause. But I was young, too young to manage the needs of my people. Seeking a vision, a way forward on the Medicine Hill, had been Fula Hatak's counsel.

Because of me, we were no more. For someone who was not acquainted with war, the sight of death sickened me. Now I would know the smell of blood, the blood of my people. The metallic odor permeated my skin and my mouth. Yes, it was as if I could taste death on my tongue. I longed to flee from this place, but how could I do that? My wife was here. The people I loved were here, but they were all silent. No fires burned, no songs were sung. There were no sounds of children.

All things were not well. Not well at all.

My toe struck something heavy, and it was no bag of sand or salt. This must be a body. As my eyes adjusted to the darkness, I squatted down and brushed the long dark hair out of the face of the dead man at my feet. Even in the faint light, I could recognize the lines of the face, the mouth opened wide—the eyes staring into nothing.

His face was bloodied and rent of all life. Whatever had happened here, the screams, the onslaught had happened quickly. There had been no chance to fight. The Dark Ones had done their evil work in the blink of an eye. A warrior like Fula

Hatak would never have given up his life without a fight. He was not the kind of man who would surrender. Yet I saw no hatchet in his hand, no blade near him. Upon closer examination of his body, I saw nothing that would lead me to believe he had lifted a hand against his enemy.

Yukpa! My wife!

Our tribe had been murdered, effortlessly and without a struggle. They had been cut down, and I had witnessed from a distance that horrible assault. The screams would always echo through my mind. Somewhere in this tangle of bodies and broken pots and precious things was my own Yukpa. Grief welled up in me like a living thing.

There were bodies everywhere! Although I was not used to shedding tears, they flowed like the mighty river that we once loved as our mother. The Waliki were no more; their souls had been stolen, taken from this world, and were now the prisoners of the Dark Ones. I must find Yukpa!
Where are you, my soul and my heart?

Ah, even the old ones were dead. Even the Waliki children. But I had no time to grieve over them, for in the distance I heard a shriek. A familiar voice. She called my name!
Yukpa!

I rose to my feet and listened carefully to determine which direction her screams were coming from. They reverberated through the forest, and the howls of coyotes echoed from somewhere close. What if she had managed to escape? What if she truly were alive? This must be her! It had to be! How could I live with myself if I did not save her? Yes, one last chance to make it right! I must save Yukpa! I began to journey through the woods, ignoring the thorns and the branches that cut my skin.

Another scream erupted from the forest. She couldn't be far now—I traveled deeper into the woods, and I would go deeper still to find her, to save her. But I was not alone.

The boy stood on the littered path before me. The clouds shifted, and the moon cast a strange light upon his face. It felt so cold here in the woods. So cold facing this creature. Fula Hatak had been right. This was the Soul Eater, and now he would eat *my* soul. To the left, to the right, the leaves began to shake, and things were moving—things I could not see. The shadow beasts rushed past me toward my wife, who continued to call my name. And the hearing of it was as if arrows were piercing my heart. I wanted more than anything to lift my voice to call to her, to promise her that I would come and save her, but...I could say nothing. It was as if my mouth had no will to obey my mind.

The Soul Eater—Nalusa Falaya! The thing with the boy's face raised his hand and showed me the sign of two folded fingers. A clear sign that I was to stay back and let him do his work. Finally, my voice erupted from my body and I screamed, "Give me my wife!"

The boy-thing waved his hand sharply, and I hit the ground as I fell on my knees. The pain in my stomach was intense, so intense that it knocked the wind out of me. To my horror, the boy walked toward me. With each step, the revulsion within me grew and I was completely undone by his presence. All the darkness. All the horrible darkness. I raised my hand above my head as if to push him back, to push him away. To stay his attack, for surely he would attack me just as he had Fula Hatak and my entire tribe. But he did not stop. He stood in front of me, and now all I could do was stare at his moccasins; my heart sank deep inside of me. It sank so deep that I knew I would never again be able to call upon it. I would die, surely, but that would be better than hearing the screams of my wife.

Why? Why have you done this to us? I did not accept your gift. It was thrust upon me!

But even as I said the words, I began to remember. I had an encounter with the Soul Eater, but I had then believed him to be a child and not the dark spirit of the woods.

I had made a deal with him...but what? What had I said? I could not quite recall it.

"No, I have been tricked," I whispered to whatever benevolent spirit might be listening. Nalusa Falaya had tricked me; it was in his nature to do so. I did not know the cost of his promise. Never would I have agreed to the murder of my people. No, the Soul Eater stole the souls of the Waliki.

Oh, but the vision. Yes, I remembered.

A chance at eternal life for you and the Waliki, Shanafila. This offer I make to you. Take my token and receive my gift.

And in my scattered state, under the fever of the vision potion, for surely that had been the reason why, I let the feather float into my shaking hand. Why else would I have ignored Fula Hatak's admonition? We were not to accept anything, nothing at all—that had been his instruction.

Seek a vision, but do not interact with the Spirits. Not all of them can be trusted.

Ah, it was too late to remember his words. The lies Nalusa Falaya told me! A promise of life for my people. I took the feather, a token of his presence and of his promise. It was in my hand again now. Where had this come from? A moan echoed from the depths of my soul. I tossed the feather away, but it didn't go far, only floated to the ground.

"I never wanted death. I never wanted this." But I could save Yukpa! I had to try. "Please, she is my life," I sobbed as tears rolled down my face. The spirit was unmoved by my raw emotion. I gathered that it enjoyed feeling them. Yes, I could see that smile of satisfaction on his face. Then the boy vanished, and another stood in his place. A man, a young man with long dark hair. His face painted with strange symbols, his clothing familiar. I was looking at myself! Nalusa Falaya had taken on my image.

No! I am Shanafila! You are Nalusa Falaya! I know what you are! You tricked me, but you cannot take me, and you cannot have Yukpa!

I screamed as the thing with my face touched my hand. I clutched it as his touch burned me. I snatched it away from him but not before the damage had been done. There burned into the palm of my hand was the shape of a long black feather. The meaning was clear to me. The contract could not be broken. I had accepted his gift.

Now he would accept mine.

He turned on his heel and ran at full speed, as fast as any wild boar or light-footed deer, disappearing into the gaping blackness. I could never run as fast as he, and never could I reach Yukpa in time. I staggered forward but did not get far. I collapsed on the mossy ground, completely consumed with my grief and with total awareness of the great sin I had committed. Fula Hatak had warned me. He had warned us all not to be fooled. We had gone to the Medicine Hill to find a way forward for our people, but instead, I had killed us all. The Waliki would be no more.

The sounds of Yukpa's terrified shrieks sealed my fate.

Forever.

Chapter Twelve—Cassidy

"Cassidy? You're a mess. Are you okay?" That was Midas' good morning to me, apparently. Before I could think of a witty comeback, he was picking up the sketches off the floor. "I didn't even hear you last night. Were you drawing all night?"

I caught a glimpse of myself in the mirror across the hotel room. Oh yeah, I looked like I'd fought a bear in my sleep. My red hair was all over the place, my clothes askew, and there were dark circles under my eyes.

"I got a few hours of sleep," I answered as I slid down the bed and joined him in picking up the pictures. "This is why I asked for two beds. I had a feeling that I would be drawing. I was so tired I crawled into bed without putting them up. Meet Shanafila."

"Shanafila? Is he connected to our case, or do you think you picked up something else? Maybe a spirit that's in the area?" Midas put the pictures on the small round table and handed me a cup of coffee. I normally didn't drink coffee, but this morning would be one of those rare occasions.

"You don't recognize him? He was in Moriah Mitchell's journal. Shanafila is connected to the Leaf Academy. Probably through the land. I don't think we're dealing with a ghost, Midas. Not in the usual sense. Jocelyn was right, this thing is strong. And it captures souls. It's called...what is the name again?" I snapped my fingers as if that would help me remember. It must have because I spit the name out without thinking. "Nalusa Falaya. That's it. Shanafila saw him; he made a deal with this spirit, but he was under the influence of a vision-inducing drink. Anyway, the Nalusa Falaya told him that the Waliki would live forever if he would accept his gift—a black feather. Oh no! Like the black feather we saw at my house, Midas. This isn't good. It can't be good!"

"Let's put these out of the way for a minute. Just take a deep breath, Cassidy, and start from the beginning."

I did as he asked. I closed my eyes and took a deep breath and then drank half my coffee before recounting what I had seen during my painting session. "Shanafila was the tribe's de facto chief. His father had been the chief, but he died suddenly. And the tribe, they were called the Waliki, they were dying off. There were many warring clans around them, but the Waliki were peace-loving people. They didn't like shedding blood, but they were in the minority. Other tribes moved into the coastal areas, their ancestral lands. The Waliki had been there for so long, but they were pushed inland into the forests. Many died in unwanted wars."

"Sounds like they had a tough time of it. How did Shanafila meet this Nalusa Falaya?" Midas drained his cup and reached for his notepad and pen.

"The tribe sent some of the young men to the Medicine Hill. It was basically a sandy hill with a ring of trees around it. Shanafila was one of those young men. They were given tea, some kind of hot drink that would supposedly open them up to see the other side. The shaman, his name escapes me at the moment, sent them to get answers for the tribe. Should they go to war and take back the land? Should they go west and hope to find new lands? They were really at a crossroads."

"Tell me more about the Nalusa Falaya." Midas jotted down a few notes on his paper and turned his intense stare to me.

"He was also called the Soul Eater; they believed he had the power to collect souls, for what reason I don't know. He is a trickster for sure because I got the feeling that Shanafila had no idea what he agreed to, and he didn't really believe in any of the stories of his tribe until this encounter. His memory of the actual encounter with the Nalusa Falaya wasn't great as a result of him ingesting that liquid. But...I hate even saying this...the entity's token was a black feather. Shanafila accepted it, and that was it for him."

"Damn," was Midas' reply. We sat in silence for a little while.

"It was horrible. Shanafila's whole tribe was wiped out by this spirit. It commanded a bunch of shadowy beings, and they helped it murder the tribe. Including Shanafila's wife." I shivered at the memory of Yukpa's screams. "Oh, and one more thing."

"You mean there's more?"

"Yes. It can take on your image. Or the image of someone you love. In some respects, it behaves like a doppelganger. I think that would explain why you saw Dominic at the Leaf Academy. You have to know that it's not him, Midas." I reached across the table and squeezed his hand. "You aren't the only one hearing things. I heard Kylie's voice. She was calling my name. I didn't see her, and I don't believe for a second it was my sister. I know she's safe. So is your cousin."

"My mind knows that, but my heart believes something else. I really hate that this thing has that kind of power. I know a few things about it. We know it can travel, since it came to your house. And it can pull things from your mind, like who you love, who you miss. And one more thing I can say with confidence—it knew we were coming. It's very intelligent."

"I would agree with all of that." I squeezed his hand again. "Do you think I should tell the team? Usually, I wait to share my sketches, but I don't think I should in this case. We can't take the risk that they encounter the Nalusa Falaya without this information. That's what I think, at least."
Midas' cell phone rang, but he didn't answer it right away. "I agree, Cassidy. Jocelyn had it right all along. Oh, I better answer this. Be ready in thirty?"

"All I need is fifteen minutes. Be right back." I grabbed my toiletries bag and headed to the restroom. Midas had stepped outside to get a better cell phone signal, presumably. I did the usual, brushed my hair and teeth and dabbed on a little makeup. As I went about my daily rituals, I thought about Shanafila and Yukpa. How did it end for them? Was Shanafila trapped in the school? What about all those Waliki souls? Not to mention the people who had been killed on those unholy grounds. Unholy was an apt description for it.

Non timebo mala. That saying was etched in stone above the doorway of the school. Somebody knew something, surely.

For the first time in any investigation, I wanted to quit. Some part of me didn't want to dig any deeper into this horrible mystery. People didn't just die at the Leaf Academy; they were murdered by this entity and the shadows that obeyed it. This wasn't your run-of-the-mill residual or a lost soul. This thing was abhorrent and hateful.

And it had Midas and me in its sights.

Chapter Thirteen—Cassidy

"You're blowing my mind, Cassidy. These are exquisite."
Jocelyn mulled over my drawings and opened Moriah
Mitchell's journal. "It's him for sure. You say his name was
Shanafila?" She pulled her camera out of her backpack. "Do
you mind if I take some photos of them? I won't use them for
anything except research."

We were huddled in the hotel conference room; my half-eaten
breakfast plate was in front of me. I really had no appetite at
all. Neither did Sierra. "Go ahead. If it helps the investigation
at all, I'm game."

"This changes things, y'all. We can't just pretend that this
doesn't change things. I'm grateful that we stayed here last
night because I darn sure don't want to bring this thing home
with me. I knew I felt a lot of anxiety, but I wasn't sure if it was
the investigation or something else," Sierra explained as she
ignored the expression on Joshua's face.

"That feather showing up on your bed could not have been a
coincidence. Well, it's made itself known to you two. It's
pretended to be Dominic and Kylie. It must plan on engaging
you. It's taken an interest in you. Let's not run back over there,
Midas. I think we should do more research first."

She licked her lips nervously and leaned forward to look Midas
in the eye. She was afraid. Clearly, she was frightened by what
she sensed. "Let's see what information we can dig up about
the Medicine Hill and that lost tribe. It's possible that in his
drugged state Shanafila imagined those shadows and that
entity. You say the Waliki had been targeted by other tribes.
Could it be possible that Shanafila was really seeing his

enemies running to the camp and only thought they were shadows? Hallucinations are not uncommon when one drinks mind-bending drugs."

Joshua eyed her suspiciously as he picked up our plates and napkins. "More secrets, Sierra? Don't tell me you were into shrooms in high school."

"No, jerk face, but my cousins were. Mostly Benny."

"That explains so much," he said as he walked away. *Wow, he's in a bad mood today.* What was up with these two? Just knowing they were squabbling added to the already tense atmosphere that accompanied this investigation.

She ignored him like she usually did, but it wouldn't last long. She'd tell him off if he kept being a smart-mouth. Midas frowned at Joshua's back but didn't involve himself beyond that. This was par for the course with the McBrides. Sierra and Joshua had their rocky patches, but they always seemed to make it through them. It was best to stay out of their way when they started bickering. They kept their cool most of the time, but not always. It was so embarrassing when they'd get this way in front of clients. At least we weren't investigating a client's house this time.

Nope. Just a spooky old building the size of Hogwarts with an entity that thrived on fear.

Midas replied calmly, "I plan to get inside those outbuildings before the sun goes down. I don't mind investigating the school in the dark, but there could be wild animals on the property."

"There are wild animals inside the building too," Sierra said as she held up her arm to show the scratch marks from yesterday. "Or have you forgotten?"

Midas wasn't going to budge on this. He was very conscious of the time constraints, and the fact that this spirit had presented itself to him as his cousin...well, that had really ticked him off.

"Tell you what, you and Joshua stay here and see what you can dig up while the three of us go check out the greenhouse and the sheds. Also, I'm curious to see if we can locate that hill. It might be that the Nalusa Falaya is tied to the land. That would make sense. See if you can find any property records, Sierra. Joshua..." Midas began, but the younger investigator interrupted him.

"I'm going too, Midas. I'm not good at research, not like Sierra. She doesn't really need me for any of that. I would like to check out the cameras. I need to pull the cards and review any captures we have. I have to be on site to do all of that." Sierra's cheeks reddened, but she didn't say a word. She left the decision up to Midas, who agreed with Joshua.

"Sierra, when you're finished, meet us at the school. Call one of us before you head out, though, so we can keep an eye out for you. I'm anxious to see what you've found."

"That's fine, and I will. Give me a couple of hours. I should be done by lunch. Tell you what, I'll bring lunch with me," she said rather too sunnily as she reached for her tablet and walked out of the conference room.

"Let's load up." Midas glanced at his phone quickly as if he were expecting a message. I felt a twinge of worry for some reason. I had no idea what was going on in his head beyond this investigation, but the wheels were turning, no doubt. He'd tell me when he wanted me to know. I wasn't going to push him.

We rode to the property in silence. It was a pleasant morning, but I found it difficult to enjoy it. I apparently wasn't the only one. I prayed that the temperature remained cool, but it likely wouldn't. At least it wasn't raining. Jocelyn mentioned that during her last investigation, a horrible storm had rolled through. I couldn't imagine staying at the Leaf Academy in a thunderstorm. Talk about ambiance. The ride ended quickly, and Midas put the SUV in park and turned in his seat to face Jocelyn and Joshua.

"Joshua, we will help you run through the footage. You set the cameras to motion detection mode, so that shouldn't take us too long. We'll investigate the greenhouse and the sheds before we make the trek to the back of the property. Everyone stay close. No taking off to check out anything. I don't care what the circumstances are—alright? This thing can take on the images of people you know. Don't be tricked. We always go with partners, got it?"

"Okay," Jocelyn grumbled, and Joshua agreed with clear relief. How could he be so mad at Sierra that he would be willing to sit inside a haunted school by himself to review the footage? They must have had a serious falling-out.

"Alright," I added as we unloaded ourselves and our personal investigation gear from the vehicle. There was no happy banter as we waited for Midas to unlock the building. I held my breath as I walked into the Leaf Academy. The equipment was fine, and nothing appeared out of place. Nothing except us.

The air had a coolness to it that I hadn't expected. I suddenly wished I'd brought my denim jacket.

Joshua didn't waste any time getting started. "Looks like the cameras on this floor are still in place. Nothing is moved. Cassidy, why don't we go check on the cameras? I just want to make sure nothing is moved and everything is where it should be. Midas, how many hits do we have?"

"Fourteen," he said as he tapped on the keyboard. "Let's not get excited yet, though. We know there are lots of living things that could trigger these cameras."

"I'll go with Joshua," I agreed. My voice echoed strangely through the bottom floor. I wondered why his hadn't...

You're making a mountain out of a molehill, Cassidy Wright. Get your head in the game!

Cassidy...

I froze on the staircase but only momentarily. "Joshua, did you say something?"

"No," he said as he turned his head slightly. We both paused, and Midas watched us from the floor below. Jocelyn was tinkering with a camera, removing the digital card or something. She didn't appear to notice.

"It was probably nothing," I said as I waved to Midas, who took a seat beside Jocelyn. I smiled awkwardly at him, and Joshua and I climbed the steps together. As we cleared the top step, I felt as if I had walked into a thick cloud of cobwebs. I yelped and swatted at the invisible web while Joshua watched.

"What is the matter with you? You're jumpier than a feral cat. You're going to give me a heart attack if you don't calm down."

"I walked into a spider web! Didn't you feel it?"

He moved his hand around but shook his head. "I don't feel anything. Turn around, let me check for spiders. God, I hate spiders."

"Me too! And spider webs!"

Joshua briefly examined my clothes and hair and gave me the all-clear. "It's weird because I don't see any webs. Not even a remnant of a web. You sure it wasn't your hair?"

"I know the difference between my hair and a spider web. I know what I felt. Let's get this over with."

He snorted and said, "You sound just like my wife."

I didn't comment. No way was I going to get between the "fighting McBrides." Brushing my hair out of my face, I hurried down the hall to check out the laser grid and the proximity sensor. They were in good working order, but I quickly replaced the batteries in both. Just in case. Better to be safe than sorry later.

"Okay, next is the camera in the teacher's room. Then we'll check the one at the opposite end of the hall." It was business as usual for Joshua, or at least that's what he wanted me to believe. I rubbed my face, wishing that feeling that I'd walked into a thick spider web would go away. Yuck! Disgusting. I shivered as my mind summoned up images of giant spiders hiding in dark corners of each room. What was wrong with me? I wasn't usually afraid of spiders. I didn't want one as a pet, but I wasn't necessarily afraid of them.

The air in McCandlish's room was cold and a bit damp. Nothing had changed, except we'd removed the stack of drawings from the room. They were downstairs near the computer. I think Midas originally wanted to use them as trigger objects before he knew anything about the Nalusa Falaya. Now, we knew we wouldn't need trigger objects—that's what we were. All of us on the Gulf Coast Paranormal team. We were trigger objects.

"Camera looks fine. I'm grabbing the card," Joshua told me as I walked to the dirty window and looked outside at the grounds below. How were we going to find Shanafila's Medicine Hill? I couldn't say exactly when he lived here, but it had to be long ago. Hundreds of years ago, way before the Leaf Academy was constructed.

Shanafila, I'm sorry for what happened to you.

"Earth to Cassidy...you with me?"

"Sure, just looking around. Let's get that other card."

"Okay, who's pulling my leg? Where is the camera?" Joshua asked me as we hoofed it down the hall. "I left it right here."

"I definitely saw you set it up, and I'm not aware of any leg-pulling." I reached for my radio and called Midas. "Hey, what are you seeing for camera four?" I eyed Joshua and asked, "Four, right?"

"Yes, that's right. What the heck?" He checked out the room beside me and the one at the other end of the hall and declared them empty.

"I see camera four. That looks odd. I can't see you two at all. But I can see the woods and from a high vantage point. Did you move it to the roof, Joshua?"

Josh shook his head and reached for the door that led to the roof. "Why would I do that?"

I radioed back. "He didn't put it on the roof. We're going up to check it out."

"Stay put. We're coming up." Midas' voice didn't convey his usual calmness. He was frazzled by this mix-up. Surely that's all it was, a mix-up of some kind. Maybe a mass hallucination? I mean, we all knew where the camera had been.

"Roger," I answered as we waited. "Hurry."

Somewhere, and not far away, I heard a door squeak.

Chapter Fourteen—Cassidy

Joshua's wild-eyed expression added to the freakiness of the moment. I couldn't stand the silence. "Are we going to pretend we didn't hear that?"

"No, but let's wait for the boss to investigate. All the more proof to me that someone is pulling our leg."

"Come on, Josh. You know that's not true." My palms felt sweaty now. "How could that have happened? Do you really think someone else came in and moved it? I don't see the neighbors trying to break into this place. Do you?"

"I thought we were supposed to debunk first. Or has the protocol changed?" Joshua's icy attitude floored me. I was glad to see Midas and Jocelyn clearing the steps and making their way to us.
"The other equipment okay? Nothing else missing?"

"No, there is nothing else missing. And I know for a fact that I did not put that camera on the roof. I haven't even been on the roof. I'm ready to go take a look at this." Joshua sounded disgusted by the whole thing. I was more freaked out than anything but also curious. Sure, I was down for debunking, but we couldn't discount Jocelyn's investigation. She wasn't one for theatrics. Come to think of it, ghosts had moved around cameras before, but not like this. In previous cases, the camera would've ended up in a heap on the floor. Not stationed in another location, and certainly not on the roof.

This was highly unusual. Maybe Joshua had the right idea. The camera's relocation seemed an impossibility unless a human agent was involved. I would have a hard time believing that any entity could relocate a camera without damaging it and set it up in a completely new location. Knocking one over? Yeah, I could see that happening.

Jocelyn led the way to the roof; her hands were clenched into fists as we made our way to the top of the Leaf Academy. The roof beneath our feet didn't look completely sound either. Any good shake and one or all of us would go tumbling through to the floor beneath. There were random patches of grass, garbage and plenty of graffiti up here. At some point, this had been a popular place for teenagers to gather. That surprised me. Maybe there were lulls in the activity here. That was certainly a possibility. The rumor was that the activity increased during the month of October. Given what had happened to us in January, I shuddered to think what this place was like in October.

"I see it! It's there in the corner!" Joshua stormed over to the camera. The equipment remained intact and standing perfectly level on its tripod. It wasn't crooked or wobbly-looking at all. Whoever relocated this camera had done so carefully.

"Wait a second!" Midas yelled at Josh before he reached for the camera.

"Wait for what? I want to take a look at this thing and get the card out. What's the matter with you?" Joshua's short-tempered attitude was beginning to grate on my nerves.

"I want to look at this before we start moving it around. Look at how it's pointed! Clearly, whoever moved this camera wanted us to take a look in this direction. I don't think that's an accident, do you? Let's just go slow here."

Joshua didn't snap back, and wisely so. Jocelyn and I looked around for any evidence of footprints besides our own but found nothing. There wasn't much soil up here except in the few places where weeds were growing, and those were nowhere near the camera.

Joshua said, "It's pointed in that direction, toward the back of the property. I think you're making too much of this, Midas. Someone is having a joke on us. Maybe Ms. Shanahan has some weird sense of humor? I've never seen a camera moved a full floor and reset without human help. Have you? Let's be real here."

My fiancé wasn't paying Josh a bit of attention now. He was busy looking through the lens and examining the camera for any damage. "Jocelyn, take a few pictures of this, and then we'll break this setup down and take the camera downstairs."

She snapped away, but there wasn't really anything to see. Just a camera on a tripod pointing south toward a faraway building. Oh yeah. I hadn't seen that before. I walked to the edge of the roof to get a closer look. Using my phone, I zoomed in on the location. "Jocelyn, how good is your zoom on that thing?"

"Pretty good. Better than that phone, I bet. Why? Oh, I see." She stood beside me and tinkered with her camera. It whirred quietly as she adjusted the lens and then snapped away. "It's a church. That's a church building, Midas. I don't remember there being a church on this property. Did you know about this?"

Midas glanced at the faded white building and then took a peek at her camera screen. She handed it to him so he could get a better look. "Nope, but I imagine there are quite a few old buildings on the property." He turned back to us and said, "I'm calling Adrian, and then we're heading over there. Just to make sure this place is open to us. Joshua, you need help with that?" Midas sounded stressed. He was only expressing how we all were feeling.

"No, I've got it. Thanks."

The trip downstairs didn't reveal much. The camera went off a few times while whoever or whatever moved, but the images were blurry. One minute the camera was on the second floor, and the next it was on the roof. There was no evidence that a person had moved it. But then again, there was no evidence that a ghost had moved it either.

Midas stalked back toward us, and we headed out to his SUV. As he walked, his feet left tiny clouds of dust behind him. "I'm going to call Sierra and tell her where we are going. I don't want anyone coming here by herself. Adrian says we have the key and that we are more than welcome to check it out. There's a road that will lead us back there. She says it's not good to travel on foot. Too many snakes and coyotes. You guys have everything you need?"

"I think so. Let's get going. I'm dying to see inside this place," Jocelyn said as she climbed inside the SUV.

I put on my seat belt as Midas turned the car to go back down the driveway.

Dying to see inside...that wouldn't have been my choice of words.

I glanced at my side mirror as we pulled away from the Leaf Academy. A little boy was standing on the porch staring at us. Only his head and shoulders were clear to me; the rest of his body was translucent, and I could see the faded red bricks of the building behind him. A flurry of crows flew past the porch, but the boy didn't flinch. Why should he?

Standing behind him was a very tall man with red hair and a neat beard. He was also translucent from the chest down, but his face...oh, his face was bereft of all emotion, all expression. He was like a doll, like a plaything for the dead. My heart sank at the horrible sight.

As I stared, I began to see more faces, more dead standing behind the boy. A woman in a deerskin dress, another woman wearing a red dress, or at least I thought they were dresses. The longer I stared, the more solidified the image became. Suddenly, I felt terrified. I closed my eyes against it. "Midas?" I whispered in surprise, but he wasn't paying attention. He was on the phone with Sierra.

I looked back, and the boy was gone. Even though I couldn't see him anymore, I could feel him watching me. Watching us. And he hated us all. I couldn't find the words to convey what I felt, what I'd seen. Had no one else seen him? No, they didn't appear to have seen anything. But they weren't looking, were they?

Midas was busy relaying to Sierra our latest find, the small white building that we all assumed was a church at the back of the property. Jocelyn was telling Joshua about how the Leaf Academy put off strange echoes. Every time she snapped photos, it was as if she heard another photographer, a phantom photographer, taking photos right behind her. And I was seeing ghosts.

Rather than break up the conversations, I closed my eyes and tried to memorize the boy's face. Thankfully, it hadn't worn the face I'd seen in the few pictures of Dominic that Midas had shown me. But this face, I had to draw it...and others.

I reached into my backpack and dug out my small sketch pad and pencil bag. I took out a pencil, just an ordinary pencil with a light lead, and started to draw.

"But that's not the worst of it. I saw several apparitions at the school, and none of them were friendly, except one. Hugh McCandlish, the schoolteacher who died there, he helped me find my keys. I don't think I would have made it without his help. But he's no match for Ollie. Not face to face. That Ollie-entity interacted with McCandlish for days, even weeks, according to Moriah Mitchell's journal."

"Its real name is the Nalusa Falaya," I corrected Jocelyn from the front seat. "And they are still there, Jocelyn. They're all still there."

Midas hung up the phone, and I paused briefly from my sketching to glance at him. He turned the SUV down the narrow road that would lead us to the building we'd targeted. "What is it, Cassidy? Why do you say that?" He put the vehicle in park; there wasn't anyone else out here on this overgrown road. Nobody would be out here at all unless they were chasing ghosts.

"The Nalusa Falaya doesn't want us here. I mean, it really doesn't." I leaned back on the seat and closed my eyes briefly, hoping that I could keep my emotions in check. How could I explain everything I was feeling? I silently counted to three in my head and opened my eyes. I totally agreed with Jocelyn. This thing had the power to trap the dead, maybe even to add to its ranks. And they were all trapped. Even Hugh McCandlish. Even Shanafila. Or maybe not. I couldn't be sure.

Midas gently pried the sketchbook from my hand, and he, Jocelyn and Joshua studied it. A boy's face peered back at us. His expression lacked innocence. Instead of innocence, I felt malevolence, hatred. I hoped that I had properly conveyed those emotions. The drawing wasn't even complete; this was only half his face. And the silhouettes beside and behind him weren't finished either.

"Let me see," Jocelyn said without a hint of fear in her voice. "Oh crap. Yeah, that's Ollie. What did you call it again?"

"The Nalusa..." Josh began, but Midas cut him off.

"A word of caution, and this is for everyone, not just you, Joshua. I don't think we should keep saying the name." Midas handed me a tissue from the console between us. I dabbed my eyes with it and accepted the sketchbook back from Jocelyn.

"Why? We're not schoolchildren, Midas. We're not playing Bloody Mary or Old Wintzell. We're conducting an investigation. It's going to be hard not to say 'Its' name." Joshua made air quotes as he used the word. "We aren't children."

Jocelyn added, "You can summon things if you use their name. Let's just call him Ollie."

Nobody said a word. We sat in the SUV for a minute until Joshua said, "Are we going to go or what?"

Midas' inquisitive expression triggered something within me. I couldn't bail on the team. The investigation at the Leaf Academy had become more than a ghost hunt. There was no need to hunt anything. There were ghosts here, but they didn't want to be here. They deserved to be free.

But what if they don't want to be free? What if what I saw were just the shadows of those souls?

No. I couldn't believe that. I couldn't believe that a soul was beyond rescuing. Either in life or in death. The fear and grief for Shanafila faded, and something else rose up within me.

Determination. I wasn't going to leave McCandlish or Shanafila or anyone else here on this property with that horrible thing. These souls had to be set free. No, I didn't know how to do it, but once again I trusted that I...no, *we* would find a way.

"Let's go, Midas. I'm ready." After giving him a brief kiss, which was totally unprofessional, I got out of the sturdy black vehicle. I shut the door behind me and made my way through the overgrown weeds to the front door of the small white building.

This was for Shanafila.

Chapter Fifteen—Midas

The key wouldn't slide into the lock no matter how many times I tried. I tried the next key, just in case. Still no luck. I checked all the keys, and none of them was the right one. "Maybe there's another door," I said as I walked around the building. Cassidy went with me, but Jocelyn was already scoping out the building with her camera. Joshua leaned against a dirty window and tried to get a look inside.

"It's dark in there. Looks like most of the windows are boarded up," he called as we walked up to the nailed-up back door. "We're not getting in here this way. Not without a crowbar or at least a hammer."

I sighed and said, "I'll try to call Adrian."

"I hope you can get a signal. I've got zero bars on my phone," Cassidy observed as she slid her phone back in her pocket.

"It's ringing," I said as we continued to pace around the outside of the building. "She's not answering. I'll leave a message. Maybe she'll get back to us soon." I left the client a polite but hurried message and then gathered the team together. "No dice, guys. I want to get in there, but I'm not going to break a window to do it. Let's do some EVP work at least and keep our eyes peeled for anything that looks like a significant hill."

"Okay," Cassidy agreed. "Let's go to opposite sides of the building and work in pairs. Jocelyn, want to come with me? Meet back in ten."

"I'm game. We'll go to the front door." Jocelyn flashed her typical grin, the one that said *I love my job*. It was good to see that again. As the women disappeared around the corner of the building, Joshua pulled his recorder out of his black bag. After adjusting the volume, he held the recorder up.

"My name is Joshua, and this is my friend Midas. We noticed the place is locked. Did you lock it?" It was an odd question, but sometimes these were the most successful. I heard nothing but the wind blowing, nothing unusual. Hearing a disembodied voice was a rare thing but not completely unheard of. "What's your name?" A crow squawked in the distance. Joshua nodded at me to step in and ask a few too.

"Did you worship here at this church? Do you know the people who did?" The crows squawked again, and I heard wings fluttering not far from us. I glanced over my shoulder and spotted a rotting wooden fence about fifty feet away. A wild cherry tree hovered over the collapsing fence line, but I didn't see any birds. We asked about a dozen more questions and decided to play back the recording. Joshua turned the volume up, and we listened to our own voices asking questions. Sadly, there were no other voices, no evidence that anyone heard us. I glanced at my watch, surprised to see that our ten minutes were almost up.

"Let's listen again. Just in case." Joshua agreed and checked the volume to make sure it was up as high as possible. We listened again, and a few seconds in, he clicked the recording off.

"Wait a second. Where are the crows? I don't hear them. Do you?" Joshua's eyes narrowed as he replayed the recording. He was right, I didn't hear the birds at all. "We should be able to hear them. I can hear the wind, the tree branches creaking, but no birds, no crows."

Before I could respond, Joshua began to wave his hands. He sputtered and jumped back and started to shout as if he were in pain. That's when I noticed the bees circling his head. The audio recorder hit the ground as he held his hands up to protect his face. He took absent swings at the buzzing cloud, but the insects weren't going to relent.

"Follow me!" When he didn't budge, I reached through the cloud and ignored the angry stings. I grabbed Joshua's shirt sleeve and practically dragged him to the SUV. "Cassidy! Run!"

A car was pulling into the driveway. Sierra! There was no time to wave her down, but I was happy to see she was rolling to a stop. Cassidy and Jocelyn were not far behind us, but the bees weren't going away. Joshua yelped in pain and swore as he continued to swing at them.

"Get in the SUV! Move it!" I opened the door and shoved him inside. Unfortunately, one of the bees followed him. He yelled again as it apparently stung him up, but he smashed the thing. I waved at the insects, but they didn't stick around. The lingering few zipped away, and the rest of us climbed into the vehicle and tried to catch our breath. "You alright? Let me look at you. Ah, dang it! You're a mess, man. Your wife is here. Let her in, Jocelyn, but wait until she's closer just in case."

"What are y'all running from?" Sierra demanded as she scurried from her car into the SUV. "Oh my God!" She climbed over Jocelyn and sat beside her husband. "Joshua! Bees or wasps?" She slid off her jacket without missing a beat.

"Bees, and I think this one has a stinger still in it." He slid up his shirt sleeve and showed her an angry-looking wound.

"Thank God. He's allergic to wasps. Would one of you mind grabbing the first-aid kit? Do we have one in here?"
"Yep, I'll get it." I glanced around the vehicle and didn't see any sign of the horrible swarm that had nailed Joshua at least three times. I quickly grabbed the bag and made my way back to the driver's seat.

A few minutes later, Joshua was breathing easier although he was largely slathered with allergy cream and smelled like rubbing alcohol. "I'm a jerk. I'm sorry, Sierra Kay."

"Let's talk about it later." She put the last of the alcohol swabs in the small plastic trash bag that I kept in the SUV for just such occasions. "Is that your way of apologizing? Because if it is, that apology sucks."

I heard them kiss, and I cut eyes at Cassidy. Before I could remind them where they were, Jocelyn shouted at me. She'd been sitting next to Sierra, her headphones in her ears as she listened to the audio she and Cassidy had recorded at the opposite side of the church.

"You have to hear this—it's a man! I swear I hear a man talking...mumbling...no. Singing! Yes, I think he's singing." She snatched the headphones out of her ears and rewound the recording. "I didn't hear anything when we were standing out there until we heard Josh screaming." She pressed the play button and turned up the volume.

Jocelyn's calm voice sounded from the small device, and then I heard the second voice. A male voice, not mine and not

Joshua's. I couldn't make out the words of the husky voice that whispered a song in the background, but Cassidy clutched my hand.

"I know that voice. It's the Crow Man—Fula Hatak! The shaman who led Shanafila to the Medicine Hill."

Chapter Sixteen—Sierra

I helped Joshua get into our own car and eased in behind the SUV as we headed back over to the school, but I wasn't sure I wanted to stay. Not with my husband's face swollen like a beach ball. Could he be mistaken about that allergy? For someone who was supposedly only allergic to wasps, his skin sure was mottled and red in several places.

"Maybe you should go back to the hotel and take an allergy pill. I saw a pharmacy not far from the hotel."

"No. I'll be fine. We can't let them go back in there without backup. I wish we'd never come here." Joshua slung his bag on the floor and leaned back, his face twisted in pain.

"What gives, McBride? You haven't been yourself since we arrived here, and now you want to act like you're all committed to the cause. I appreciate your public apology, but you've got some explaining to do." Joshua and I had had our troubles in the past—some were his fault, and a lot of them were mine—but I thought we'd put all that behind us. Evidently not. He was harboring some ill will for whatever reason. To my surprise, he didn't pretend I was being paranoid.

"I don't know what it is. I just feel off. Angry for no reason, and I know it's not me. You and I both know I'm not the sunniest person, but the Leaf Academy...I don't like it. Actually, I hate this place."

I took his hand and squeezed it. "I'm not a fan either. And if we were here for any reason other than to help someone, I would say let's go to Midas right now and tell him we're out. But I can't. Neither can you."

He shook his blond head and frowned. "What do you mean we can't? Adrian Shanahan wants to bulldoze this place to the ground, and I can't say I blame her. Yeah, I know that's not what a paranormal investigator should admit, but places like this...they don't need buildings attached to them."

"We're not here for Adrian Shanahan. We're here for all the others. They are stuck here, Joshua. Can you imagine being enslaved to something like this...thing? Forever? I can't walk away. Midas needs my particular skill set."

"Let's think about this for a minute. You've been attacked by crows, I've been attacked by bees, and you want to set a school full of ghosts free. Are you nuts, Sierra Kay?"

I stared past him and took in the sight of the crumbling Leaf Academy. Even with its faded bricks and boarded windows, it was an intimidating sight. Although I hadn't yet seen the bevy of ghosts hiding here, I knew that they were there. And that there was no peace here at the Leaf Academy. None at all. "Yeah, probably. If you're coming with me, then come on. Before something else comes after us." Midas waved at us quizzically as we all pulled up and parked, and I waved back. Joshua's swollen face broke my heart, but I wasn't lying to him. I had to help these lost souls.

With a heavy heart, I walked with Joshua hand in hand back into the school. I glanced at the stone above the door and reminded myself of that half-forgotten Bible verse. *I will fear no evil.*

How long did that stone help these people? Ten years? A year? A day? Or had it just been an empty dream keeping the entity that they knew resided on this land out of this building? No, it had been an empty promise to all the students who had come here, and to Hugh McCandlish.

"What about your research, Sierra? Did you uncover anything that will help us?" Midas asked as we gathered in the small room that used to be the headmaster's office. Joshua tinkered with the computers and pulled up the monitors for the cameras. Everything appeared to be in good working order. At least for now.

"Only a few news stories. Mostly about this Holloway character. He was kind of a bad seed, and his family more or less disinherited him because of his rough lifestyle. He burned through the family fortune in a space of three years before his brother stepped in."

Jocelyn gasped at Sierra's news. "All of it? Ms. Shanahan didn't say anything about that to me. I got the feeling that they were still very wealthy."

"Oh yeah, he didn't do any permanent damage but enough to get him ousted. He was found dead here. The coroner ruled it a suicide. I guess you all know he jumped off the roof. Hey, did someone leave a radio going around here?" I tucked my hair behind my ear and strained to hear the music.

"I hear it too," Cassidy said quietly. Apparently, no one else heard a thing. Joshua and Midas immediately went into debunk mode and began searching rooms and even looked outside, but there was nothing that could have caused that music. No passing car was going to blare classical piano. Once they returned shaking their heads, I decided it was time to get back to investigating. Someone wanted to talk to Cassidy and me. As we were the only sensitives here, it would have to be us.

"Since we're the only two hearing it, I guess we have to check it out. Sun is still up, but it's dark down that hallway. Cassidy, do you have a flashlight?"
"Yep. The thermal will be useless in there, since there's still light coming through that broken ceiling, but we can take the proximity meter and..."

I reached into a nearby black box and took out my rag doll. It wasn't just any doll; it was rigged to light up and interact with anything that touched it. "I've been dying to try her out." Midas laughed. "A girl toy in a boy's school? You should definitely get some attention, but I wouldn't want to be that doll if one of those schoolboys shows up. Might get kicked around a bit."

"Exactly. Let's hurry, Cassidy."

We trekked down the hall cautiously and entered the auditorium without any fuss. The back of the room was raised slightly; it was built this way, in a kind of funnel, to amplify the sounds coming from the orchestra pit and the stage. I thought it was wild that a boys' school would have an auditorium like this. From what I read, they allowed the town to use the property for many elegant events. But why would they do that knowing it wasn't safe here?

I walked carefully down the steps toward the stage, keeping my eye out for birds that might be waiting to attack me. There were broken sections of chair rows everywhere as if a giant had visited the auditorium and had a big ol' fit. Kind of like our daughter, Emily, who had the McBride temperament. Unfortunately.

Stay focused on the investigation, Sierra. Don't think about anyone you love right now. You know this creature plucks things out of your mind.

"Let's see. Where's a good place to put our rag doll? Would anyone like to play with her?" I asked. Cassidy clicked the audio recorder and put it next to the doll. We did our best to prop her up neatly, but she kept falling over on the stage. "Do you like my doll? I tell you what—I will lay her down here. If you want to, you can touch her hair or her feet or..."

I feel cold, the doll said pitifully.

Cassidy's wide eyes matched mine. "That didn't take long. Are you cold? You can play with my doll. I don't mind."

I feel cold.

The doll repeated the phrase, but the voice sounded a bit off. Kind of like the batteries were low. Cassidy shivered and walked the edge of the stage with her flashlight pointed at different things.

"What's your name?" I asked despite the lump I felt in my throat. "If you're cold, maybe we can help you." The doll went quiet, and I followed Cassidy around as she checked out a few areas. It was easy to see shadows here with the sun going down and the debris everywhere. "Look! I think I see a room down there. Shine that light between the boards, Cassidy."

The LED light illuminated a room we hadn't seen before; obviously, this was a room that had been used for housing props and costumes. "Look at that! I have to get in there. Do you see a door?" We searched for a door but had no luck. However, the boards were easy to move; they were so rotted that they practically crumbled in our hands.

"Should we tell Midas?" Cassidy asked cautiously.

"We should but after we check it out. Low bridge in here. Watch your head. On second thought, let's go one at a time. If this thing collapses, you go get help. May I borrow your flashlight?"

Cassidy agreed, but by the tone of her voice, I could tell she didn't like this idea...either because she wanted to go first or because she would much rather Midas be in on every detail of the investigation. "Damn, I should have brought a camera. Look at all this. There are literally trunks everywhere. A wooden rocking horse. God, I hate those things. I don't see any musical instruments at all. I wonder who was playing music...Cassidy, can you hear me?"

"Loud and clear." I could see her squatting down and peeking inside the room at me. "I'm right here. The first sign of trouble, you get out, okay? Stay where I can see you."

"Sure, Mom," I said playfully as I waved the flashlight around and visually plundered this room.

I couldn't stand up all the way; the ceiling was too low, and that was a strange sensation for me since I wasn't that tall. Swinging my light around, I nearly screamed when I saw a shadow crouching down on the far wall. It was a mirror and the image was Cassidy, but I gasped and then laughed at myself for being scared.

"What is it?"

"Just a mirror. Who puts a mirror under a stage? So weird."

I'm cold...

The doll sounded off again, but it wasn't the usual doll's voice. It sounded deep and growly, the phrase drawn out and menacing. Like it was mocking us.

"Uh, did you hear that?"
Before I could answer Cassidy, I heard the doll's voice again. But it wasn't coming from the stage this time. The voice was in my ear.

I'm cold...

And then I saw the figure crawling away on its hands and knees. A black shadow, boy-sized and moving too quickly to be human. A living human, anyway.

"Time to go," I said to no one in particular as I scrambled like a madwoman to get out of the storage space. Just as my hands breached the door, I felt a tug on my foot. A definite, painful tug. "Quit!" I screamed as it dragged me back a few inches.

Apparently, this ghost wanted to play, but I was pretty sure I wouldn't like these games. Not at all. "Cassidy! Help me!" I forced myself to keep my emotions under control. That's what this thing wanted more than anything—to generate and feed on fear. Oh yes, this was a powerful entity. And this was no damn ghost!

"Get off me!" I said as I felt a second icy cold hand reach up higher on my leg. I kicked my sneakered shoe at the air; my foot didn't make contact with anything, but the thing did release me. "Holy hell!" I shouted as I climbed out of the dirty hole.

"What is it? What grabbed you?"

"I think you know. I don't think you should go in there. Nobody should go alone. You were right, Cassidy. Let's get the—where's the doll?" I handed her the flashlight and checked the ground in front of the stage.

"It was just there. I wasn't watching it; I was watching you."

Midas and Joshua entered the auditorium and called out to us. "Hey, you two. What do you think you're doing? We can't see you on the camera when you crawl around like that. What's going on?"

Cassidy said, "We found a room; Sierra found it, actually. She took a peek inside and made contact with something. It grabbed her leg? Ankle?" I nodded as I wiped the dust off my clothes.

"The doll started putting off weird voices, and now we can't find it. It was just right here. Oh, look."

I hadn't noticed it before, but it was there now. As clear as day. A large black feather. Did this thing believe that we'd made an exchange, the doll for the feather?

"Sierra Kay, are you alright?"

"Yeah, I just need to get out of here. Tag, you're it, Midas."

Without waiting for permission, I left the auditorium with Cassidy beside me. No way was I ever going back in there.

I would be lucky to leave here alive.

Chapter Seventeen—Cassidy

"Deadsville, huh?" I asked the guys as they returned to the headmaster's office. "Nothing at all?"

"There were a few anomalous sounds, but I'm not sure I would classify them as paranormal. They sounded like the noise we heard upstairs yesterday, the footsteps, but they weren't steady. You know what I mean. Thumps but with a bit of metal, like spurs. Or biker boots, like Jocelyn said."

Sierra's eyebrows raised. "No sign of the doll?"

"No. Anything on the camera, Jocelyn?" Midas asked hopefully.

"You aren't going to believe this, but the camera shifted. Like, a couple of inches, enough to cut out that part of the stage. I can see you two looking around, and I can see when you find the hidey hole. But a few minutes after, it shifts. Look at this." The team crowded around the largest monitor and watched as Jocelyn scrolled back the camera feed. "Could anyone have bumped it?"
I shook my head in disbelief.

"I don't think so, but I guess we can't rule out animals. Birds. I think we would have heard an animal, though. Don't you, Sierra?" She shrugged and continued to watch the loop. "The only other alternative is that an intelligent being moved it. Anywhere else, I would say that was highly unlikely." My investigative partner didn't offer any other suggestions, just looked unbelievably pale. "Tell the truth, Sierra. Are you sick? Is this place making you sick?" It wouldn't be the first time she had a physical reaction to spiritual activity.

"Yeah, but it's not unmanageable. Not yet. Things are just weird. Like I said before. It's not natural to have this kind of vacuum, and I guess I'm a bit rattled about my encounter." Joshua put his arm around her and kissed her forehead. His face hadn't quite cleared up yet, but at least they weren't fighting anymore.

Midas frowned and said, "Listen, if this place is too much, for any of you...if you want to leave, I'm okay with that. Everyone has their limits. I am not asking any of you to put yourselves in a bad position. Not on my account. Not for anyone."

Joshua squared his shoulders and said, "Nobody said anything about leaving, Midas. If you're here, we're here." Sierra didn't disagree with him, but then again, she didn't quite agree either. If I could get her alone anytime soon, I planned on picking her brain about what unseen things were happening. "Then let's turn our focus to the second floor. Maybe we'll find the doll up there. Stranger things have happened." Midas' grim expression surprised me. Why the sudden shift in the atmosphere here? Were the spirits of the Leaf Academy making themselves known by affecting our emotions? Our thoughts?

"Cassidy and I will head up first." Armed with digital recorders and the thermal camera, we journeyed up the stairs side by side. The treads were dirtier than I remembered. It seemed like with as much foot traffic as this staircase had seen recently, there wouldn't be any dust here. It was as if the dead were trying to cover up the footsteps of the living.

Man, this place was a dirt pit.

"You say something?" Midas half-turned to me on the top step.

"No, but I was thinking loudly," I said with a smile, hoping to lighten his intense mood. There wasn't a hint of happiness in his eyes.

"Funny," he whispered with a certain air of impatience.

"I thought it was," was my tart reply, but then I heard it too.

Midas!

I clicked on the audio recorder as Midas pointed his camera toward the hallway to the right. The air crackled with electricity—like a powerful thunderstorm was growing and about to descend on the Leaf Academy. And all those inside it. This floor in particular. My hair raised up, including some of the hair on my head, like I'd rubbed my feet on thick shag carpet wearing slipper socks.

"This entire hallway is hot. Look at the camera!" Midas whispered to me in an excited tone. The screen displayed vibrant orange and red colors. I'd never seen this colorization on the thermal camera before. I suddenly wished Jocelyn were here to make sense of all this.

I reached for my walkie-talkie. "Hey, are you guys getting this?"

"Yes, we've got it," Jocelyn answered. "Proceed with caution. I can't say what that is, Cassidy. Ask Midas to step back and pan to the right."

"You heard her," I said as he did just that.

Midas! Midas! Come and find me!
Yes, that was a child's voice. It was sing-songy. As if the name-calling were some sort of game.
Midas remained in position, but he was too close to the stairs. Definitely too close... I reached out to touch him, to pull him back from the edge, when I heard the voice again.

What are you? Chicken?

That's when I saw the camera's display change. The colorization returned to normal levels, but there was a blue dot about ten feet away from us. Blue indicated cooler temperatures, not something living. Like a draft or ice. There wasn't any ice up here, and it wasn't drafty. In fact, it was incredibly stuffy. I wanted to get out of here, or at the very least open a window and let some air in.

And then maybe jump. You should do that, Cass. Then you can be with me.

"Stop it!" I said in a hiss. Midas appeared transfixed by whatever waited for us in the hall. The voice that addressed me didn't come from the hallway. It rang in my head. I knew only I could hear it. The voice wanted me to believe that it was Kylie, but she would never suggest something like that. Never.

My heart pounded as I shifted my eyes from the screen to the hallway in front of us. I felt him before I saw him.

A boy—a boy with a familiar face. This thing wanted us to believe that this was Dominic Demopolis, a child who'd been dead for at least twenty years. "Dominic?" Midas' grip weakened on the camera, his hand wavered, and he wobbled on his feet. As he staggered, I snatched him by his shirt and pulled him closer to me.

"Midas! Please! You know that's not Dominic! Snap out of it!" I yelled as the image fluttered before us like it was a projection by an old camera that clacked as it worked and occasionally blurred the film.

The image shifted slightly, or at least the thing's face did. His frame and height remained the same. This was Ollie! I recognized the evil child's face from Shanafila's encounter.

Mi-das! Come play with me!

"You aren't here." His voice sounded rough and broken like he didn't truly believe it. Was he entertaining the idea that this was actually his cousin? The boy's face shifted again into a twisted mask of anger. I pulled Midas even closer. My fight-or-flight instincts were kicking in, but my fiancé's feet weren't moving. For a moment, for one terrifying moment, the façade vanished. No more Ollie. No more Dominic.
The creature had burnt black skin. I detected a strange glimmer to it, like it had scales. What was even more shocking were the yellow eyes that didn't blink. They stared and hated and stared some more.

"Nalusa Falaya!" I said without thinking. Then it smiled and showed a pink mouth and white teeth. Sharp white teeth. "Midas, step away!"

The thing issued a hiss and a growl, all rolled into one. I couldn't think, I could barely speak, and more than anything I wanted to cry my eyes out. But all I could do was hold on to

Midas and watch it all unfold. The creature flickered away, and Dominic returned.

Dead and bloodied Dominic.

I heard Midas catch his breath. He saw him too! The thing raised its arm slowly in strange, puppet-like movements. I couldn't fathom what it could be doing, but then I saw the feather in its hand. The Nalusa Falaya offered Midas a feather. A black feather.

The walkie-talkie went crazy with static as Sierra's voice crackled. I heard Joshua's boots running up the stairs, but I couldn't look away. Instead of a scream I shouted, "I know what you are—Nalusa Falaya! I know what you are!"

Suddenly a huge boom shook the school. Even what was left of the window glass rattled, and I heard the sound of breaking glass in the rooms to the left. Whatever happened, however it happened, I realized that a great surge of energy was just released. And it was coming our way. But to what end? Would it kill us? Would it kill Midas?

Another boom hit us, and the recorder I held clattered to the ground.

"Stop!" I heard a wailing banshee scream as she dashed past me. I could barely breathe as I picked myself up off the floor. Somehow, I managed to snatch Midas to his feet too. But it was too late.

That hadn't been Joshua's boots I'd heard coming up the stairs. That had been Jocelyn!

A wild wind whipped down the hallway, and then everything stopped. The air lightened, and my hair wasn't standing on end anymore. The thing was gone.

And so was Jocelyn.

Chapter Eighteen—Jocelyn

I heard him before I saw him. Gary Holloway flicked a switchblade as he paced back and forth a few feet away. How I ended up in a heap on the ground I couldn't say, but I wasn't staying here. With a surge of fear-fueled adrenaline, I clambered to my feet and stepped away from the menacing spirit. Only he wasn't a spirit. He seemed so much more real than he had before. Even during that first encounter, when I hadn't detected that he was anything but a homeless guy dressed in vintage rags hanging out in an abandoned school. Not so weird in today's society. I glanced around and was surprised to see that Midas and Cassidy had vanished, and so had the cameras and anything related to the Gulf Coast Paranormal investigation.

I was by myself here! What had I been thinking running up those stairs?

"Ah, you again. Can't stay away from me, can you?" He flicked his knife again and grinned.

"I'm not supposed to be here. I can help you, Gary. That's your name, right?" I held up my hands to show him I wasn't armed. And I wasn't. Even my radio had vanished into thin air.

"You know my name, honey. How about telling me yours? Let's get acquainted. You look like a real peach," he said in a deep, threatening voice. I couldn't believe the detail with which he appeared. Black boots with metal chain accents. A pair of dirty jeans with thick cuffs. A ragged t-shirt and a moldy leather jacket. "But you can't fool me, Honey. I know you aren't human."

"Yes, I am, Gary. I am very human. See?" I held up my hands to show him my palms. What was I thinking? How far was I going to get with this guy?

"Oh no, you're not. And you know what that means." He took a step toward me, swung his knife lazily and shouted, "Boo!" as I screamed and nearly threw up.

"You don't have to obey him. He's not your master, Gary. You made a mistake, but you don't have to pay for it forever. Not forever, Gary Holloway. Please, I can help you. My friends can help you. That's why we are here; you have to believe me." I was near tears now. A moan welled up from deep within me. "My name is Jocelyn Graves. I'm not your enemy."

"I can smell you." His smile widened.

"No, Gary! Listen to me. Your brother passed away recently, and Adrian owns this place. She would be your great-niece— she called us because you're trapped. She knows you're trapped, Gary! Please, listen!"
Gary stopped pacing and bowed his head slightly, but his eyes never let go of me. Oh, this was no optical illusion. I was with a dead man, a crazy dead man who had every intention of killing me. His greaser hairstyle sagged a bit as he bent his neck even deeper. Then with a blast of angry and profane language, he slammed himself in my direction.

I almost missed the blade. Almost. I screamed as the knife made contact with my arm, but I flung myself ahead of him and raced toward the door at the end of the hall.

There was nowhere to go but up. As my heart beat crazily and the world fell silent except for Gary's curses, I fled up the stairs to the roof. All the while, my mind raced with what I should do next. If I could get to the edge of the roof, maybe I could signal someone, catch someone's attention. But then again, I had the strangest sensation that I had slipped not only to another time but to another place, another world.

"Don't run from me, honey. You'll only make it worse. So much worse. Come on, sweet plum. Gary ain't gonna hurt you. Not much." The ghost of Gary Holloway enjoyed this deadly cat-and-mouse game far too much.

I found it hard to breathe; my lungs were burning as if I had run a mile or two, not just traveled up a couple of stairs. My hands were sweating. All proof that I remained very much alive. And I was looking to stay that way.

I reached for the doorknob, expecting that it would stick like it did the last time I came up here, but it swung open easily and I nearly spilled all over the ground. That would be bad because Gary Holloway was right behind me, not fifteen feet. I didn't bother trying to close the door. He was coming after me.

I screamed as loudly as I could, "Midas! Cassidy! Anyone!"

Nobody answered. I couldn't hear a car anywhere, nothing but birds. Crows or ravens, I couldn't be sure.

And then Gary was there. He spotted me and swung the knife as he bit his lip with pleasure.

"Oh, I'm going to enjoy this, honey. Time to let ol' Gary see if you're human. Don't make it hard on yourself," he purred as he began to walk toward me.

All I could do was scream.

Chapter Nineteen—Cassidy

"Take my hand, Cassidy. We have to work together. I need your help!" Sierra was screaming. Joshua and Midas were still running around looking for Jocelyn, and Midas was near tears. I couldn't explain it; I'd never seen anything like it before. Jocelyn Graves had vanished into thin air right in front of me.

"She just vanished, Sierra. She's just gone."

"Snap out of it, Cassidy! It's Ollie, you know it is. He made it happen, but now he's weak. Too weak to keep all the balls in the air without taking another soul. We can't let him have Jocelyn. He thought he would take Midas. It's the anniversary of Dom's death. I knew he wasn't in the right state of mind for all this, but I didn't say a word. I'm responsible for this, and I have to make it right. Hold my hand, Cassidy, and give me your energy."

"How? I'm not a sensitive, Sierra. Not like you. I'm an artist. What do I do?"

"Look at me and control your breathing. I want you to imagine yourself wrapped in purple light. Think about the light, Cassidy. Just do that. As you think about it, make it brighter and bigger and stronger. Just do that and leave the rest to me."

"Okay," I whimpered as I focused on my task. All I wanted to do was cry. Or call the cops, but what good would that do? I could hear Midas yelling for Jocelyn.

He's never going to find her, she's not here.

"Focus, Cassidy. And don't open your eyes."

"What? Why?" She didn't answer me, so I took a breath and did what she asked. I had a hard time focusing on anything at first, but it got easier by the second. I wanted to ask a dumb question like what kind of purple, but Sierra was squeezing my hand and doing her thing.

Stop being an artist and just focus.

Lavender. I could see it all around us. I imagined it easily.

Sierra began to speak in a confident tone. "I am calling out the spirits trapped in this place. You have been here too long. You have been separated too long from your family. It's time to go now. You deserve peace and rest. All of you. Leave while you can! I call on the families of these souls trapped in this place, come now! Help your loved ones return to you! Please, come now!"
Through my closed eyes, I imagined the colors changing to a deep indigo. A wild, throbbing color full of life and love. I heard strange sighs around me and felt the wind whip my hair, but Sierra's voice never wavered. "Children, you may go to your parents, to your grandparents. Your loved ones are here now!"

I heard giggles and laughter, and the air felt lighter every second.

Suddenly Joshua was with us, holding on to both of us as the wind continued thrashing us. And Midas was there, and I could feel his hand in mine. *Stay focused, Cassidy*, I imagined Sierra whispering to me. I focused on the indigo color and pictured it wrapping around us like a living thing. It protected us from the rage that was about to be unleashed on us. Oh yes, the Nalusa Falaya hated Sierra McBride. It hated us all!

"Hugh McCandlish! Moriah Mitchell! Shanafila! You are free! Go to your rest now!"

As soon as the air shifted, I felt the angry presence of the creature.

"We can't make him leave since he is not human, Cassidy. He was never human, but we can push him back. Midas, go find Jocelyn!"

Joshua said, "He's dangerous, Sierra Kay! I'm not leaving you."

Suddenly it occurred to me. I knew where she had to be. In fact, I could almost hear her screaming my name. "She's on the roof. She's on the roof!" The four of us hurried to the roof door, clambered up the steps and found the door wide open.

Jocelyn! But she wasn't alone! There was a man with her; it was Gary Holloway, and he was doing his very best to kill her. Gary pushed her to the edge of the roof by swinging his knife at her. Her clothes were blood-soaked, and she was screaming for help.

"Midas!" she screamed as he took another swing at her.

"Cassidy, just like before! Help me!" Sierra wept as she reached for my hand again. I couldn't tear my eyes away from the horrible spectacle, but in my mind I could see the purple energy around us. Only briefly. I couldn't do it. Gary reached for her as she began to fall backwards. He raised his hand as if to deal her the death blow before she tumbled over the side, but then he vanished.

Just as Jocelyn had vanished earlier.

But then Midas was there, reaching for her. She caught his hand before she fell. He had her! I looked at Sierra and said, "We did it!"

I heard Midas say with some relief, "I've got you, Jocelyn." But as he turned around with her in his arms, he was not prepared for what waited for him.

Ollie had returned with feather in hand. He was offering Midas a deal. But who could trust the Nalusa Falaya? It felt as if time stood still. The message was clear. *Take the feather or you'll both die. I can kill you both now.* My legs wouldn't work, and clearly no one else could move either. All we could do was watch in horror.

Midas was weighing his options; his mind worked on solving the problem. And then Ollie changed his mask. He was Dominic Demopolis again, and he was crying pitifully, "Help me!"

Sierra made a hissing sound as if she wanted to speak, but Ollie raised his hand and silenced her. There was nothing and no one that could help our friends. Tears rolled down my face, and before I could come up with any solution, it all came to an end.

In one agonizing, awful moment, I saw Jocelyn grab the feather and plunge off the roof. The Nalusa Falaya melted into the night air as Midas' scream echoed through the dark woods around us.

Jocelyn Graves was gone for good.

Epilogue—Cassidy

"She would have liked it, Midas. She really would have loved it," Sierra whispered in Midas' ear as she tried to comfort him. He was a shell of himself. I could count on one hand how many times he'd actually spoken in the past week or eaten a meal.

Joshua hugged him tight and patted his back. The sight of my fiancé's sagging shoulders and red-rimmed eyes broke my heart. "I'm here for you, boss. Whatever you need, you call me." Joshua hugged me too, but I resisted the urge to emotionally crumble although that's what I wanted to do more than anything. Jocelyn Graves was dead, and her death had broken all of us. Midas most of all. That's all Midas needed was for me to lose it. I couldn't believe that her family hadn't attended. I mean no one.

Except Aaron.

The lanky investigator observed the service from the back of the chapel and made no effort to speak to Midas or his former teammates. His message was clear—he blamed us for Jocelyn's death. He left without a word to anyone, not even Joshua, who was making his way to him. Joshua glanced back at me, and the confusion and sadness on his face said it all.

"Midas, I'm sorry about Jocelyn." Sara rubbed his arm gently, and he hugged her momentarily. The funeral announcement had drawn people from near and far; Jocelyn had apparently touched many people in her short life. Sara didn't behave inappropriately or pile on the accusations. Thankfully, she didn't accuse Midas of all the things he was accusing himself of like being reckless, putting his team in danger. I'd heard those things from his own lips, and although I disagreed with him, I knew he believed it.

"Sorry to have to see you again like this, Cassidy." Sara stretched her hand out to me, and I shook it. She hadn't changed much since I met her at that first meeting in the Gulf Coast Paranormal offices. Sara and Midas used to be business partners, and personal partners as well, but they'd broken up when she accepted an offer to participate in a paranormal reality television show. Her presence here was just a testament to how great Jocelyn was. Sara didn't overstay her welcome, leaving us alone to receive the remaining attendees. There was no sign of Peter Broadus. I would have bet money on him being here since he and Jocelyn had been an item for a little while. Hopefully, he wasn't knee-deep in a bottle somewhere.

Even Papa Angelos had come to pay his respects. "Jocelyn was a lovely girl. You come to the diner when you're done here, okay? I'll wait for you. We'll have the place to ourselves. I'll see to that."
"I can't, Papa. I'm going to California to meet Jocelyn's mother. She's been pretty sick and couldn't come. I need to go."

Papa's eyes watered and his thin mouth quivered as he hugged Midas tight. He was so small compared to his grandson, but he was still the family rock. He comforted Midas as he cried and then patted him lovingly before kissing my cheek and leaving with Jimmy, one of Midas' many cousins.

After the service, there was no time to do anything except take Midas to the airport and beg one last time for him to let me go with him. "I love you, Cassidy, but I need to do this. Alone. I hope you understand." I didn't really agree, but I told him that

I understood. I walked with him to the security checkpoint and then a half-hour later watched his plane take off. He'd only be gone for a day, but I knew I'd spend every minute thinking about how to help him through all this. Sierra texted me as I left the airport inviting me to dinner. I turned her down but promised to come see her in the morning.

We needed to stick together; we needed to talk about it. We were still a team, I hoped. But for how long?

Oh, Jocelyn. I'm so sorry. I'm really sorry.

I drove home from the airport in an emotional fog. Maybe I should go see Sierra? To comfort them, for the three of us to comfort one another. No, I was going to stick to my plan. I didn't ditch Sierra because I wanted to be alone but because I wanted to paint. If Jocelyn were around, maybe she'd present herself and I could paint her. Maybe what she showed me wouldn't be terrible, and maybe I could show it to Midas.

That's a lot of maybes, Cassidy Wright.

Domino met me at the door. He'd gone completely crazy at Midas' house for those few days we were gone, and he was still in a wild-I-can't-believe-you-left-me mood. He smacked me with his paw as I rearranged his food dish. He had a habit of pushing it around the kitchen like it was a toy. I spent a few minutes coaxing him to come out from under the dining room table before I gave up.

After changing my clothes, I returned a few phone calls— Helen was in New Mexico with Bruce at another of his archaeology conferences. She sent her love to Midas and promised to come see me as soon as she arrived back in

Mobile. She took the news about Jocelyn pretty hard. I hung up the phone feeling completely alone.

No family. No Midas.

Domino continued to rebuff my attempts at hugs, so I grabbed a quick sandwich and headed off to my studio. Domino meowed to complain about my leaving, but he wasn't interested in coming with me. I suspected he'd find something of mine to chew on or otherwise destroy. There was always a level of punishment involved in this cat-human relationship. Always from his side, of course. I shut the door and ignored his plaintive cries.

Too late, buddy boy.

Opening the studio door, I instantly felt peaceful, the kind of peace that accompanies all creatives when they dive into their work. Creativity strengthened me, and I needed that right now. I set a new canvas on the easel and brushed it off with a soft, clean paintbrush. I ransacked my paint-splattered table and found a good pencil, then stood in front of the canvas waiting for inspiration to strike.

"Jocelyn, please...if you're here, help me see. Let me know you're okay." I waited for what seemed an eternity without hearing anything or seeing a single image. My hand hovered over the canvas because sometimes that helped engage the source of my visions, but nothing came to me.

No images of Jocelyn. Feeling defeated, I plunked down on the chair and finally let the tears fall. I couldn't carry them any longer. Jocelyn, young, intelligent, spirited Jocelyn, died this week. A beautiful soul left this world, and what had she left behind? Just her dog and a massive catalog of photos.

Sierra beat me to the punch and adopted Sherman; the poor dog was having a tough time with the loss. Midas offered to send Jocelyn's possessions, her many cameras and notebooks full of ideas, to her mother, but she didn't want them. That seemed even worse to me. Jocelyn had no siblings, no extended family beyond her sick mother.

I cuddled up with my butterfly pillow and sobbed until my eyes were swollen. The garage-turned-studio suddenly felt cold, and I reached for the throw and cuddled up with it. I replayed the investigation over and over again in my mind. The horrible crows, the bees that attacked Joshua, the creepy jackboots that everyone heard echoing through the hall. And the terrifying Nalusa Falaya. Whatever classification one might put him in, he was a trickster from the word go. As far as I could tell, he would still be there, on that piece of land, long after I was dead and gone. The Nalusa Falaya had won, and we had lost our Jocelyn.

Midas had been right to tell Adrian to bulldoze the place, level it. Tear it down. Not only that, but he instructed her to salt the land and abandon all hope of using it for anything commercially or residentially. No one should be there. Ever. But at least the other souls were free. The Nalusa Falaya didn't have Shanafila anymore, or any of the Waliki. And McCandlish and the others, they were gone too. I'd been with Sierra, held her hand, and we'd done it together. Well, it was mostly Sierra; I was more moral support than anything else.

Yes, they were gone. Hopefully, Jocelyn had left too.

Oh please, God. Don't let Jocelyn be trapped in that awful place.

That was the closest thing to a prayer I could muster. I didn't want to believe that she was still there, but it was a possibility. The entity's power had been weakened, but broken? No. Not broken. I fell into a deep slumber but not for long. When I woke up, it was still light outside. I felt groggy but tossed the pillow away and pushed my hair out of my face.

I had a dream, and from that dream, I had an image to work with. Not of Jocelyn but of Shanafila!

I tossed the blanket to the side and walked back to my canvas. Before I knew it, I was drawing long lines, long limbs. I sketched out a face and then another. Without much thought, I reached for my palette and my brush. I filled the jar with water and then began rummaging through my paints for just the right colors.

Yes, that's right. Not quite that dark, though.

I brushed the canvas lightly at first, the darkest shades and then the lightest. Then the blending. Time passed, and the light in my studio shifted. I turned on the overhead lights and continued. I glanced at my watch briefly. Four hours had passed, but I had a long way to go. I would need days to finish this. I needed to add much more detail, like the thick black forest and the crackling fire in the distance. I wiped tears away as I studied my work with the freshest eyes I could muster.

Yukpa held Shanafila's hand, and together they were walking toward me, away from a warm campfire. They were happy, smiling, loving one another. Always together. Yes, this was right. Maybe more light on Shanafila's face. Yukpa's fingers should be longer. Just a little longer. Yes, I would have to change that but tomorrow. Not now. I needed to call Midas; he should be on his way to Jocelyn's mother's house by now.

One more thing.

I picked up the pencil again and carefully avoided getting my arm wet. No contact with the paint today. I didn't need to spy on Shanafila and Yukpa. I knew this had been the end for them. They had crossed over together.

Goodbye, Shanafila.

I scratched at the canvas with my pencil; I wasn't sure what my sketch would reveal, but the figure quickly came into view. Yes, she was there holding her big black camera. It was pointed at Shanafila and Yukpa, pointed at me.

Jocelyn was still there, but she wasn't trapped.

She was free and doing what she loved. Only from the other side. I put the pencil on the easel and stepped back to take it all in. Jocelyn's face was obscured by the camera, but it was clearly her. She'd done it. She'd made contact.

My hand shook as I put my fingers to my mouth. "Jocelyn," I whispered. My hand hovered over the canvas, but I knew I wouldn't connect with her. There was no paint on her part of the painting. Not yet.

One day I would finish this painting, and it would be a tribute to my friend and to all those who had been captured for so long by the Nalusa Falaya. I would paint her, in full living color. But not today.

Today, I needed to let her go, and that meant living. Not lingering in the past with the shadows and the ghosts and all the other things that dwelled there. I had to leave this for a day or two.

Maybe a month. I couldn't say. But the peace returned, and I knew what I needed to do.

Love my family and help them through this gut-wrenching time. I shed my smock and put my brushes away, not even pausing to glance again at the happy, retreating couple.

I turned off the lights, closed the door and left all the ghosts behind.

Return to the Leaf Academy

Book Eight
Gulf Coast Paranormal Season Two
By M.L. Bullock

Prologue—Sierra

The night was already thick with tension, the kind that makes your hair stand on end and what I was about to do was only going to make that worse. Out of habit, I tugged at my messy bun, pulling on the zebra stripe elastic to tighten it up. My hair was getting kind of long and even though it was October in south Alabama, it was quite warm. Once I adjusted my sloppy style, I took a few deep breaths to clear my mind.

It was as if the atmosphere around me was woven from *threads of unease*. I read that in a fiction novel recently and the description sort of stuck with me.

Yeah, this was all sorts of uneasy but it had to be done.
I sat alone in my dimly lit room, incense smoke twisting like ethereal snakes in the air around me. Burning incense wasn't necessary but setting the mood helped me ease into the otherworld. It was kind of ritualistic but it brought me comfort so there was that. I eased into a comfortable sitting position. It was important to relax because the more fear I brought into the session, the more I would attract fear during my psychic walk.
I was about to do something I rarely did anymore—a remote psychic session.

But not just any session; this was an astral dive into the Leaf Academy, a place with a history so dark it could eclipse the freaking Alabama sun.

As I closed my eyes, I felt a magnetic pull like the undertow of a dark ocean. A dark, endless ocean.
My surroundings vanished, and suddenly I was walking through the deserted halls of the Leaf Academy.

Wow! That was quick. I didn't have to struggle at all. Weird.

The air smelled of must and decay; the walls were textured with the peeling paint and the graffiti written by a hundred lost souls. *Geesh, Sierra. You've got to lay off the late-night novel reading.* Each step echoed as if announcing my intrusion to unseen watchers.

Something was off.

With every step, I felt a disturbing realization creep over me like ivy on a gravestone—I was walking, yes, but these weren't my steps. Not at all.

I was in someone else's leather shoes, experiencing their dread, their fear. My heart raced, not with my anxiety but with the urgency of another's hidden terror. I was tall and powerful—I was a man, but for some reason, my blood coursed with fear.

Who am I? What is my name? What am I afraid of?

I glanced down at my manly hands, but my feet would not stop moving. No, I wasn't directing this remote walk at all. I was in this man's shoes, looking through his eyes.

Keep calm, Sierra. Breathe and focus.

Up ahead, a flicker of movement—just at the edge of my peripheral vision caught my eye. I was standing at a hallway intersection. *Yes, I could see someone sitting to my left. Should I turn? Dare I look?* The feet carrying me hesitated as if the person I was synced with also felt the presence.

And then it hit me. A name flashed in my mind as if whispered by an unseen mouth just inches from my ear. *Ollie. Could this be Ollie?*

No. That's wrong. This man knew who Ollie was--he'd seen him before and he feared him. By the style of his clothing--I could see his reflection in the doorway glass. Yes, I'd stepped back in time. And not just by a few decades. I studied the face that shone back at me, but I didn't recognize the man.

This was not Hugh McCandlish. This was no one I recognized. "Who are you?" I whispered.

He didn't answer, but I felt him move as if startled. And then in a flash, I snapped back to my room, gasping for air as if I'd just broken the surface of a deep, suffocating pool.

The incense was acrid now, biting at my senses, as I realized the danger of the dark path I'd placed myself on. The Leaf Academy had come alive and was ready to share its secrets, but what waited there was powerful and prepared for my arrival. Ollie was not afraid of me, at all.

Sweat trickled down my forehead as I contemplated whether to go back into that dark, ethereal realm.
My fingers tingled with a lingering unease, a residual echo of the fear that wasn't mine. I glanced down at my wedding ring. Studying the precious item brought me comfort.

What did I have to be afraid of? Joshua was in the living room. He would be checking on me soon. It's not like I'd get lost.

I shook off the sickening fear. I had to. The image of Jocelyn falling off that roof lingered in my memory. I couldn't allow that to happen again. Our return to the Leaf Academy was imminent, and I needed to understand the lurking dangers—psychic or otherwise—that awaited us. Not only for me but for the entire Gulf Coast Paranormal team.

With a steadying breath, I closed my eyes again. Once again, the transition was instant.

I was back in the dusty, dimly lit halls, my feet took me deeper into the haunting maze. I was standing close to the location where I'd been stationed earlier. I didn't focus on the reflection in the glass door, but instead, turned my gaze to the child.

Yes, I could see a child. A child in a wheelchair, sitting alone in the corridor. A blanket was draped over her lap, its frayed edges suggestive of many a lonesome night in this place worrying over the hem. Why would a disabled child be abandoned in the Leaf Academy?

Oh hell no. This ain't right at all.

Confusion washed over me. "There were no disabled children at this school. Certainly not girls," I thought.

My borrowed feet moved closer to the child. With each step, a gnawing suspicion grew within me. As I neared, the blanket shifted. In the dim light, I could see a strange, serpentine movement underneath the material—something was off.
My skin went cold, my breathing shallow.

I—or the person I was linked with—wanted to run, to flee this horrifying vision. But we couldn't. It was as if some invisible force held us there, captive spectators to an unfolding nightmare.

"Child? Is that you? Mary Ellen?"

But the child would not lift her head. She whimpered, her chin on her chest, the blanket still moving. What is happening? Am I dreaming? The man's fear came through strong.

He'd known this child. Loved her. After a moment it became clear. *She'd been his child! Oh no!*

Summoning a courage that wasn't my own, my hands reached for the blanket.

In a single, swift motion, I yanked it away. My eyes widened, and my stomach turned.

Rats. Dozens of them.

They had consumed the child's lower half. There was nothing left but a grotesque mass of writhing vermin where legs should be.

The child's face twisted in torment, her scream piercing the silence, "Help me, Daddy!"

It was the last straw.

The words were a jolt, shattering my tenuous hold on the trance. I was yanked back to my reality, gasping for air, trembling from head to toe. My eyes flew open, yet the child's desperate plea echoed in my ears, a chilling reminder of the grim and horrific mysteries that lay ahead.

The Leaf Academy was an abyss of terror, a maze of soul-shattering horrors. I had returned with a dreadful knowledge that I couldn't shake. Whoever that child was—yes, I remembered her name, Mary Ellen, she wasn't just a lost soul. She was a sign, a grim harbinger of the dark and complicated tapestry we were about to attempt to unravel.

Again.

The Leaf Academy was more than haunted; it was a Pandora's box of despair and malevolence. And we were about to open it. The October People had returned to the Leaf Academy. They were walking the halls still and they were waiting for us.

I staggered to my feet, shaking off the lingering dread that clung to me like a cold mist. Blowing out the candle, I felt the light's absence intensify the shadows that filled the room. But it was done. I had stared into the haunted abyss, and I knew what we faced.

Now it was time to share it.

Exiting my meditation room, aka the spare bedroom, I found Joshua in the living room, poring over some old case files. He looked up, concern filling his eyes when he saw my expression. "I was just about to peek in on you. Sierra? What happened? You look like you've seen a ghost—or worse. You made a connection then?"

I moved closer, sinking into the sofa next to him. "I walked the halls of the Leaf Academy in someone else's shoes. A man, but

I'm not sure who he is, Josh. It's worse than when we left it. Much worse."

He took my hand, his grip a comforting anchor in a sea of unease. "Tell me what you saw, Sierra. Don't leave anything out."

With a shuddering breath, I recounted the haunting vision, the rats, the pitiful child, the blanket of dread that suffused the air.

The man and his wretched daughter. Joshua listened, his expression darkening with each detail.

"Did you sense Jocelyn there?" he asked, his voice tinged with hope and apprehension.

I shook my head, a heavy sadness settling over me. "No, I didn't. But remember, Ollie is stronger now. He could be holding her back, keeping her from reaching out."

Joshua raised an eyebrow. "Stronger than a maelstrom? He was already that."

I nodded, my eyes meeting his. "I know. But it's as if the boundaries between our world and whatever hellish place he comes from are growing thinner. We're not just facing a ghost or a lost soul. We're up against a tidal wave of darkness, and it is a gathering force."

He squeezed my hand, reassuring yet firm. "Then we'll face it together, as we always have. With the whole team."

A storm was coming, a storm of shadows and screams, and it was headed straight for us.

"I've got to figure out who the girl is and fast. If I can do that, I should be able to identify the man. I need the file. Is it on this jump drive?" I asked as I slid on the floor and commandeered his open laptop.

"Should be. What was her name again?"

And just like that, Joshua and I were lost in the prep work for the next investigation. Thankfully, Midas would be taking the lead on this case, as he should, but I couldn't slack off.
We weren't going to the Leaf Academy to be entertained. This wouldn't be a weekend of fun paranormal investigation. Once again, we would engage in a battle of wills with the darkness.

This time, I would make sure we all came back home.

Chapter One—Midas

The air in the Gulf Coast Paranormal team's headquarters was thick with tension and anticipation. Old maps and files covered the table, surrounding the whirring gadgets and custom devices that had seen us through countless hunts. As I looked around at the faces of my team—my extended family—I felt the weight again of what we were about to undertake.

"Okay, guys," I began, forcing my voice to stay steady. "We're all aware of why we're here today. It's been a long time coming. We're going back to the Leaf Academy. The objective is to verify the presence of Jocelyn's spirit and if she's there, we will help her. In whatever we can."

I couldn't believe I was saying this but I was convinced that she was indeed trapped there. If not her, then some sort of trickster was using her memory to pull us all back. I'd seen her from time to time out the corner of my mind. Cassidy drew her constantly these days and Sierra mentioned more than once Jocelyn's spirit was hanging around.

If she was truly trapped, I wouldn't abandon her and allow her to be captured by evil.

A ripple of unease swept across the room. Cassidy shifted uncomfortably in her chair, Sierra glanced away, her expression unreadable, and Macie gripped the arms of her chair so tightly her knuckles turned white. Chris, sitting near the end of the table, cleared his throat. We all knew why we'd come here but to say it, it made this investigation even more real.

I was thankful that everyone was approaching this task with a mature air of seriousness.

"Um, about that, Midas," he said, meeting my eyes with a blend of embarrassment and regret. "Jericho and I did a little recon. We went to the Leaf Academy. We thought we'd get a feel for the place before the team headed in."

"You did what?" I felt my temperature rise, a boiling mix of anger and concern. "Chris, that's not protocol. And where is Jericho now? Is this why he isn't answering my calls?" I had a litany of questions for him but I restrained myself from any verbal bombardment. I could feel my jaw popping. That always happened when I was tense. Or angry.

Chris looked down, his face a mask of guilt. "Jericho got attacked. I swear, we were just doing some recon, and something got him. He's... well, he's out of commission. He won't be coming back anytime soon." He took a deep breath and described the terrifying moments when he couldn't find Jericho and his condition when he did spot him.
His shirt had been ripped and there were three long gashes on his back. They heard an audible voice command them to leave.

"Can you describe the voice?" My wife Cassidy asked quietly as she tapped her pencil on her closed notebook.

Without hesitation, our newest team member answered her. "Uh, not human. That's the best description I can come up with. It was loud and it resonated, like inside my chest. It had a vibration to it. Make of that what you will. I've heard disembodied voices before but that was something else."

The room fell silent, each of us processing the gravity of Chris's words. I turned to find Macie's eyes locked onto mine. "I know what he's talking about," she confessed, her voice tinged with fear and steel. "I've been there too. I know you asked me to stop going, but Jocelyn is there. I know it."

My eyes met Cassidy's. Her face was absent her usual easy smile, her straight, shiny red hair tucked behind her ears. She watched me with steady assurance. What good would it do to crack on my team about solo investigating? They were all adults and Macie had a compelling reason for going there. Chris and Jericho not so much, but again, what was I able to do about it? They weren't children. I couldn't ground the team.

I looked around the room, taking in the solemn nods, the clenched fists, the air heavy with resolve. "Jocelyn gave her life for us, for me. If she's still there, if any part of her remains, we have to set her free. I understand why you all went but as I've reminded everyone, multiple times, the Leaf Academy requires the whole team."

"What's done is done," Sierra added, her voice soft with resignation. "Let's focus on the here and now. Whatever's in that forsaken place, it's time to go back. And when it's over, that will be the end of the Leaf Academy. No one else will suffer because of it."

I couldn't help but notice Macie, her face a study in anguish. "I hate to hear about Jericho. He's not answering my calls either, y'all. I guess I know why." Her eyes glistened, holding back tears that were threatening to spill. The room seemed to respond instinctively, the atmosphere shifting from focused resolve to one of warmth and support.

"Hey, Macie," Sierra began, her eyes filled with compassion. "Why don't we do a quick drive-by later, just to check up on Jericho? We can keep it discreet."

Macie shook her head, trying to manage a smile. "No, let's give him his space. If he's not coming back, if he doesn't want to talk, he must have his reasons. I have to respect that."

We all nodded, not pressing the issue any further. But the room seemed to grow heavier with unspoken words and shared concerns until Joshua decided to break the silence.

"Alright, everyone, let's shift gears a bit," Joshua said, directing our attention to a small, sleek case he was holding. "Chris and I have been working on something new, a piece of tech that could be a game-changer for us."

He opened the case to reveal a headset, its design compact and sophisticated, with a series of intricate sensors and lenses. "Meet RYDER," he announced, a hint of pride shining through his serious demeanor.

"RYDER? That sounds mysterious. What does it do?" Cassidy asked, her interest piqued.

Joshua looked at Chris, who took over the explanation. "RYDER stands for Resonant Ylem Detection and Entity Recognition. Resonant because of the usage of frequencies associated with the supernatural. Ylem refers to the essence of the soul. So that's how it works, through frequency identification. The headset allows us to scan for possessions or any supernatural attachments in, on, or connected to the living. Given what happened to Jericho and considering the nature of Leaf Academy, this will be invaluable, I believe. We think we've got most of the glitches worked out."

"Wow," Macie whispered, her eyes meeting mine. "That's trippy if it works like you describe. Sounds like something you'd see in a science fiction movie."

"Right," I agreed, impressed by the ingenuity of my team. "Let's make sure we take it with us. Anything that gives us an edge, we'll need it."

As I looked around the room, I saw a mixture of awe and renewed determination on everyone's faces. We were gearing up, not just with technology but with the unity and resolve that had always been our greatest asset. And with RYDER as our new wildcard, I felt a flicker of hope that we might survive what lay ahead.

"Demonstration time," Joshua announced as he and Chris carefully unzipped a black case and pulled out the headset. It did indeed look like something out of a sci-fi movie, sleek and filled with mysterious tech. "This is her—meet RYDER. It's designed to alert us of supernatural presences."

"Who wants to go first?" Chris asked, grinning from ear to ear, clearly excited about the new gadget.
Macie volunteered. She put on the RYDER headset, adjusting the straps. "Why does it have to be a her? I don't get that."

"Ready for initiation?" Joshua asked her without answering her question. She nodded her head in response. After a few seconds, she gasped in surprise.

"What? This is crazy! I see shadow overlays. Not solid though. In different colors. I see you, Midas. You're clear. And that must be Cassidy and wow, look at everyone. The colors are so vivid." She took it off and handed it back to Chris. "Like I said, trippy," she commented, eyes still wide.

Sierra, however, shook her head when Joshua offered her the headset. "I don't need it, honey," she said softly. "I see plenty already."

"What did you see on your walk, Sierra?" Cassidy questioned; her artist's eyes full of curiosity.

Sierra took a deep breath. "Earlier today, I did a psychic remote walk-through of the Leaf Academy. And I saw something—someone—rather unsettling. I walked in Moriah Mitchell's shoes."

"Wait, the headmaster from the late 1800s?" Midas interjected, concern lining his face.

"Yes," Sierra continued. "And I saw a child in an old-fashioned wheelchair. It was his daughter. I recognized her from this photo," she said, showing the team a printout of an old, sepia-toned photo from the late 1800s.

The room went silent, tension thickening the air. Each of us felt it—an escalation of stakes, a tug toward a reality more twisted and sinister than we'd ever realized.

"I think Ollie was using the girl, Mitchell's daughter, to threaten him. To manipulate him," Sierra said, breaking the uneasy silence. "I could feel the tightening of Ollie's grip. Moriah Mitchell knew all about this being." We discussed the implications of this information a little more until I glanced at my watch.

"Time to go, guys. We have work to do," I said, my voice heavy with the weight of our collective responsibility. As the rest of the team began packing up the RYDER headset and other equipment, I motioned for Macie to join me in a quiet corner of the room.

"This is it. We're going back but I need you to keep your head about you. Especially after hearing about Jericho. No doubt this thing knows who you are and it may target you," I started, my eyes searching hers.

Macie nodded. "Of course, I plan on keeping my head in the game, as you say. But you aren't pushing me out of this investigation."

"I have to keep you safe, Macie. I owe that much to Jocelyn— and you."

Her eyes met mine, a complex swirl of emotions—fear, determination, and something else—flickering within them. "I understand," she finally said. "I'll stick with you. I won't cause trouble. Promise."

Just as we were about to join the others, Cassidy walked over to join us. She smiled at the two of us and gave Macie a warm, supportive hug. "Ready for this?" she whispered.

"As ready as I'll ever be," Macie whispered back, her voice tinged with both trepidation and resolve.

We made our way to the SUV. I decided to leave the van behind. It was emblazoned with the bold GCP—Gulf Coast Paranormal—logo. Everyone would know what we were doing if we went rolling up in that. I couldn't risk putting any other lives in danger.

Macie, Chris, and the rest of the team piled in, the atmosphere heavy with anticipation and uncertainty. I took one final look at the group before climbing into the driver's seat of the SUV.

Cassidy leaned over and briefly kissed my cheek. The scent of her perfume comforted me as I cranked the vehicle up.

"All right, guys," I said, glancing at each of them through the rearview mirror. "Let's do this. Next stop, the Leaf Academy."

Chapter Two—Cassidy

I sat in the passenger seat of the SUV with the sketchbook in my lap. I closed my eyes briefly to focus on the spirit that hovered nearby. The road to Orange Grove stretched before us like a long, ominous tunnel.

I had an hour to kill—might as well use it productively.

Midas had music blaring over the radio. It helped fill in the silence that settled over our usually lively group.

I switched on the map light, flipped open the sketchbook to a blank page, and began to draw. My hand moved almost autonomously as if some invisible force guided the pencil. It wasn't like that for me. This wasn't automatic writing. Not like Macie. It was just drawing, usually whatever popped into my head. At first.

I was thinking about my son, Dominic, back at home. He'd been teething, and there'd been nights of no sleep and days filled with drool and fussing. I hoped he was doing okay with the sitter. He was my little light, and it was tough leaving him, even for something as important as this. Midas felt the same way. Father and son were nearly attached at the hip. He was always toting our son around, spoiling him rotten. Like I didn't do that enough.

As the SUV hummed along, my sketches began to take shape.

Faces emerged, but they weren't familiar to me. I drew a woman with hollow eyes, a man with a weathered forehead, and a child, no older than ten, with an eerie stillness in her expression. Could this be Mary Ellen? I didn't show it to

Sierra. She was staring out the window while Joshua tinkered with RYDER beside her in the third row.

Chris and Macie sat awkwardly next to one another in the second row. They weren't touching or talking, but you would have to be blind to not see the potential attraction between them.

Focus on your work, Cassidy. Mind your own business.

I paused and took a hard look at what I'd drawn. A chilling realization washed over me.
I was drawing the lost souls of Leaf Academy. The faces staring back at me were cries for help etched in graphite. I felt a cold shiver crawl up my spine. The weight of what we were about to face settled deep in my bones.
My sketches weren't just drawings; they were warnings, a glimpse into the spectral world we were driving toward. Feeling uneasy about the faces I'd just sketched, I flipped to a new page.

My pencil began to move in wider, more chaotic strokes this time.

What emerged on the paper was not a face, but a swirling vortex—the maelstrom, the thing Sierra had described as a soul-eating entity. Only now, it seemed larger, more menacing than before. At the center of the swirling chaos, I saw and drew an enigmatic figure, its form barely distinguishable, yet unnerving.

I paused and took a deep breath, reminding myself to stay grounded.

I had my secrets to bear, knowledge that felt like a burden at times. I knew something the others didn't. Midas had bought the Leaf Academy. Adrian Shanahan, the former owner, had promised to destroy the place, but tragedy had kept her from following through. Now it was up to us, and that responsibility weighed heavily on me.

Yeah, her bad luck had to be connected to inheriting the run-down old school. Lost her grandfather, and her mother and even experienced a bad breakup. Coupled that with a house fire and a car accident, I didn't blame her for selling everything and moving to Ireland.

And now the devilish place belonged to us. I'd tried to talk him out of purchasing the property, not for any reason other than my fear of an unholy inheritance. We weren't related to the Shanahans at all, but sometimes unfortunate property owners inherited ghosts and worse.

Say it, Cassidy. You can't be afraid to say it. I shook my head as I studied my face in the mirror. *Curse. I don't want us to be cursed and I do believe in them.* I wouldn't say the word out loud, but I sure feared it. Hadn't I already walked under some sort of curse? I mean, my entire family was gone. I could not bear the thought of losing my husband or son.

The maelstrom I had sketched loomed ominously, like a storm cloud ready to break open. And the figure in the middle? It was almost as if it was daring us to come and find out what lay at the heart of the darkness.

I closed the sketchbook, tucking my pencil away. My heart pounded in my chest, a rhythm of anticipation and dread.

As the van and SUV pulled into the gravel lot in front of Leaf Academy, I felt a weight settle over me. The place looked just as foreboding as ever, its windows like empty eyes staring back at us. We unloaded our gear, setting up basecamp right at the entrance.

"We've got a long night ahead of us," Midas announced, looking over the equipment. "I want to get as much done as we can while we still have daylight."

Sierra nodded, her eyes meeting mine briefly. She looked uneasy but resolute. "I'll get the thermal cameras and EVP recorders set up in the east wing," she said. "Macie? Will you come with me? Midas, I could use her help. I'll keep her close."

Midas agreed and if Macie disapproved, she didn't say so. The team began to dig into the electronic gear cases.

"I'll tackle the west wing with Chris," Joshua added, hoisting a case containing the newly minted RYDER tech. "Let's test this baby out."

"That thing is legit creepy," Macie muttered again, looking at the RYDER headset case with a mix of awe and apprehension. "So, this is going to tell us if there's anything... out of the ordinary here? You've tested it out in spaces? Not just on people, right?"

"Yep," Chris chuckled. "The primary design is to process shifts in energy around the living but we've had some success in situations absent a person. A living person that is. It'll hopefully let us see what's lurking in these corners. I wish I would have had her when Jericho and I visited."

"We need to cover as much ground as possible," Sierra interrupted, reminding us to get back to the business of setting up. "We don't know how much time we have before Ollie...well, let's just say things get complicated."

I saw Chris shoot a concerned glance toward Macie. The emotional undercurrent between them was hard to miss.

"I'll head to the auditorium," said Midas, turning to me with a serious expression.
"Cassidy, you're with me."

I hesitated for a moment, my thoughts drifting to the sketches I'd made. The faces, the maelstrom, and that enigmatic figure. Was it a warning or a portent of things to come? Either way, we had a job to do.

"Alright," I agreed. "Let's see what secrets Leaf Academy is keeping this time."
We gathered our equipment, a sense of urgency hanging in the air. The night would fall soon, and with it, whatever spirits, entities, or otherworldly phenomena Leaf Academy was harboring would become more active.

The October People were back and so were we. Hadn't we learned anything?

As we dispersed to our respective investigation sites, I couldn't shake off the sense of dread that clung to me. *Oof.*

I suddenly felt chilled to the bone. Leaves shuddered in a sudden breeze that sailed through the oaks that surrounded the landmark. I zipped up my jacket and looked up at the broken windows one last time before we splintered off.

The sense of responsibility, of owning this accursed place, weighed heavily on me. What had we gotten ourselves into? With the setting sun casting long shadows across the grounds, we stepped into the haunting embrace of the Leaf Academy.

In the dilapidated auditorium, Midas and I tread carefully, our footsteps echoing in the emptiness. Dust and disarray were our only company but thankfully I could hear Joshua's loud mouth out in the hallway. The atmosphere was thick, and oppressive, as though the air itself remembered what had occurred here before. Spotlights and stage curtains hung in tatters, remnants of better days and happier performances.

Midas moved ahead, his flashlight sweeping across the room. "It hasn't gotten any friendlier. That's for sure. I can't believe we came back."

"Nope. Not friendly at all?" I replied, my thoughts drifting to the showdown we'd faced here. "It feels like...the epicenter of hell."

Midas glanced at me with a knowing look. "It does, doesn't it?" He touched my shoulder as if he wanted to comfort me. I shivered instead. There was no comfort to be found in the Leaf Academy. There never would be.

I hesitated before asking, "Are you planning on going up to the roof again?"

He paused; his face shadowed by the dim lighting. "I've been thinking about that. Why?"

"No reason," I lied, trying to keep my voice steady. "Just curious." But deep down, the thought of Midas returning to the roof made my skin crawl. It was almost as though the very structure of the Leaf Academy was baiting us, luring us back to confront what we had barely escaped last time.

Midas seemed to read my thoughts. "We have to go where the investigation takes us, Cassidy. Even if it means going back up there then so be it. But I won't put the rest of the team in danger. Never again."

"Well, you sure as heck aren't going alone, Midas Demopolis. Not as long as I am here. Don't even think about it."

"Okay, honey. Let's get this done." He nodded, gripping the cases tightly. I knew he was right, we needed to get the cords down, but the dread that loomed in my heart was hard to shake off. "Let's keep moving," Midas said, breaking the silence that had settled between us.

As we ventured deeper into the auditorium, I couldn't shake off the nagging feeling that the Leaf Academy was waiting for us.

And whether it was on this ground level, or up on that eerie roof, something told me we were inching ever closer to another showdown.

I set the cases down and I tugged at my zipper again.

It's an exercise in futility, Cassidy Demopolis. You can't keep the darkness and cold out. Not here.

I ignored my intuition because I was determined to stay with Midas.

I hoped I didn't live to regret my love and loyalty.

Chapter Three—Moriah Mitchell

I found myself again seated at the oak desk that filled a considerable corner of my office. This space, adorned with faded floral wallpaper and old mahogany bookshelves, represented my daily imprisonment.

How hopeful I had been when I first arrived here at the Leaf Academy. The fanfare, the respect, had it all been worth it?

No. It had not been worth it at all.

Coming here, accepting this position had been akin to selling my soul, but I had not intentionally done so. I knew nothing about the local legend about the October People, the strange entities that possess this land every year. From what I heard, these beings invaded the area for only for a few days, but to be safe, the administration had long ago decided that the facility would close for the entire month every year.

My title as Headmaster of Leaf Academy was once a title that I wore proudly.

But now the role had become an unbearable weight around my neck, dragging me closer to an abyss I dare not peer into. The scent of old leather, ink, and lingering moisture of this aged room suffocated me as if they were wrapping invisible hands around my throat.

Such morbid thoughts, Moriah. Take your medicine. You know your mind tends to wander.

With shaking hands, I opened my desk drawer and retrieved the medication I needed. I swallowed a single pill without drinking any water. I'd forgotten to request a tray for my evening meal. I was quite sure the kitchen staff was gone by now. It was late in the day and it was a holiday. In a few days, the shadows would gather and if the lore was to be believed, the October People would return. I had no plans to be here for that.

The thing that walked the halls now was bad enough.

It had only been a year since my appointment as headmaster of Leaf Academy, and yet it felt like a lifetime trapped in purgatory. The once grand edifice of learning had become a tomb of unsettling quietude and veiled malevolence.

The hallways, lined with old portraits of former teachers, headmasters and notable residents, watched me. Yes, their dusty painted eyes seem to follow me. Especially now that the school was nearly empty. The halls were now filled with an eerie silence, broken only by the echoing footsteps of invisible presences.

Or so I imagined. Sure, I am imagining such noises. Or it could be some of the staff doing the last of their tasks before they leave. Loading coal, sweeping floors and all the other things that go into taking care of a large school like the Leaf Academy.

No. I saw them leave.

Whispering winds circumvented the labyrinthine corridors, carrying with them a cacophony of soft cries and hushed voices—sounds not of this world but of the spectral entities that make this academy their haunting ground.

No, I was not only hearing things, but I was also sensing them too. Even now, my scientist's mind pushed against this idea. Ghosts, spirits, curses. I had never believed in any of this, but that was before.

Before I saw the boy crawling on the ceiling. Before I woke up and found him hovering above me. Before he pretended to be my daughter and came to my room at night. This monster, that's what he was—he was as real as the devil.

As far as I knew, he could be the devil.

I continued to walk the halls, turning off lights and closing doors. The classrooms, supposed crucibles of knowledge, felt like sanctuaries for the darker arts. Lights flickered erratically even when there was no possible breeze. The shifting light cast unsettling shadows on the walls—shadows that moved and danced as though celebrating some malevolent rite.

I shivered in the darkness.

Before most left for the break, students and faculty alike went about their days with a sense of resignation, their faces pallid, eyes sunken. Yes, the school's temporary closure was affecting everyone, only everyone wasn't seeing the monster.

As we inched toward October, laughter and youthful exuberance had become alien here. Everyone whispered about shadows and strange sounds, but no one spoke about it openly. The terror was an unspoken yet universally shared experience, a secret pact sealed by fear itself.

And then there was the library, a repository of both human wisdom and arcane secrets. The old texts with their leather-bound covers and brittle pages seem to hold more than just ink and parchment.

No one else would notice such things but I, Moriah Mitchell, Headmaster of the Leaf Academy did see it and I saw it all clearly.

At night, the darkness here was overwhelming, as if the academy itself swallowed the moonlight. Sleep offered no respite; nightmares invaded the dormitories, leaving even the bravest souls waking in cold sweat, their screams dissolving into the eternal night. The children couldn't wait to leave for their fall break, bless them. I was glad to see them safely exit the property.

The very walls of the academy seethed with a dark energy, emanating an oppressive aura that sought to break my will, to bend reality itself.

It wanted what it wanted and it wanted that so badly! I imagined that it wanted to be free. It wanted to go home with me. Leave with me. Yes, go to my home. I would never agree to that. No matter how many feathers the beast left for me.

Despite its veneer of civility and education, the Leaf Academy, in its essence, had become an otherworldly cage. One which I, as headmaster, held the keys to—but never the means to truly escape. *Oh, but I had plans to do just that. I only had a few more things to do.*

It was a horrible task, one that I must do if I wanted to save Mary Ellen.
Save my family. Yes, I knew what I had to do, I think I always knew, but I refused to consider it.

I reached for the pen on my desk, but my hand hovered over it for a moment. I was reminded of that terrible event that marked my first days here. It had left an indelible mark upon me, transforming every shadow in these halls into a stalking phantom and turning every creak of the floorboards into a harbinger of unspeakable dread.

I had just finished reviewing the disciplinary reports late one evening when I heard a whisper—a soft, almost melodious murmur that slithered into the room from underneath the closed door.

Curiosity piqued, I opened the door only to find the hallways dark and empty.

The academy's corridors, which were normally filled with the lively voices of students, had gone deathly quiet, except for that insidious whisper that was growing louder, more insistent. It beckoned me, pulling me toward the eastern wing—the oldest part of the academy, abandoned due to its state of disrepair. Thankfully, there was a construction project going. That should soon set everything right.

There, in a room veiled in a thick cloak of darkness, I felt it—a presence so malevolent that it consumed all warmth and light, leaving only an inky black void.

I couldn't see the presence, but I felt its gaze, heavy and penetrating, fixed on me. I dared not breathe. My heart raced as I realized I wasn't alone. Whatever was in that room was ancient, malevolent, and unforgiving.

The entity whispered words I didn't understand, but they reverberated in the depths of my soul. These were words not meant for human ears to understand; they were words that seemed to twist reality itself. And then, just as suddenly as it had come, it retreated, leaving me alone in that suffocating darkness.

I fled, never speaking a word to anyone about it, but the malevolence remained—a spectral occupant in the very walls of this cursed place.

I shook my head, trying to dispel the memories, and finally picked up the pen. There was work to be done, but the haunting past lingered, never fully retreating into the shadows.
The unforgiving clock on my office wall ticked away, each second grinding at my already frayed nerves. I found my gaze drifting towards a stack of applications on my desk—a motley pile of resumes and letters of recommendation.

We needed a new teacher for the literature department, but my mind had been far too occupied with darker thoughts to give this the attention it required.

It was an impossible task, really. How could I invite another person to join this dance of shadows? But the clock ticked, and the students needed educating. Life had to go on. So, I sifted through the pile with a hesitant hand.

That night, I locked the hiring folder away in my desk drawer. But the names on the resumes haunted me in my sleep, morphing into ghastly specters that pulled me down into an abyss of indescribable horror.

When I returned to my office the next day, my breath caught in my throat. The drawer was ajar, and the hiring folder lay wide open on my desk. The applications were scattered, as though tossed by some invisible hand, but one sat perfectly centered, as if presented for my inspection.

Hugh McCandlish.

The name sent a shiver down my spine, as unfamiliar as it was foreboding. I didn't recall ever seeing this application in the pile. My eyes were drawn to his qualifications; they weren't impressive. Then my gaze fell upon the feather, and my blood ran cold. The feather didn't belong here. Not on my desk or in the folder. The message was clear. Hugh McCandlish was the one they wanted.

The October People had chosen this man. Poor man. Chosen by evil.

The October People had made their choice, and the dread within me deepened, pulling me further into the pit I had hoped to escape. At that moment, I knew. I was not simply hiring a teacher; I was inviting a new chapter of horror into the annals of the Leaf Academy.

I was sentencing a man to a life of torment. In fact, I had chosen my replacement.

I picked up the pen and started writing the acceptance letter to Hugh McCandlish. My hands trembled as I formed each letter, each word. With every stroke, I felt as though I was sealing not just his fate, but my own.

It was a path from which there was no turning back; this was a chain of events set into motion that would spiral beyond my control.

With a heavy sigh, I pressed the ink to paper and began to draft the letter to Hugh McCandlish. "Dear Mr. McCandlish, it is with great enthusiasm that the Leaf Academy extends an offer of employment for the position of..."

My hand moved mechanically, each word a ghostly echo of the formalities I'd penned countless times before.

Yet, as I finished the last sentence and laid down the pen, I felt a hot tear trickle down my cheek and splatter onto the letter, smudging the ink like a dark omen. My shoulders trembled, racked with silent sobs. I was committing something unspeakable here unearthing a malevolent seed that would quickly take root within these already cursed walls.

Why do it then? A voice within me whispered, as if attempting to justify this macabre act. But deep down, I knew why. It was for Mary Ellen, my daughter, my little light. *If I couldn't keep these shadows at bay, who would protect her?*

My tears fell freely now, for McCandlish and Mary Ellen and for all the damned souls I'd just drawn deeper into this labyrinth of dread. Just as I was lost in this lament, a subtle creak snapped me back to reality. The hairs on the back of my neck stood on end.

Slowly, I lifted my gaze to the doorway and saw him—the boy standing there, peering in through half-open eyes. Oh, but he was no mere boy. He was something far more sinister. His stare was unnerving, cold, and yet somehow filled with an ancient understanding.

As if he knew what I'd done, as if he had witnessed my tragic fall from grace, he grinned at me.
He did not speak but the weight of his presence hung thick in the air, a palpable darkness that even the morning light streaming through the windows failed to dispel. He stepped back into the shadows and vanished. Long fingernails scratched at the walls of the hallway but to my relief, the sound seemed to get further and further away.

Yes, please let this be over. I have given you what you wanted. He will come and you will have the one you want. Then I will leave. Leave forever! You cannot stop me! I obeyed you!

Suddenly I rose from my chair and shouted at the monster, "I obeyed you. I did what you asked! Now leave me alone!"

I can't say what persuaded me to take such a stand, but I did. I needed to. I need to feel as if I were in control of my life, my future, and my family's safety. I hurriedly left my office and went to my room to pack. A month away from here would make all the difference. Yes, it would.

I wouldn't think about November. I wouldn't think about welcoming the new teacher, or about offering him up to the monster. I wouldn't think about that at all. But I cried as I packed my clothes. I cried as I drove away. I didn't want to return but I had to. I had to see this thing through because the monster knew where I lived.

This thing knew what my daughter looked like and she'd never been to the Leaf Academy. It must have followed me or read my mind. I couldn't be sure, but now...now I had done an evil deed to placate it.

What have I done?

Yes, I would return to the Leaf Academy and I would give the monster what it wanted. For now, it wanted Hugh McCandlish.

I screamed and banged my hands on the steering wheel as I eased away. I glanced at the school one last time and shook my head at the mockery of the motto engraved over the door.

I will fear no evil.

When they built this place, they must have known what they were doing. When they designed the Leaf Academy on this hellish land, they had to have seen.
I will fear no evil.

The founders knew, but they did it anyway. They tapped into the evil and now I served it.

I pulled over on the side of the road and threw up.

Chapter Four—Sierra

I shook my head violently as if the motion could dispel the ghostly images that had invaded my thoughts. The vision had been so sudden, so intense like someone had thrust me into a whole other world for a moment.

"Are you okay?" Macie's voice broke through the fog in my mind. She looked at me with concerned eyes, clearly sensing that something was off.

I took a deep breath, trying to steady my racing heart. "I'm fine, just a little dizzy," I lied. I didn't want to confess that I had just lived an entirely different moment within seconds.

Macie was a medium too. She'd get it, but I didn't want to influence her in any way. We needed her gift of automatic writing to work without being influenced by anything I might say or do.

As we stepped into the hall of the Leaf Academy, a wave of unease washed over me. The intricate wood carvings, the ancient chandeliers, the murals that told stories of a past long forgotten—it was far too familiar.

I had been here before. More than once, but this eerie old building always took my breath away.

I couldn't shake off the feeling that something—or someone—was watching me, reaching out from the hidden corners of the academy, corners steeped in mysteries I couldn't yet comprehend. But I knew one thing for sure--Leaf Academy was haunted, and my psychic senses were its newest playground.

My phone vibrated in my pocket, pulling me away from my thoughts. It was Joshua. I quickly excused myself from Macie, telling her I'd catch up later, and I retreated to a more secluded area.

"Hey, Joshua. I'm glad you called. What do you need?" Yes, I was glad to hear his voice,
"Sierra Kay, have you seen the SLS camera? The handheld one?"

I glanced around and spotted the case. "Yeah, we got it. Do you need it? Let's trade. I want to use RYDER."

There was a brief pause, then my husband said, "Are you joking?"

"No. I can't say why yet but I need to try it. Just for a little bit."

"Of course. I'll be there in a few minutes."

Joshua arrived sooner than expected, carrying the black case that held RYDER. It was cutting-edge technology, designed to capture psychic energy and other supernatural phenomena. Joshua set up the device in the empty classroom, his fingers deftly connecting wires and calibrating the settings.

"Alright, it's all yours," he said, stepping back. "Remember the charge only lasts twenty minutes. Use it wisely. If you feel sick, take the headset off."

"Sick?" I asked in surprise. "What kind of sickness?"
"It's got a virtual reality component to it. I know that always makes you sick. Macie should keep an eye on you."

"Great. We got it. Thanks. Macie? Are you ready to spot me?"

The moment I turned on RYDER, a rush of images and emotions overwhelmed me—faces I didn't recognize, desperate cries for help, and intense feelings of despair. I staggered back, gripping the edge of a desk to keep myself from falling.

"You okay?" Macie asked, concerned.

"Yeah," I muttered, regaining my composure. "RYDER's more sensitive than I understood."

The walkie-talkie squawked in Macie's hand. I could hear Joshua's voice. "I'm monitoring the readings from here. They're spiking, fluctuating in a way I have never seen before. I'm going to record the activity. It will also record what you're seeing, Sierra," Joshua shared, barely hiding his excitement. "Stay focused, Sierra; take RYDER off if you need to."

"Macie? Walk with me, okay? Don't let me fall down a flight of stairs or something." I laughed half joking, trying to sound lighthearted when I felt anything but. "I see blue shadows. They're moving all around me. I want to follow them."

I heard Joshua answer me over the radio. "Um, okay. Blues are considered neutral entities, at least according to the limited data we have."

"Macie?"
She touched my hand. "Hold my hand and I will lead you. I won't leave, I promise. I thought we were going to set up first. Midas is going to be pissed."

"I know, I know. I'll take the heat. Blame it on me. I'm just... I need to test the equipment," I answered as I tried to keep my breathing steady.

"Now?" She asked not convinced. I offered a shrug as my answer.

Still gripping Macie's hand, I powered forward. The RYDER device turned my vision into a haunting panorama of the spectral realm. But amid this ghostly chaos, one figure detached itself—a less twisted form that seemed to cry out in sheer desperation.

"Do you hear it?" My voice was a shaky whisper.

"Hear what?" Midas' tone was wary, skeptical.

"The ghost is begging for help," I said, almost entranced by the mournful words echoing in my ears. "This one can speak, and I can hear it."

The ghost I was following seemed different from the rest as if it had retained more of its humanity amid its spectral existence. It wasn't just a cloud of energy or a distorted figment; it appeared more defined, almost solid.

Draped in tattered, time-stained clothes that hinted at an era long gone, the ghost had hollow eyes that spoke of untold sorrows. Its face was twisted in a perpetual grimace of torment and yearning, but when it looked at me, the eyes seemed to soften for a moment, pleading.
Oh, it seemed very human. A very real and entirely dead human. This was not an inhuman entity. Even RYDER agreed with me because my guide remained shadowed in electric blue.

The spirit's form wavered like an old film reel, flickering in and out of my enhanced vision, but its outline was sharp—a paradox that set it apart from the other apparitions.

Wisps of ethereal fog trailed behind it, remnants of unfulfilled dreams, or perhaps lost thoughts. But this was no wandering ghost. It moved with purpose, almost urgent, leading us through the twisted maze of the academy's hidden recesses.

"Don't move so fast, please!" I pleaded, but the spirit paid me no mind.

This ghost's presence carried a different kind of energy, a pull that was impossible to ignore. Its voice resonated in a low, mournful timbre that could only come from a once-human throat. When it spoke, its words were both a whisper and a scream—a paradoxical sound that burrowed deep into my soul.

No, I couldn't make out the words. Not at all. But it did have a voice. What was it saying? Or was it merely moaning?

As I followed it deeper into the bowels of the academy, I felt a mix of dread and compassion. There was something about this spirit, a gravity that held me captive. It was as if it had chosen me to confide in, to lead to its long-hidden secrets.

I couldn't help but wonder what tragedy bound it so tightly to the haunting labyrinth that was Leaf Academy.

Moriah Mitchell? Is this you?

No, couldn't be. It didn't feel like Moriah.

The ghost was an enigma wrapped in a mystery, a chilling yet pitiable figure, and it was leading me to a place I wasn't sure I wanted to go, but I felt compelled to see. It was a siren's call I couldn't resist, no matter how terrifying the path became.

With no doubt dubious glances exchanged between them--I still couldn't see them with this headset on, Macie and Midas followed me.

 The specter led us to a winding stairwell that was hidden behind an aged statue of the school's founder, his eyes seeming to follow us as we descended.

"He wants us to go down here. Midas? Did you know this was here? How many times have we walked these halls? I've never seen it. Uh, oh. I think I should take off my headset, but I'm afraid I'll lose him."

"Leave it on as long as you can. Step by step, Little Sis. This looks like it is a narrow stairwell. How have we missed this? I can't believe this. I don't remember seeing this on any plans either."

As he said that, the temperature plummeted, and each step we took was accompanied by the deafening silence, shattered only by our footsteps. It felt as though the walls of the stairwell were trying to suffocate us in a tomb of eternal darkness.
The ghost suddenly appeared again, this time stopping before an ancient, rotting door, but that door was phantom. It didn't exist anymore. I guess this is what it looked like in his time but how long ago was that and who was this spirit? There was a more modern-looking door standing in its place.

With a trembling hand, I pushed the door open. A foul stench of decay wafted out, and what lay before us was not just a room—it was a sanctum of nightmares. The room beyond screamed dread; it was a void begging to be filled, an unanswered question that loomed in the thick air. Dusty tomes, faded letters, and black-and-white photos of people long gone were strewn about. But what caught our eyes were the symbols etched onto the floor and walls—cryptic, arcane markings that seemed to writhe and shift when looked at directly.

"Trippy," Macie whispered, her voice tinged with awe and fear. "We aren't supposed to be here. I wish I'd brought my notebook. Boy, I could do some automatic writing here, for sure. Is the ghost still here?"

I nodded but didn't say anything. The ghost was still there, but only a part of him. Half his face had vanished and the electric blue shadow was vanishing. Had he used all his power to lead us here?

"Hey, don't go. Tell me your name. Why did you bring us here?"

It opened its mouth, and as it did, the eyes elongated like they were made of rubber. I wasn't sure what to expect, but I was determined to see this through. A powerful burst of energy hit me as the ghost's mouth moved and the eyes vanished into nothing.

Curse...

Midas looked pale, his usual stoicism cracking for a moment. "Even I heard that. Let's move the team into this room. We'll get back to the original plan eventually."

"We're here thirty minutes and already off plan. If it wasn't me that created this havoc, I'd be ticked," I confessed as I removed RYDER and fixed my messy blonde hair with my fingers.

Midas reached for his walkie-talkie and with a grin, summoned the team to the newly found room.

"Wow. I can't wait for you to see the footage. Joshua recorded it all." As I disconnected from RYDER from her power box, the specter vanished but its unspoken gratitude permeated the air like a fleeting wisp of sanity.

Standing in the room, it felt like we had crossed a significant threshold, an entryway to the malevolent secrets that the Leaf Academy harbored in its bowels.

I hope I haven't made a huge mistake by finding this place.

Yeah, this might be a big mistake.

Chapter Five–Midas

Cassidy was normally quick to delve into mysteries, especially those of the supernatural kind. Today, however, she seemed to be taking her time. Holding my radio, I called her again, but with a tone of gentle urgency, "Cassidy, you'll want to bring your sketchbook. What we've stumbled upon defies imagination. A hidden room, behind the statue in the courtyard."

As I awaited my favorite redhead's arrival, my feet carried me around the strange room, each step reverberating like a distant, haunting drum. The atmosphere felt thick, almost sentient, as if the very walls were aware of the secrets we'd uncovered.

What exactly have we found here?

A shiver traced its way down my spine, an unshakable sense that the building itself was brimming with anticipation—or was it a warning?

Just then, Joshua and Chris appeared, their faces a complex mix of excitement and caution. They were loaded down with mysterious gear, gadgets, and gizmos.

"Jesus," Chris muttered as they cleared the stairs. "You guys know this was here?"

"Nope," Joshua answered as he scanned the room with the SLS. "Nothing in here now. "How's my girl?" He was at Sierra's side and together the pair walked off to speak quietly.

Bypassing formalities, Chris promptly unzipped his laptop bag and set it on a nearby table, his fingers flying over the keys as he brought up various interfaces.

I had to ask. "Talk to me about RYDER. How's it performing? How did she do? Any glitches or odd readings we should know about?"

The weight of my question hung heavy in the air, adding another layer of intensity to an already electric atmosphere. It was clear that even these veteran paranormal investigators sensed that we were on the verge of something both extraordinary and unnerving.

"Better than expected, boss. You should see what Sierra recorded," Chris replied, still on edge from the sensory onslaught we'd experienced in that accursed room. The McBrides came to join us. Chris immediately started skimming through the footage. His eyes widened at the sight of the electric blue apparitions and fluctuating energy readings.

"Whoa, this is incredible, but also...kind of terrifying," he admitted. "Take a look. Is this what you were seeing, Sierra?"

"Yep," she answered as she slid her arm through Joshua's. "Exactly like I saw it. See that? That weird blue light, you called it electric blue, it was bright with this guy. I still can't make out who that was, it's possible we will never know. Old, I mean like ancient old."

Just then, Cassidy appeared sketchbook in hand. "Sorry, I'm late. Couldn't find my pencil bag. I found it in your backpack," she nudged me with a questioning stare.

"Pulling pranks on me, Midas?"

I frowned at that idea. "I didn't touch the pencil bag. If it was in there, you put it in there."

Cassidy tilted her head curiously, but she believed me. We weren't the kind of people who played pranks on one another. If I told her I didn't do it, she could take that to the bank.

"Chris, what's your take on this place?" Joshua asked, trying to find a logical explanation to anchor himself.

"It's older than the rest of the academy. Looks like it's been hidden for a reason," he mused, scanning the walls and floor with a handheld device that looked like something out of a sci-fi movie.

We were all engrossed in our tasks—me observing, Cassidy sketching, Joshua and Chris with their devices, and Sierra taking pictures of the strange grooves in the stone floor.

Wait... Where's Macie?

Suddenly, a piercing scream echoed through the Leaf Academy, bouncing off the arches and penetrating straight into our souls. The sound was gut-wrenching, a wail filled with anguish and terror.

"Macie!" We all shouted in unison, our hearts pounding in our chests like frantic drumbeats. Whatever relative calm we had managed to maintain shattered in an instant, replaced by a palpable sense of impending doom. We turned toward the direction of the scream. Macie was gone. The room suddenly felt even darker, and the weight of the unknown settled upon us, heavier than ever. It was as if the room itself was issuing a stark, unspoken warning.

You're not alone, and you're not safe.

And just like that, the exploration took a sinister turn, one that we couldn't back away from.

We decided to take the path that led us deeper into the academy's older sections. The air grew colder as we moved, and a strange mist seemed to form around our ankles, swirling as though it was leading us.

I knew exactly where this would lead us. Where it always led us. The auditorium.

Finally, we arrived in the large, disturbing room, its doors creaky and swollen with age. Pushing them open, we found ourselves standing at the back of the dimly lit space. Rows of old, worn-out red velvet seats faced a stage veiled in darkness. The air was thick with dust and stale perfume, and it was chillingly quiet—except for the soft, erratic breathing echoing in the space.

"There," Joshua pointed to the front row. "She's there!" There was Macie, slumped over in one of the seats, unconscious but seemingly unharmed.

Cassidy rushed to her side, checking for a pulse. "She's okay, just fainted. We need to get her out of here."

But as we prepared to lift Macie and leave, I couldn't shake the feeling that this auditorium, this school, was watching us. It was as if we had stepped into a sentient trap, and we were now part of a dangerous game whose rules we didn't understand. "We have to go, now," Sierra's voice trembled as she spoke.

"Cassidy, help me with Macie. We're taking her outside for some air," I ordered, not willing to take any chances with her well-being. Together, Cassidy and I carefully lifted Macie from her seat and made our way out of the auditorium.

"Midas? What happened?" Macie sounded frightened as her eyes blinked open. I didn't stick around to wait to explain to her what I didn't know.

"It's going to be alright, kiddo. Cassidy and I are taking you for a bit of a break," I glanced at my wife as we hurried to the front door.
Sierra, Joshua, and Chris remained behind; last I looked, their eyes were fixated on the grand piano at the corner of the stage. I gave them a nod before I left, acknowledging the unspoken agreement—we needed to find out what was going on, even if it defied all reason.

As Cassidy and I stepped outside into the courtyard, the contrast between the fresh air and the heavy atmosphere inside the building was striking. It was like crossing the boundary between two worlds—one normal and the other profoundly unsettling.

We were not alone.

And we were not safe.

A few minutes later, Cassidy assessed the investigator and gave her the all-clear. I looked at Macie, her face pale but slowly regaining its color. "Are you feeling a bit better now?" I asked softly.

"A little, yeah. Thanks, Midas." She managed a weak smile.

"Can you recall anything? How did you get to the auditorium?"

"All I remember is wanting my backpack. I wanted to do some automatic writing. The next thing I knew, I was pushing open the auditorium door. I saw...I saw...I can't remember but it was horrible."

I listened intently and waited to see if Macie could recall anything else. She insisted that she could not.

"Cassidy, would you mind staying with her for a bit? I need to go back inside," I said, my eyes meeting Cassidy's. She nodded, understanding that the investigation couldn't wait.

"I'll stick with Macie," Cassidy reassured her as she took a seat next to her on a courtyard bench.

Taking a deep breath, I turned to head back into the academy, my hand clutching the radio just a bit tighter than before. Each step back toward that building felt like a step further away from reality as if I were entering a realm where anything could happen. And with every step, I grew angrier.

As I reached the grand corridor that led to the auditorium, something caught my eye. At the far end of the hall, barely illuminated by the flickering overhead lights, stood what looked like a little boy.

Ollie. But he was no little boy. My feet froze, anchored to the floor as if by some invisible force. The radio in my hand felt suddenly heavy, its weight a grim reminder of the paranormal energies we had awakened in our search for answers.
For a brief moment, Ollie and I locked eyes. And in that moment, I felt a chilling recognition—a message sent across the void that separates the natural from the supernatural.

He had been waiting for me. Waiting and waiting. He'd been waiting a long time.

As our eyes remained locked, Ollie's lips stretched into a smile—except this was no ordinary smile. It was large, oversized, unsettlingly so. His mouth seemed to widen unnaturally, revealing an excessive number of teeth, each one more menacing than the last.

Just then, piercing through the air, I heard it—a baby's cry. My heart stopped for a moment; it sounded just like Dominic, my baby boy. But as my eyes remained on Ollie's grotesque grin, a shiver ran down my spine. I knew it was a trick, a deceitful lure into the dark web of this haunted place.

Ollie's smile seemed to confirm my worst fears, an evil acknowledgment that he knew just how to pull me into his twisted game.

I was not alone. I would never be alone again, or so he threatened.
I chose you. Just like I chose them.

The boundaries between what was real and what was unimaginable were dissolving rapidly.

This was far from over—and it might already be too late.

Chapter Six–Sierra

I approached the piano with caution. With a handheld device in one hand, Chris scanned the air around the instrument. "No electromagnetic fluctuations. This doesn't make sense."

"Everything okay?" Chris asked, still back at the tech station.

"Yeah, but... this isn't adding up," Sierra chimed in. "If there are no readings, then how did—"

Before she could finish her sentence, a single, discordant note echoed through the auditorium, its reverberation unsettlingly loud. They all turned to look at the piano. No one was near it. Another note followed, and then another—forming a melody that was both melancholic and eerie.

"Again?" I asked absently as we stared at the piano, our eyes wide with a mixture of fear and fascination. We couldn't deny what we were witnessing a piano playing with no one at its keys, an act so blatantly paranormal that it defied all our instruments and prior experiences.

As the final note resonated, fading into an unsettling silence, the three of us knew that we were in the presence of something far beyond our understanding.

That's when I heard it. The sound of a baby crying. "What in God's name?" I asked as I raced toward the open door. Joshua and Chris were on my heels, each holding cameras. There were no babies here at the Leaf Academy.

That's when I saw Big Brother on the ground. He was on his knees and he appeared to be crying. "Midas!" I yelled as my boots stomped on the dirty floor. I slid as I arrived before him. I glanced around but didn't see anyone else.

Not Cassidy or Macie. Certainly not a baby.

"Midas, hey! Can you hear me? Are you okay?" I knelt beside him, concern flooding my voice.

He looked up, his eyes refocusing. "Sierra, I heard...I heard a baby cry. It sounded like Dominic."
My heart clenched. "We all heard it, but there's no baby here. No way was that your son! This is escalating. Is Macie okay? Are you okay?"

Midas nodded and stood up. He rubbed his face with his tan muscular hand and shook his head in an obvious attempt at clearing the cobwebs, so to speak.

"I saw Ollie. He is here. Everyone stay alert," was all he said as we quickly made our way back to the auditorium. I didn't ask questions but my hackles had hackles. He reached for his radio and called Cassidy.

"When Macie is feeling steady, y'all join us in the auditorium. Let's keep everyone close."
"Roger that, Midas," Cassidy's warm voice answered.

"Please don't tell her what I told you about hearing the baby."

I offered up a pinky. "I won't, Big Brother. I promise."

We'd barely made it into the auditorium when Cassidy radioed back and said they were coming in. Macie appeared sheepish. "How are you feeling, Macie?"

"Still a bit shaky, but I'm okay. I just... can't remember why I fainted," Macie responded, her voice tinged with confusion. "I don't think I've ever fainted before. That was a first."

"Any new readings?" I asked Chris and Joshua as I reminded myself why we'd come there.

"Zero. Zip. Zilch," Joshua replied, shaking his head. "It's like the piano wants to keep its secrets now that the gang's all here."

Chris chimed in, "It's not just the piano. It's the whole building. It's as if something's protecting it. Shielding it. Maybe we should head back to the hidden room. Perhaps Macie's fainting spell and the piano were merely distractions. No offense to Macie."

"Soon. He's here—Ollie that is. Only he's hiding," Midas added, his voice somber.

"Sierra, let's examine that piano again. Something doesn't add up. Cassidy, anything?"
"I have my sketchbook, but I'm not feeling anything. Macie?"

She nodded and dug into her bag. It was a leather backpack with a sugar skull on the front. "I'll try to do some writing. I've been dying to try since I got here."

"Cassidy, grab the panoramic and record them. Chris, if you'll keep your eyes peeled. Keep your head on a swivel. The more cameras the better. Let's give that piano a good look and then we'll head back to the new location." I headed back toward the grand piano with Joshua. We both took out our handheld devices and started scanning again. Strangely enough, there were odd readings with the thermal. Like someone had been sitting on the broken bench as if a phantom piano player had worked over the keys. The heat signature was fading fast though.

That's when Joshua noticed it—a hidden, cryptic symbol etched into the wood.

"It's a leaf with a letter carved into it. What is that? An A? A V?" The team slowly gathered around to get a better look.

"Whatever it is, it's probably a warning," I said, taking a snapshot with my camera.

"Either way, this is a clue we can't ignore."

Midas came over to us. "What's the verdict?"

Joshua showed him the photo. "Look at this. You were right. This piano is significant. Check this out." Joshua snapped a few photos as Cassidy got closer to the panoramic.
Midas looked intently at the etched marking. "We need to dig deeper. This might come into play, but it also might be vandalism. Whatever it is, time is of the essence."

Just then, the room was plunged into darkness, and a chilling whisper wafted through the air. It was still day, but it was as if a giant cloud now hovered over the auditorium. There were plenty of broken windowpanes in here and usually lots of light, at least during the daylight hours.

Leave!

A voice spoke so softly we could almost convince ourselves we'd imagined it. But we hadn't. No way. I glanced at my husband who paused his picture-taking. Midas clenched his fists. "We're not going anywhere. Not until we figure out what's happening here. We are here for Jocelyn. If you have her, let her go!"

Despite what the spirit was saying, I knew it would be perfectly happy if Midas stayed here alone. It wanted him. Badly. Why? Why had Ollie targeted Midas again?

As if to punctuate the spirit's determination, another note from the piano reverberated through the auditorium, like a distant echo challenging our resolve.

Suddenly, the previously quiet stage curtains began to flutter, though no breeze was present. From the darkness, an indistinct, shadowy figure formed just beyond the curtain's edge, its shape barely discernible. The team's devices began to buzz and whir in unison, signaling a massive surge in paranormal activity.

Chris, turning pale, pointed to the stage, his voice a shaky whisper, "Do you guys see that?"

Before anyone could respond, a ghostly hand reached out from behind the curtain, beckoning to them. The air grew icy, and every light in the auditorium simultaneously flickered on and went out. Which was strange because I was quite certain there was no power on for this building.

"Sierra, stay close to me," Joshua whispered urgently.

Suddenly, the disembodied voice of a young woman, presumably Jocelyn, sang out softly from the surrounding blackness, her melody intertwining with the haunting notes from the piano.

Why did you come here? Why did you wake me?

The chilling words echoed, leaving the team in frozen silence, surrounded by an oppressive weight of unseen watchers and the ever-present, haunting song of the piano.
No, that's not Jocelyn. Merely an impersonator.

The air grew thick with tension as Midas's words hung in the stillness. For a few heartbeats, everything was silent. And then, that voice, deeper and more malevolent than before, responded.

You can't send us back. Not the October People, not me.

From the darkness, laughter erupted, not just from one source but from many. But it was Ollie who stepped forward as if he were truly made of shadow. He appeared as before, as a small boy with dark hair and questioning eyes. We were not truly seeing this entity's face.

Suddenly it was as if the auditorium was filled with countless spirits, all mocking Midas's bold declaration. Whispers began to overlap, creating a cacophony of voices that seemed to come from every direction. Some even swore at him and cursed Midas in entirely indecent ways.

"We've been here far longer than you know," another voice sneered.

"And we have no intention of leaving," a childlike voice, eerily like Jocelyn's, echoed.

Sierra's device started to beep wildly, signaling a massive surge in supernatural activity. Chris's laptop began to glitch, and the recordings played backward, distorting the voices into something otherworldly.

Out of nowhere, a dense, cold mist began to fill the room, reducing visibility to nearly zero. From the fog emerged fleeting images of ghostly apparitions—figures from different eras, all with hollow, haunted eyes and twisted expressions of torment.

The grand piano began to play once more, louder, and more frantic, with keys moving violently on their own. The unsettling tune resonated, creating an eerie harmony with the chorus of whispers and laughter.

And then, as abruptly as it began, the mist began to clear. But in its wake stood the most chilling sight of all—Ollie, no longer the image of an innocent boy, but a twisted, sinister version. His face contorted in an impossibly wide grin, revealing rows upon rows of sharp, jagged teeth, his eyes deep voids of blackness.

"Are you human? You know what I like to do to humans. Jocelyn knew," Oliver's voice echoed, dripping with malevolence as he turned to face Macie. "She knew and it terrified her, but she could not escape. Neither can you, *M A C I E*. This is just the beginning for you."

Macie was on her feet and ready to run. I couldn't blame her. I waited in Midas. We exchanged glances, but I could not read his expression. I can count on one hand how many times I've seen Midas terrified.

Oh yeah. Big Brother is beyond afraid. We all are! "Midas?"

With a final, ear-piercing scream, the apparition vanished, leaving the team in chilling silence, their breaths visible in the still-cold air, each one feeling the weight of the dark challenge that had been issued.

"Calmly, move to the door," Midas continued to face the stage, he watched as Ollie became shadow again and disappeared into the floor. "Move! Now!" He shouted without looking back.

We did as we were told. We walked quietly to the back of the auditorium leaving our equipment and Midas alone.

This was a very bad idea.

Chapter Seven—Midas

The darkness enveloped me, pressing in from all sides. An overwhelming sensation of being observed washed over me. Then, from the black void, came a voice, soft as a whisper but cold as the wind on a winter's night.

Come, Midas. Join us.

I took a deep breath to steady my racing heart. "I'm never going to do that," I asserted, my voice echoing in the vast room. "I am here for Jocelyn. If you have her, release her now!"

The silence was palpable, and then the grand piano played another melancholic note. But what followed was even more chilling. A gust of cold wind blew through the auditorium, and though no windows or doors were open, the curtains on stage billowed as if caught in a storm.

From that darkness, laughter emerged, sounding from what felt like every corner of the room. But among those myriad voices, one voice stood out—Ollie's.

I strained my eyes, trying to pierce through the shadows, and there he was. No longer the innocent-looking boy, but something far more malevolent. He had a big, creepy smile showing lots of pointy teeth. His eyes looked like empty black holes.

"You can't stop us, Midas," he taunted, his voice echoing around me. "No one can. You don't understand our power. Do you know why they call us the October People?"

In a bold move, I took a step forward, trying to show no fear. "I'm here for Jocelyn. Tell me where she is. I don't want to hear anything else you have to say. "

Suddenly, the space around me filled with the dense, cold mist, making it nearly impossible to see.

In the thick, chilling mist, shadowy figures from long ago started to rise. Their eyes, empty and haunted, seemed to hold the pain of centuries. I could feel their anguish, their despair, and their anger. But among them all, Ollie stood out, watching me with that same chilling grin.

"You think you can save her?" he mocked. "You think you have the power to face us? There's only one way to save her, fool. A trade."
The fog grew thicker, the whispering voices louder, and the weight of unseen eyes pressed down on me. Feeling trapped and overwhelmed, I tried to find a way out. But in every direction I turned, there he was—Ollie, his grin wider and more malevolent than ever.

Suddenly, all the voices merged into a unified chant, growing in intensity. The room started spinning, and the floor seemed to tilt beneath me. Just as the overwhelming sensation threatened to consume me, a voice, clear and distinct, broke through the chaos.

"Midas!"

It was a plea, a call for help, and I recognized it immediately— it was Jocelyn's voice. As the room continued its disorienting spin, I reached out toward where I believed the voice originated, trying to make sense of the swirling chaos.

Then, with a jolt, everything stopped. The fog began to lift, and the room returned to its eerie silence. Standing before me was Jocelyn, or at least her apparition, looking just as terrified as I felt. Behind her, the shadows shifted, and Ollie's grin became even more sinister.

"You want her? Come and get her," he taunted, before both he and Jocelyn vanished into the darkness, leaving me alone in the deafening silence of the auditorium. "Join us, Midas. I could use a strong one like you. You will serve me well."

The room seemed to close in on me. A heavy pressure settled in my chest, making it harder to breathe. Was I going to have a heart attack? I could still hear Ollie's voice echoing, taunting me. My heart raced faster, the weight of his words sinking in. He wanted me to become one of them, one of the October People.

Every instinct in my body told me to run, to find a way out, but I was rooted to the spot, paralyzed by an unseen force. The darkness seemed to grow thicker, wrapping around me like chains. I could feel the cold tendrils of the mist reaching out, trying to pull me further into the void.

A whisper, just behind my ear, sent chills down my spine. "You can't resist us forever, Midas." I could feel the cold breath of the unseen speaker, and I knew without looking that it was Ollie.

Desperation set in, and I mustered all the strength I had left to shout, "I will never join you! Release Jocelyn and leave this place!"

The room began to shake as if reacting to my defiance. The grand piano played a frantic tune, its keys moving on their own, matching the increasing tempo of my heartbeat. And then, from the center of the room, a blinding light erupted, cutting through the darkness.

As the light intensified, I could hear the October People wailing, their cries of anguish echoing around me. The fog began to recede, and the oppressive weight lifted, replaced by a newfound sense of hope.

But as quickly as the light appeared, it faded, leaving me in near-complete darkness once again. I strained my eyes, trying to adjust, but I could barely make out the silhouettes of the auditorium's seats.

And then, I heard it.

A soft, rhythmic thudding sound, slowly growing louder. Footsteps. They seemed to be coming from every direction, converging towards where I stood. The realization hit me: I was not alone.

They were closing in.

The last thing I remember before everything went black was the chilling sensation of cold fingers wrapping around my arm and Ollie's voice, now a mere whisper, "Welcome to the fold, Midas."

I blinked awake, the glaring sun momentarily blinding me. The sensation of cold, rough concrete pressed against me, was jarring and unsettling.

As my vision cleared, an overwhelming realization hit me: I was on the roof of the Leaf Academy. The sprawling grounds stretched out beneath me, but the sickening height wasn't what made my stomach churn—it was the dizzying edge just inches away from where I lay.

From below, muffled calls reached my ears. "Midas!" "Big Brother, where are you?" My team. They were searching for me, but here I was, trapped in this nightmare.

I wasn't alone. A few feet away, Jocelyn's ghostly form shimmered, a beacon in the daylight. And right beside her, casting a dark, contrasting shadow, stood Ollie. The playful innocence he once embodied was gone, replaced by something dark and twisted.

He took a step closer, that unnerving grin still on his face. "We can do this again, you know. I'm willing to make a trade. You for her." He gestured toward Jocelyn. "What do you say?"

Her eyes, filled with a mix of sorrow and urgency, locked onto mine. "No! Midas, listen to me! It's a trap! I'm already dead! You can't do this! You mustn't! Think of Cassidy."
Cassidy. My heart ached at the thought of her. Memories flooded in—her laughter, the warmth of her touch, the security I felt in her embrace. I couldn't let her down.

But something else was happening. A cold, persistent pressure built against my back. It pushed me closer to the edge, urging me on. The wind whispered promises, enticing me to just let go.

Inside my mind, Ollie's voice echoed, seductive and chilling, "Yes, this feels right. This is how it should be. Do the right thing, Midas. Just one more step."

The pressure grew, guiding me toward that endless void. With Cassidy's face fresh in my mind and Jocelyn's desperate pleas echoing around me, I found myself teetering, balanced between the world of the living and the haunting pull of the abyss.

I tried to push back against the force urging me to the edge, but it was overwhelming. Despair crept in, the feeling of helplessness becoming all too real.

My foot teetered on the precipice, the yawning void below promising eternal darkness.
Suddenly, a force yanked me back, away from the edge. Jocelyn, her ethereal form glowing brighter than before, had intervened, her ghostly hands gripping my arm. Her eyes met mine, determination battling fear.

"No, Ollie!"

Ollie hissed, his malevolent eyes fixed on Jocelyn. "You'll pay for this."

But Jocelyn stood her ground. "No more death, Ollie. No more innocent lives."
With a final, haunting scream of rage, Ollie vanished. Jocelyn looked at me one last time, her eyes brimming with gratitude and sadness. "Protect them, Midas. Protect them all." And with that, she too faded away, leaving me on the roof, my heart pounding fiercely.

Suddenly, the door to the roof burst open. Cassidy raced toward me; her eyes wild with fear. Before I could react, she threw me to the ground, her fingers clutching at my shirt. Tears streamed down her face.

"What were you thinking? What are you doing? Did you even think about me? About Dominic?" I couldn't say a word. I was a wreck. The weight of my actions, the gravity of the moment, hit me. I wrapped my arms around Cassidy, pulling her close. Our tears merged as we held each other, her sobs echoing my remorse.

Sierra approached, her face pale but her voice strong. "Does anyone need to be convinced now? We're up against the devil here. The straight-up devil. I'm calling it for tonight. We need Jericho and Aaron on this one. We're not coming back without some holy men on our side."

She paused, taking a deep breath to steady herself, then continued, "Come on, Midas. Let's go. Forget about the equipment. Forget everything. We need to get out of here. Now."

With Cassidy still wrapped in my arms, the weight of our task heavy on our shoulders, we left the Leaf Academy behind but the battle was far from over.

The ride home was somber. The chilling events of the night pressed on us all, creating a silence that no one seemed eager to break. When the car finally pulled into our driveway, I took a long, steadying breath, trying to dispel the heavy shadow that clung to my spirit.

Upon entering the house, my first instinct was to seek out Dominic. I quietly stepped into his room. His peaceful sleep was a stark contrast to the chaos of the evening. Bending over, I placed a gentle kiss on his forehead. The simple touch, the warmth of my son, grounded me amidst the swirling uncertainty.

Cassidy joined me, her arms wrapped around her middle as if she were hugging herself for comfort. "Promise me, Midas," she whispered, her voice tinged with raw emotion, "that we'll never let the darkness touch our home."

I pulled her close, trying to convey reassurance and determination in the embrace. "We won't. I swear it. We're going to get to the bottom of this, and we're bringing in the best."

Moving away from the haven of Dominic's room, I made my way to our home office.
First on the list was Jericho. When he picked up, I laid out the night's harrowing events. By the end, he was on board, understanding the depth of the threat.

Aaron was next. Convincing him required more persuasion, but eventually, the gravity of my account won him over. He'd join the fray.

With a renewed sense of hope, I made the most pivotal call of the evening. Dialing Dr. Elena Martinez, the esteemed demonologist whose expertise was legendary. She listened, her silence making it clear she was weighing every word. When my recounting was done, she responded with an assertive, "I'm interested but I'm not sure I can make it. I'll have to get back to you, Midas."

Setting the phone down, a surge of determination bolstered my spirit. We were amassing a formidable team. Whatever lay in wait at the Leaf Academy, we'd confront it head-on. United, we would put an end to this horror.

For Jocelyn, and for every soul ensnared by the October People's malevolence.

Chapter Eight–Sierra

Exhaustion weighed heavy on my limbs as I found myself curling up on the couch, with Emily nestled closely beside me. Her rhythmic breathing acted as a soothing balm, driving away the evening's traumatic memories, if only for a short time.

Across the room, Joshua was engrossed, his eyes darting back and forth as he poured over camera footage on his laptop. The dim glow from the screen cast shadows across his face, highlighting the creases of worry and concentration. His fingers flew over the keys, pausing, rewinding, and playing particular segments of video over and over.

His devotion to unraveling the mystery of the Leaf Academy never ceased, even in the wake of the danger we'd experienced.

Feeling the pull of sleep, I surrendered and drifted off with Emily's soft snores as my lullaby.

When I awoke, the living room was veiled in darkness, save for the residual light from Joshua's laptop. My neck was stiff from the awkward position on the couch, and Emily was no longer by my side. With a groggy mind, I made my way to our bedroom, thinking I'd catch a few more hours of uninterrupted sleep.

But the moment my head hit the pillow, sleep was the furthest thing from my mind.
A rush of images, sounds, and emotions overwhelmed me.

Oh no! Is this happening right now? I'm not ready. I'm not grounded! Crap!

The surroundings were eerily familiar, yet foreign—the Leaf Academy, but decades, perhaps even centuries ago. I found myself standing outside, watching as young children played.

Among them was a boy, distinct from the rest, with jet-black hair and curious eyes—Ollie. His laughter was infectious, drawing the other children to him.

But beneath the mirth, I sensed a darkness, a heavy burden that he carried. I followed his journey, watching as he transformed from a carefree child to a brooding, tormented soul. I watched as the sun rose and set, rose and set.

The days flew by in the vision. I could see Ollie's friendships erode, replaced by solitude and shadows. Suddenly the boy was no longer smiling. It was as if his life's essence had been stolen from his very bones.

I saw the allure of forbidden rituals and the pull of the occult, as Ollie and a group of followers dubbed "The October People" danced around bonfires, chanting incantations, and beckoning forces beyond comprehension.

These October People were not human and they had slowly but surely wrapped their talons around Ollie's soul. They were dark spirits bound together for one purpose. To choose another face, another body, another persona, and this boy, this Ollie, he was almost empty of life, of his humanity.

He would make the perfect monster.

Dear God! That's what they are—monsters! The October People are monsters in the darkness.

The more they led Ollie into their darkness, the more the darkness consumed the lonely boy, it made him a conduit for entities beyond our realm. *How was I seeing this? How was I allowed to see this?*

Ollie's transformation was dramatic.

He became their favorite possession. A toy for a particular demonic entity—the devil himself. His youthful curiosity and inherent power made him the ideal vessel, a mask for the devil to wear, granting him dominion in our world.

As the vision evolved, I saw the tragic fate of those who crossed Ollie's path.

An ever-growing list of souls, including Jocelyn Graves, each ensnared by the October People's malevolence. This was their sole purpose. They existed to kill and to claim. They existed to curse and torment. That was all they wanted. They did not want help. They did not want anything good or kind to interfere with their dark work.

The vision culminated in a chilling confrontation between Ollie and an older woman, a seer like me. She'd known him in life. Tried to help him. She felt love for him and pity, but it was too late. She'd been killed by the thing that wore Ollie's face.

I could see that last day. Mary was her name. Mary warned the boy of the cost of his actions and the eternal torment that awaited him. But Ollie, or rather, the entity controlling him, merely laughed, a sound devoid of any humanity.

"I am eternal," he boasted, his eyes black voids of malevolence. "I am the devil's chosen."

Jolted awake, I found myself drenched in sweat, the weight of the revelation pressing heavily on my chest. My heart raced, realizing the depth of the threat we faced. Ollie was no mere specter; he was a conduit for the devil himself, making our mission at the Leaf Academy even more perilous.

As I tried to calm my racing heart, Joshua entered the room, concern evident in his eyes. "Sierra? Are you okay?"

I nodded, swallowing the lump in my throat. "We need to talk. I've seen things... things about Ollie and the October People. It's far worse than we ever imagined." Even as I relayed the visions to Joshua, the heavy weight of it all pressing on my chest, there was a sudden, yet soft knock on our front door. My senses immediately heightened.

It was past midnight, and we weren't expecting anyone.

The room's ambiance shifted dramatically. The dim light seemed to quiver, and I felt a chill that wasn't from the evening air.

Slowly, a spectral form materialized. It was the ethereal presence of a man, poised with authority and grace, even in death. Moriah Mitchell—the former headmaster of the Leaf Academy.

"Joshua, be still and remain calm," I whispered as I felt him tense beside me.

I instantly felt a connection with this entity, at least a possibility of a connection. At the very least, an avenue for communication. I closed my eyes momentarily, grounding myself to best use my psychic ability. I held Joshua's hand to comfort him and remind him to be quiet.

"Moriah? You're Moriah Mitchell, aren't you?" I whispered tentatively. "What message do you bring?"

There was a brief silence, and then, as if carried by the wind, I heard his voice in my mind. I hoped he would speak to both of us, but I was the psychic medium. I was okay with this. If Moriah felt more comfortable talking to me, the psychic, and not my husband, the investigator, I would respect that. His voice sounded distant yet unmistakably clear. "He wants him, he's been watching for a long time. He always picks the ones he covets most. He never truly yearned for the girl. He wanted him all along.

What? Who? I asked in my mind. Why was I asking dumb questions? I knew what Moriah was saying, what he was talking about. He was most certainly talking about Midas.

Ollie wanted Big Brother. Moriah kept crying and talking. As if he were being forced to share this message. Maybe Ollie sent him here.

Inform him of the trade—he will exchange the girl for Midas.

Understanding dawned upon me. Jocelyn was never the true target. She was merely bait. The actual prize, the one they truly sought after, was Midas.

My thoughts raced, and I uttered, more to myself than anyone, "But why Midas?"

Moriah's energy wavered with a melancholic tint. "I cannot know Ollie's complete intentions. However, he chooses with purpose. The October People, are his legion. They are not merely the dead. There are others in their numbers. He covets Midas. He wants to vanquish Ollie and eat his soul, but he cannot do that until he has a new soul, a new face to wear."

The weight of Moriah's revelation was palpable. Joshua squeezed my hand and it comforted me. The urgency in Moriah's spectral voice continued, "My efforts to stop Ollie from continuing on his malevolent path were in vain. He has returned to consummate his dark ambition. I have done horrible things. I have done horrible things..."

He began to weep sorrowfully. Was he trapped too? I wasn't sure if he was truly trapped or not. He was beginning to fade, so much so that I could only see him in my mind's eye now. Moriah's fading energy prompted my urgency.

I reached out mentally, "How can we halt their advance? How can we shield Midas?"

A pregnant pause ensued, thick with anticipation. "Your vision is a beacon," Moriah's voice grew weaker. "Rely on it, Sierra. Display fortitude. They thrive on and exploit terror. Mask your own, always." With that, Moriah Mitchell's form dissipated, merging with the shadows, and leaving behind a thick air of foreboding. We were forewarned, and we had to prepare.

The adversaries we faced were unlike any other, and the danger they posed was all too real.
A hushed silence settled over the room. Joshua and I exchanged glances, the weight of the situation settling heavily upon us. Each moment felt elongated, suspended in time. I

relayed to him everything Moriah told me and he believed every word.

Suddenly, the hum of electronic equipment came alive in the adjacent room. The soft beeping of the equipment grew frantic, and the digital recordings from the Leaf Academy started playing on their own. Ollie's laughter, that chilling, malevolent giggle we had grown to dread, echoed throughout our home.

Inching towards the doorway, the hairs on the back of my neck standing on end, I peered into the room. The screens of Joshua's equipment displayed the same chilling image: Ollie, his eyes hollow and black, with the words, "See you soon," scrawled eerily below his visage.

Before I could react, the power abruptly cut out, plunging us into darkness. Emily's soft cries reached us from her room, and instinctively, Joshua and I moved together, hand in hand, toward the sound, ready to protect our family.

A cold wind blew through the house, despite all the windows being shut. The whisper of an old song from the Leaf Academy's past played faintly in the background, the lyrics impossible to make out, but the melody all too familiar.

The realization hit us both simultaneously—this was far from over.

The October People, especially Ollie, were just getting started.

We were in their crosshairs, and it was going to take everything we had to protect those we held dear.

Especially Midas.

Chapter Nine--Macie

The walls of my room seemed to close in on me, the weight of recent events suffocating in their magnitude. Every time I tried to catch a moment of respite, memories of my sister, Jocelyn, would flood my senses.

Her infectious laugh, the secrets we shared, the way she'd tease me—every moment, every memory was like a dagger to my heart. What I wouldn't give to have just one more day at the beach with her. I'd do whatever dumb things she wanted to. I'd even let her put cornrows in my hair.

"I love you, Jocelyn. You were such a sweet sister. I should never have treated you like I did. You were trying to live life to the fullest and I was jealous. Jealous of your zeal. Jealous of your sense of wonder. I was just jealous. God, I wish I could see you again. Be with you again. I love you, Jocelyn."

I cried on the couch in the fetal position. It did not make me feel any better, but I couldn't help myself. I'd often heard people say that time heals all wounds, but the trauma of grief felt fresh and raw, never truly scabbing over. Instead, my grief throbbed with an incessant ache.

And now, knowing what I did about Ollie and The October People, the wounds felt as if they were being torn open anew, a constant, cruel reminder of my sister's fate.

Hell no, she was not resting in peace!

Why had I pushed to return to the Leaf Academy? Was it my return to the school that stirred things up? Why did I have to be so damn nosy? Why hadn't I heeded the initial warnings, the unease that churned in my gut?

Yeah, this one was on me. It was my fault. Deep down, I knew Ollie had come for Midas, but the burden of being the catalyst, the one who brought them back to that accursed place, gnawed at me.

I had helped the devil do his dirty work and hadn't even known it.

In a desperate attempt to connect, to find some semblance of closure, I took out my journal and placed it next to a cherished photo of Jocelyn. Hoping to bridge the chasm that now separated us, I began an automatic writing session—a technique I'd often practiced in hopes of reaching the other side.

As my pen made contact with the paper, I tried to quiet my mind, letting the words flow without conscious thought. Almost immediately, the pen began to move.

"Jocelyn, speak to me. I'm right here. It's Macie..."

Scribble, scribble, scribble. Nothing. I turned another page and drew more circles just waiting for some sign that she was there. Nothing until I was about ten pages in. That's when I felt the unnatural warmth in my fingers.

Yes! A message!

My heart leaped as the scribbles became words, tears brimmed in my eyes as I felt a surge of emotion. *It was her; it had to be! It must be!* But as quickly as the warmth spread, it turned chillingly cold. The handwriting shifted, becoming jagged and erratic.

He won't let me go, Macie. Darkness everywhere. He wants him. He wants Midas. Run, Ma...

A shiver ran down my spine. Jocelyn's gentle message had been hijacked, replaced by something much more sinister. My hand began stabbing at the notebook, the black pen poked and poked the paper punching holes in it. I struggled to regain control of the paper.

"No! Stop that!"

Dropping the pen, I crumpled to the floor, sobs wracking my body. The sensation of being watched, of malevolent eyes boring into me, was inescapable. My heart ached not only for my lost sister but for the looming threat that now hung over all of us, especially Midas.

Desperate for solace, for any form of comfort, I reached for my phone to call Mom. But there was no answer, just the haunting silence of the void on the other end. How long had it been since we spoke? I couldn't even remember.

Panic gripped me, and in my flustered state, I began rummaging through my backpack for my phone charger.

Maybe if I tried to call her work, she'd answer.

My fingers brushed against something soft, yet coarse. Pulling it out, I stared in horror.
A black crow feather lay in my palm, its dark sheen gleaming under the room's light. The symbolism wasn't lost on me. Crows were often seen as messengers from the other side,

omens of change. And right now, it felt like a clear message—a sign that the October People, with Ollie at the helm, were closer than ever.

They gave me a gift. They would respect one in return.

"NO! I never accepted it. That doesn't count, you bastard! Do you hear me?"

Staring at the feather, I felt a cold dread creeping up my spine. What do I do with it? I had to get rid of it. No way was I keeping this thing.

The silky, obsidian strands were undeniably a token from the October People—a warning, perhaps, or a vile promise. I recalled reading somewhere that crows were sometimes associated with death and transformation. In this situation, its meaning felt all too clear. They were telling me that they were watching, always present and lurking in the shadows.

Sherman, my big white dog with a black nose and deep, soulful eyes, seemed to sense my distress. He nuzzled against me, seeking comfort and offering solace.

Jocelyn had loved her dog, and after her passing, he'd been my constant companion. Every time I looked into his eyes, I saw a piece of her—a silent guardian, ensuring that her love for me endured. I took the unholy feather, opened a window, and dropped it outside.

There you go, you bastard!

The night was already deepening, and in just a few hours, the investigation's second night would commence. I shut the window solidly and locked it. A whole night loomed ahead, waiting to unfold its dark mysteries, and yet, here I was, still haunted by yesterday's nightmares, sleep remains elusive.

Driven by a mixture of hope and desperation, I once again placed the journal beside Jocelyn's picture and embarked on another session of automatic writing. Maybe, I thought, I could reach someone else—someone with insight, guidance, or even just a glimmer of hope. My hand moved across the page, forming words I hadn't consciously thought of.

You seek answers. I hold them.

Um, this wasn't Jocelyn. It felt different—older and laced with authority. The words of the former headmaster, Moriah Mitchell, came to mind. Was I connecting with him?

God, I hope so.

However, as my pen glided further, the tone began to shift. The script became more aggressive, malicious, even.

You're a curious little thing, aren't you, Macie? I've been watching you. I've seen your dreams. Soon, I'll peel you apart, layer by layer. Your sister? She's all but bones now. But you... you'll be a delightful new toy.

My heart raced, the malicious intent behind each word piercing through me. I screamed as I threw the pencil across the room.

This wasn't Mitchell; it was Ollie, cruelly taunting me.

His malevolent energy was palpable, even through the veil that separated our worlds.

A loud knock jolted me from the trance. I snapped my journal shut, hastily wiping away tears. Rising unsteadily to my feet, I approached the door with caution, but nothing could've prepared me for what awaited.

Upon opening the door, I was met with the familiar face of Jericho. However, there was something startlingly amiss—his cheek bore a fresh, angry scratch, blood still fresh.

Without uttering a word, I wrapped my arms around him, pressing my lips to his, allowing the warmth of the embrace to momentarily chase away the chilling events of the evening. I don't think he knew what to do. I had shocked him, yet I knew he wanted me as much as I wanted him.

Sherman, sensing the tension, let out a low whimper, and slunk away to find a spot on the couch.

Pulling back from Jericho, our eyes met, reflecting mutual concern and unspoken understanding. "I love you, Jericho. I should have told you that before. I love everything about you."

"Macie, are you..." My mouth was on his again. I did love him, at least in that moment.

I loved that he was alive and not a dead thing. I loved his warm, dark eyes, his tanned skin, and the softness of it. I loved his pure heart. Jericho stepped inside, and as I shut the door, the reality of our situation loomed larger than ever.

The October People were closing in, and we were right in the eye of the storm. Before I went back to the Leaf Academy to face the devil and his minions, I would at least have this. At

least know the warmth of Jericho's arms, feel his chest rising with mine.
And if that is all there is to my life, at least that would be enough.

Yes, it would have to be enough.

Lost in Jericho's embrace, I felt a fleeting moment of warmth and safety, almost allowing myself to forget the terrors that seemed to be mounting around us. But that ephemeral comfort was abruptly shattered as a bone-chilling breeze swept through the room.

We pulled apart, our eyes darting to the window I had securely locked after discarding that sinister crow feather. Now, it stood wide open, its curtains dancing wildly with the wind.

On the windowsill, an unsettling sight awaited. A row of sleek black crow feathers were meticulously lined up as if placed with deliberate intent. My heart thudded loudly in my chest, dread weighing heavily on it. But it was the frosty inscription on the window that truly sent icy shivers down my spine.

We are watching, Macie.

Outside, the haunting caw of a crow echoed, mocking the false sense of security I had momentarily felt.

I clutched Jericho tighter, a sinking realization dawning.

The night, with all its lurking horrors, was far from over.

Chapter Ten—Cassidy

I watched Midas from across the room. The dim lighting cast gentle shadows on his handsome face, but tonight, my husband looked more tired and drawn than usual. The lines of stress were evident, etched deeply into the furrow of his brow and the tightness of his jaw.

It was clear that the weight of responsibility and looming danger pressed heavily on him.

Silently, I moved behind him, placing my hands on the tense muscles of his neck and shoulders. Gently, I tried to knead the anxiety and stress away, hoping to give him even a momentary reprieve. But the rigidity persisted, making it all too evident how deeply he was affected.

"Darn. My magic hands have lost their touch, I see."

He let out a deep sigh, tipping his head slightly. "Are you kidding me? What would I do without those magic hands? And those magic lips?" I leaned in, placing a soft kiss on the top of his head to show my appreciation, wishing with everything in me that I could shoulder some of his burden. I couldn't of course, but I was his wife and I would sure as hell try.

The doorbell rang, breaking the somber ambiance that had settled in the room. Midas looked up, almost relieved for the distraction. "That should be Aunt Lila," he mentioned, pushing himself up from the chair.

When I opened the door, Midas's aunt stood there, her face lined with concern. Aunt Lila was a comforting presence, her eyes always warm and understanding. She gave me a brief, tight-lipped smile, no doubt sensing the palpable tension in our home. "Cassidy, dear," she greeted, her voice soft and gentle.

As Aunt Lila stepped inside, Dominic fussed in his highchair. No doubt he loved her deeply. The feeling was mutual. She sauntered over to tidy him up, he already had his arms up. It warmed my heart to see him find solace in her presence.

"I'll take good care of him," Aunt Lila promised, her eyes locking onto mine. "Don't you worry. I've already got teething rings in the freezer. Poor little man. He'll get those teeth in soon." Aunt Lila glanced at Midas, her face betrayed her worry. "Just take care of this one."
"I'm trying, Aunt Lila. Thank you."

Her reassurance was comforting, but the thought of letting Dominic go, even for a short while, made my heart clench. Midas joined us, placing a hand on Dominic's head. "Be good, buddy," he whispered, his voice shaky with emotion.

The next few minutes I flew around the house gathering my son's necessities. The act of doing so brought a tear to my eye. I was happy he was going to Aunt Lila's, but more than anything I wanted this Leaf Academy case over. And I wanted us all to be safe.
After they left, the house felt eerily quiet, the absence of Dominic's cheerful energy was deeply felt.

Midas seemed to sag, the weight of the upcoming night weighing him down even more. He'd fallen down the rabbit hole in his research. The laptop shone in his face and he was pounding coffee, which was weird because he'd given coffee up not that long ago. Again. I unsnapped a water bottle and took a sip while I sighed. Neither one of us talked about eating. Honestly, I wasn't the least bit hungry.

I needed to distract myself, so I turned to my sketchbook. As my pencil glided over the paper, I tried to channel my feelings, my intuition, attempting to capture Ollie's essence.
Sketch after sketch, I drew the face that haunted our lives, hoping to find some insight, some clue in the lines and shades. Each image seemed to reveal a different facet of the dark entity that lurked behind Ollie's visage. It felt like a desperate, silent plea to understand the force we were up against.

As I sketched, Midas sat nearby, working his phone tirelessly, talking to contacts, discussing plans, and arranging for support. I could hear snippets of his conversations, the urgency in his voice, and the occasional sigh of frustration when a call didn't go as planned. Each call he made seemed to chip away at his usually unflappable demeanor.

"This place has quite the reputation. I'm tempted to bulldoze it today."

"You know we can't yet," I warned him. "Jocelyn..."

"I know," he interrupted me. "I know." Taking a momentary break, I watched him, really took him in.

The light from his phone illuminated his handsome face, now appearing even more tired and drawn. I could see the depth of his worry in the furrows on his brow and the slight tremble in his hand as he dialed the next number.

Hadn't he already found a demonologist willing to come tonight?

"Shoot. She's not going to make it. It's just us, and Aaron and Jericho."

My heart ached for him. Here was the love of my life, standing at the precipice of something unimaginably dark and dangerous, and there was so little I could do to ease his burden. He turned to me, his eyes searching mine, and I could see the silent plea in them.

"And that will be enough. It's going to be okay," I whispered, even though a part of me was uncertain. My words were as much for him as they were a mantra for myself. We sat there for a moment, drawing strength from each other, bracing ourselves for the storm ahead.

We kissed, but neither one of us were at a place where we could let go. Lovemaking wouldn't help us. Well, it might help me, but that would have to wait.

Turning back to our makeshift command center in the living room, my eye caught my sketchbook. Its pages were filled with numerous attempts to capture Ollie's visage, but something always felt off.

Maybe it was because the true nature of Ollie was something beyond the physical, something that couldn't be captured by mere pencil strokes.
Determined, I decided to give it another try, hoping that by understanding and portraying him visually, I could somehow find a way to help Midas.

With each drawing, I delved deeper, trying to get past the physical appearance and capture the essence of Ollie, the malevolent spirit we were up against. The room was silent save for the soft scratching of my pencil on the paper. I could feel Midas watching me occasionally, but he respected my process and kept his distance.

The time seemed to blur, and as I sketched, I felt a strange connection forming, as if I was being pulled into the paper. The sketches took on a life of their own; details emerged that I hadn't consciously observed.

Images of the Leaf Academy, Ollie's transitions, the children he played with, and the rituals with the October People.

One particular drawing stood out: a haunting image of Ollie, his eyes eerily hollow, standing at the forefront of the October People. Behind him, in faded lines, was a monstrous entity, its form almost imperceptible, but its malevolent presence was palpable.

It was as if Ollie was not just a puppet, but also a doorway for something much darker.

Suddenly, I felt a cold draft caress the back of my neck. Goosebumps pricked my skin. The room's atmosphere had shifted, thick with an oppressive energy. As I looked down, the last sketch of Ollie seemed to pulse, the lines vibrating ever so slightly as if alive. The eyes in the drawing appeared to be watching me, studying me.

Panicking, I slammed the sketchbook shut, my heart pounding. Was it possible that in trying to understand Ollie, I had inadvertently invited him in?

Even with the unsettling feeling from the drawing, I forced myself to take a deep breath, trying to regain some semblance of control. Midas must have noticed the tension in my posture, because he approached, placing a gentle hand on my arm.

"Cassidy? You okay?"

I nodded slowly, not trusting myself to speak immediately. His touch, warm and grounding, was a stark contrast to the chilling sensation that had enveloped me moments before. "I... I think I drew something I shouldn't have."

He raised an eyebrow, his face etched with concern. "What do you mean?"

"I'm not sure," I whispered, not daring to open the sketchbook again. "But I felt... watched. It's as if the more I tried to understand Ollie, the closer he came to understanding me."

Midas's face grew more serious, the lines of his handsome features even more pronounced in his worry. "Maybe you should take a break. We can't risk letting him in any further."

I knew he was right, but part of me still wanted to dive back into the drawings, to find a way to gain an advantage. Yet, the lingering sensation of being observed was too overpowering. I needed a distraction.

"That might be a good idea," I conceded, attempting a smile. "Any suggestions?"
Before Midas could respond, there was a soft knock on the door. We exchanged puzzled glances—no one was expected at this hour. As Midas moved to answer it, I couldn't shake the ominous feeling growing in the pit of my stomach. This day,

filled with so many ups and downs, was far from over. And whoever was on the other side of that door could very well be our next challenge.

As Midas opened the door, a gust of wind blew in, momentarily blurring the figure standing on the threshold. When the dust settled, a familiar face came into focus, but it wasn't one we were expecting. It was Jericho, looking more haggard than I'd ever seen him. And he wasn't alone. Macie was with him, and for the first time in forever, they were holding hands. She'd brought Sherman, too, but that wasn't unusual. He often traveled with Macie.

"Jericho?" Midas queried; surprise evident in his voice. "What are you doing here?"

His gaze flitted between the two of us, a sense of urgency in his eyes. "I had a feeling, an instinct. I couldn't shake it off. I felt like I needed to be here, with you guys." He paused, catching his breath. "I was already coming, even before the phone call. There's a storm coming, Midas. And I'm not talking about the weather."

I glanced out of the window, noting the darkening skies and the first few droplets of rain that had begun to fall. It was as if nature itself was mirroring our turbulent emotions and the impending doom we all felt.

Jericho continued, "I've been doing some digging of my own. And while I know you two are hell-bent on facing this, there are things you should know. Things I've discovered about Ollie, about the October People, and how deep this all goes."

"You two, come inside," I felt a cold shiver run down my spine. Here we were, already neck-deep in a nightmare, and now there was more? I glanced at Midas, whose face was a mask of determination, but I could see the worry in his eyes.

"We need to regroup, get everyone together," Jericho stated firmly. "We can't go back blind."

I nodded in agreement, my resolve strengthening. Whatever was coming our way, we would face it together. And with Jericho now by our side, perhaps, just perhaps, we might stand a chance. After Jericho's revelation, the room felt heavy with tension, like the charged moments before a storm. The low hum of the AC did little to quell the stifling atmosphere.

I watched as Midas, our ever calm and collected leader, seemed to momentarily crumble under the weight of it all. He paced back and forth, his fingers rubbing his temples.

Seeing him so troubled, I felt an urge to reach out and provide comfort. I gently took his hand, entwining our fingers together. "Midas," I whispered, trying to break through the fog of anxiety clouding his thoughts.

He paused, his deep-set eyes meeting mine. "Cassidy," his voice wavered just a touch, "I thought I knew what we were getting into, but with each revelation, it feels like we're just scratching the surface."

I squeezed his hand reassuringly. "We'll get through this. Together. We always do."

Jericho cleared his throat, drawing our attention. "We need a plan. A real, concrete plan. We've got resources, knowledge, and determination. We just need to put it all together."

"He's right, y'all. I'm sorry I dragged you back into this, Midas. You too, Cassidy. I'm really sorry." Macie brushed the dampness from her eyes.

Nodding in agreement, I pulled out my sketchbook and began laying out a makeshift map of the Leaf Academy. "Let's strategize, step by step," I said, determined. "If we're going to face the devil, let's make sure we send him back to hell."

With everyone huddled around a makeshift map, we started hashing out our plan of action. As we debated our approach, the room was filled with a mix of seriousness and determination, punctuated by brief moments of levity as someone cracked a joke to ease the tension.

Midas occasionally glanced my way, his eyes searching mine for reassurance. I called Sierra and Joshua, and of course, Chris. I couldn't get a hold of the new guy, but the McBrides came right away.

As the hours wore on, my sketchbook became more than just a canvas for artwork. It transformed into our blueprint for the night, filled with annotations, symbols, and notes.

Sierra and Jericho pointed out potential hotspots, while Midas and Joshua provided insights into the structure and layout of the Academy. Macie and I didn't say much, but we were paying attention to everything.

While I scribbled down their input, Midas's phone buzzed with incoming messages. Information from Aaron and others familiar with the Leaf Academy poured in, giving us invaluable insights. But amidst all the planning, a shadow of dread hung over me.

Every time I sketched Ollie's face, trying to capture his essence, a cold shiver would run down my spine. It felt as though he was watching, aware of our every move, waiting for the perfect moment to strike.

Shaking off the unease, I focused on the task at hand. We were a team, and together, we were formidable. And as the final pieces of our plan clicked into place, I felt a renewed sense of purpose.

"We've got this," I whispered to myself, flipping to a new page in my sketchbook, ready to face whatever lay ahead. As the night drew closer, the atmosphere grew thick with anticipation. Eventually we headed to the Gulf Coast Paranormal office.

Our equipment was meticulously checked and rechecked, ensuring everything was in working order. Joshua and Sierra went through a series of drills with the team, making sure everyone knew their role and position for the night.

In one corner of the room, Jericho and Macie practiced their communication techniques. Macie's sensitivity would be crucial tonight, and she was sharpening her abilities with Jericho's guidance.

Midas pulled me aside, taking a moment away from the chaos. His handsome face, even more tired and drawn than before, softened as he looked at me. "Cassidy," he began, his voice soft, "I know I haven't said it enough, but thank you. For being here, for standing by me, for... everything."

I placed a gentle hand on his cheek, "This is our fight, Midas. Together, always."

The room was abuzz with a mix of tension and resolve. Everyone knew the stakes; everyone understood the risks. And yet, amidst all the apprehension, there was a unified spirit of determination.

Sherman, sensing the intense mood, trotted over to where I was sitting and nestled beside me, offering his own form of comfort. I gave him a gentle pat, taking solace in his warmth.

The clock ticked on, each second a reminder that the time to face the October People and their enigmatic leader, Ollie, was drawing near. The impending confrontation was almost palpable, and as the hour approached, I took a deep breath, bracing myself for what was to come.

As Midas locked the office door, the crisp air rushed in, indicating the onset of the late evening chill. Before either of us could question who it might be, an urgent ringtone cut through the silence. Midas quickly grabbed his phone, his face paling as he answered.

"We need to get to the Leaf Academy. Now!" The voice on the other end was panicked and unfamiliar. I followed closely, my heart racing. Whatever was happening, it wasn't good. "Aaron is going to meet us there."

The drive to the academy was tense and silent. The looming structure of the Leaf Academy soon came into view, its imposing silhouette casting long, eerie shadows in the pale moonlight.

As we approached the main building, a horrifying scene unfurled before us. From the roof of the academy, a figure plummeted downwards. Time seemed to slow as I squinted at the form, revealing it to be none other than Jocelyn. Her short blonde hair and leather jacket fluttered around her like a ghostly aura.

Just like in that moment, that horrible night.

Midas slammed on the brakes, the car screeching to a halt. Macie, who was in the seat ahead of me, struggled with her seatbelt, her scream piercing the night. The echo of that scream seemed to linger, reverberating with the anguish and pain of a sister witnessing the impossible.

"No, Macie! Stay in the car!" I told her from the backseat. It was too late.

We were here at the Leaf Academy. Everyone was piling out of the vehicle and rushing towards Jocelyn, but before we could reach her, she vanished, as if swallowed by the ground. There was no impact, no body—just an empty space where she should've been.
Clearly, we'd seen a vision only. A horrible, cruel vision.

Confusion and fear settled over the group. We stood there, shell-shocked, as the chilling realization hit us.

The October People were not just sending us a message; they were playing with us, taunting us with their ability to manipulate and distort reality.

Macie, tears streaming down her face, looked up at the roof, then back at where her sister had been moments before. "They have her," she whispered, her voice hoarse. "And they'll do anything to keep her."

Sherman was beside her licking her face and then he was gone. He ran barking into the open doors of the Leaf Academy.

Already, we were off track and off plan.

This isn't what I expected.

Chapter Eleven—Aaron

The air was crisp and cool, carrying with it a sense of foreboding. On my way inside the imposing doors of the Leaf Academy, I paused under the ominous Fear No Evil motto which was carved into the stone, in Latin no less. So many occultic signs here.

Yeah, rituals went down here. Clearly. The Nalusa Falaya doesn't randomly show up for no reason.

I journeyed inside the school and climbed the grand staircase. As I traveled up, my mind turned to my late girlfriend's death. Memories of that fateful day, the day Jocelyn left, rushed back, flooding my senses.

It felt like only yesterday that we, the Gulf Coast Paranormal team, were called in to investigate strange occurrences at this very institution. The owner, Adrian Shanahan had been charming but I always sensed she'd been withholding information. Sadly, I'd been correct in that observation.

The entire Leaf Academy was shrouded in a heavy, oppressive energy. But amid that palpable darkness, one memory stood out vividly—my Jocelyn. I will never forget her vibrant energy and infectious smile, she was a beacon of light in that gloomy place. Such a free spirit. A truly free spirit. She'd never been the true target.

I miss you, Jocelyn. My soul still sings your song and it always will.

I prayed I never heard her voice, cries, or laughter echoing in these hallways. I, too, believed she remained here and not by her admonition. She was a prisoner of the Nalusa Falaya, or what some call the October People.

I could still hear the anguished screams, the frantic footsteps, and then the deafening silence that followed her fall.

I had raced to the scene, my heart had pounded wildly, fearing the worst. And there she was, lying lifeless, her once-sparkling eyes now vacant. The memory remained a gut punch, an indescribable pain that left a lasting scar on my soul.

It would forever be burned in my memory.

Now to discover the truth—that she was still here. Why?
Merely to lure Midas?
Questions swirled in my mind, mingled with a torrent of grief and anger. The image of Jocelyn's lifeless form haunted my every waking moment, a constant, cruel reminder of the fragility of life and the lurking dangers of our profession.

As the memories played out, a weight settled in my chest. How had I let it happen? Why couldn't I protect her? The guilt gnawed at me, a relentless specter reminding me of the past's unforgiving nature.

As I tried to push past the overwhelming emotions, I pulled out a small leather-bound journal from my backpack. This was no ordinary notebook; it was a compilation of native legends and folklore passed down through generations in my tribe. My grandmother had entrusted it to me, saying it contained knowledge that could aid in my investigations. And she had been right; time and again, the tales and rituals inscribed in its pages had provided invaluable insights.

Today, I hoped it would offer some answers about the Nalusa Falaya, a dark entity that I had spent quite a bit of time studying. I had heard stories about them before I lost Jocelyn, but the depth of information in this journal was unparalleled. Before her death, a part of me didn't believe the ancient stories.

How could demonic shadows be real?

According to the legends, the Nalusa Falaya, also known as the 'Long Black Beings,' were a malevolent shadow creature. They preyed on the weak and vulnerable, sapping their energy and dragging them into its realm of darkness. Its power was said to be formidable, capable of influencing minds and bending wills. Even some of our tribe's strongest braves had been unable to resist its influence.

I flipped through my book as I waited on the team.

A fleeting memory of Jocelyn resurfaced. A conversation we had late one evening, where she spoke of feeling watched, of shadows that seemed to move on their own, of whispers that called out to her in the dead of night.

Back then, I had dismissed it as the usual fears that come with investigating haunted places. But now, given what I was reading, I wondered if there was more to her words. If only I had paid more attention, and taken her more seriously.

I let you down, my love. I failed you in every way.

A deep sense of regret welled up, threatening to drown me. We were supposed to protect each other, to have each other's backs. And in Jocelyn's most vulnerable moment, I had failed her. The weight of that guilt was suffocating, and for a moment, I felt paralyzed by it.

Taking a deep breath, I tried to refocus. Dwelling on the past wouldn't help. I needed to ensure that what happened to Jocelyn didn't happen to anyone else. Especially Macie. An innocent, so much like her sister. I walked to the second-floor windows that overlooked the driveway.

This would be a great place for waiting on the team. Resolved, I delved deeper into the text, hoping to uncover a way to counter the Nalusa Falaya.

The journal spoke of rituals and rites used by the tribal shamans to ward off dark spirits. One ritual in particular seemed promising. It was a protective circle invoking the power of ancestral spirits to shield against malevolent entities. The process required specific ingredients, some of which I had in my possession, like sage and sacred ash, but others, like the feather of a red-tailed hawk and special stones, might prove more challenging to obtain.

Suddenly, a particular entry caught my attention.

It spoke of a chant, a series of words handed down through generations, believed to repel dark spirits when spoken with conviction. The chant was in the old tribal language, and even though I wasn't fluent, I recognized enough to understand its essence. The problem was, if you misspoke one word, the Nalusa Falaya could pounce. You had to get the phrases right, just right. These beings, and there was more than one, although there was always an alpha.

If I misspoke once, they would take my mistake as a weakness and then strike.

Better practice, Aaron.

I repeated the words softly, letting them roll off my tongue, feeling the power in their syllables. My skin seemed to grow warmer, the dense atmosphere lifting slightly. I was encouraged; I realized that this might be the key, a weapon against the shadows that haunted the Leaf Academy.

As I began to mentally compile a list of the items I would need for the protective circle, a memory of Jocelyn flashed in my mind. She had once gifted me a pendant, a beautiful moonstone encased in silver. She said it was to keep me safe during our investigations.

A bittersweet smile tugged at my lips. The irony was not lost on me. The very stone I needed to protect the group was a gift from Jocelyn herself. I reached into my pocket and felt its smooth, cool surface, drawing strength from its presence.

As the sun began to settle, the sky was painted in hues of orange and purple, and the distant sound of tires on gravel reached my ears. Looking out of the window, I saw the GCP vehicle pulling up the driveway of the Leaf Academy.

As the GCP vehicle approached the entrance of the Leaf Academy, the headlights illuminated the grandeur of the historic building. But just as the vehicle came to a stop, they froze in place.

They were pointing and screaming. I looked where they were looking and I wanted to puke. From the roof's edge, the translucent figure of Jocelyn was teetering, her arms flailing, and then, heartbreakingly, she plummeted to the ground.

The scene was surreal, like a nightmarish replay of that fateful day. I screamed—I couldn't help myself.

Everyone poured out of the vehicle, their faces a mixture of horror and disbelief. Midas's face turned ashen, his eyes wide with shock. Macie's hands covered her mouth. Jericho had his arm around her. The rest of the team stood motionless, their expressions reflecting the gravity of the vision they'd just witnessed.

I noticed that Chris was missing, I'd met him briefly the other day. Had he quit already? I couldn't think of anything except seeing my dead girlfriend die again.

I sprinted down the stairs and out the doors. I raced towards them, my heart pounding in my chest. "Did you all see that?" I yelled, trying to make sense of the ghostly apparition.

Midas nodded slowly, tears glistening in his eyes. "It's exactly as it happened...every haunting detail."

"But why are we seeing it again?" Cassidy questioned, her voice trembling.

"He's threatening us," I replied, my voice filled with urgency. "Our suspicions are correct. Jocelyn's spirit is trapped; she was forced to replay her final moments, and the Nalusa Falaya is feeding off her anguish—and ours."
The team exchanged worried glances. It was clear that this investigation was not going to be like any other we'd encountered. We were dealing with forces far older and more malevolent than we'd ever imagined, and Jocelyn was right at the heart of it.

I stood under the looming structure; the shadow sent a shiver down my spine. Finally, I would face Midas. I mean, we'd kind of made up, but I'd been a bastard to him. Our eyes met, and for a moment, the weight of our shared history hung heavily between us.

Midas approached, extending a hand. "Aaron," he greeted, his voice holding a hint of hesitation. "Thanks for coming."

Taking his hand firmly, I nodded. "Midas. I'm glad to be here. It's time to make this right."

His eyes darted briefly to the academy, then back to me. "I can't believe we're back. It's time, I think."

"So do I," I replied. There was nothing else to add to that. The team hugged one another, all of us still reeling from the horrible replay we'd all witnessed. There wasn't a dry eye amongst us.

We didn't linger long. We began unloading equipment, our actions methodical and purposeful. Among them, Macie seemed particularly affected, her eyes constantly drawn to the upper floors of the academy, no doubt haunted by memories of her sister.

"We've got to be careful," Midas whispered, leaning closer. "More than ever."

I nodded in agreement. Together, we made our way inside, ready to face the shadows of the past and the present. As we ventured further into the academy, the weight of its history pressed in on all sides.

The air was thick with silent tension, the shadows seeming to shift and move just beyond the corner of my eyes. We set up the standard equipment and discussed the plan for the night. After a half hour of hard work, checking cameras, and changing out batteries, thankfully nothing appeared to have been disturbed.

But I needed to investigate on my own. Midas gave me the nod and I walked away. I wouldn't be long, I just need to finish my recon. I retreated to a quiet corridor. With the dim light from my flashlight, I began to scan my journal. I was tempted to speak the ancient words here and now. But I resisted the urge. Hearing footsteps, I looked up to find Macie standing at the entrance of the corridor. Her face was a picture of mixed emotions, but there was a clear thirst for knowledge in her eyes. She had every right to understand the entity that may have had a hand in her sister's demise.

"What are you doing, Aaron? We're supposed to stay together."

"Reviewing my journal. Did you know, that the Choctaw believe that the Nalusa Falaya can absorb a person's shadow and even influence their actions and thoughts," I continued, glancing at Macie. "While many modern accounts describe shadow beings as malevolent, the Choctaw understanding is more nuanced. Yes, the Nalusa Falaya can bring harm, especially if one opens themselves to their influence, but it can also serve as a reminder of the balance between light and darkness, good and evil."

Macie stepped closer, her voice barely above a whisper. "My sister's murder was all in the name of balance?"

I flinched at her words. "That's not what I meant. Not at all. I am sorry for the way that sounded. I'm just looking over my material to be sure I have everything we need for protection."

Macie stepped closer, Sherman was by her side. "Is there truly a way to protect ourselves from it? No way am I letting Sherman stay here. I'm about to put him in the SUV. I probably shouldn't have brought him but I was afraid something would happen to him. Jocelyn loved him so much."

"Yes, she did. Strange how he just showed up on her doorstep one day. It's like he was meant to find her. He's a very empathic dog."

She scratched his head and sat beside me. I flipped to another section of the journal. "What's in there?"

"There are rituals and protections that the Choctaw used. Believe it or not, unity of purpose is a strong protection. I think we have that. But I have something for you, Macie."

Reaching into my bag, I pulled out several small stones. "These are protection stones, blessed by a Choctaw shaman. They'll help guard us against the influence of the Nalusa Falaya." Handing one to Macie, our fingers brushed momentarily, and there was a fleeting connection, a shared understanding of the weight of the night ahead.

"We need to distribute these to everyone," I said, gathering up the rest of the stones in a velvet bag.

.

She accepted the bag and agreed to pass them out. I decided to return with her. I even volunteered to put Sherman in the

SUV. The poor dog was happy to leave the Leaf Academy. I didn't blame him. I wouldn't want to be here either but for Jocelyn.

Everyone accepted a stone and I felt a bit better.

Macie gave me a thumbs up. She missed her sister so much and I could feel her pain. I could feel it and hated it for her. Night had settled, casting the Leaf Academy in an eerie tapestry of moonlit silhouettes and deep shadows. The ever-present chirping of crickets was abruptly interrupted by the distant hoot of an owl, a harbinger of the unknown events that lay ahead.

The team regrouped in the main hall, our faces illuminated by the soft glow of solar lanterns and flashlights. We'd set up cameras, audio recorders, and other paranormal equipment. Midas and Cassidy were discussing strategies, their heads close together, while Macie appeared deep in thought, clutching the protection stone I'd given her.

The main hall's grand staircase, though aged and covered in dust, still maintained a semblance of its former glory. Glancing around, my eyes met Jericho's. Though he was relatively new to the world of the supernatural, his determination to uncover the truth was evident.

"I've been thinking, Midas," I broke his conversation with Cassidy. "I want everyone to understand a few things about the Nalusa Falaya... the shadow entity or more likely entities. This is a collection of these beings. There is one leader, one stronger than the others. No one must accept any gifts. No one picks up feathers, paper, or anything. The stones I gave you, should keep them away for a bit."

"Tell us what you know," Sierra encouraged me. I did as she asked. I told them everything I knew.

"The entity is drawn to negative emotions, to turmoil. Jocelyn's death was undoubtedly a traumatic event, and such events can act as beacons for entities like the Nalusa Falaya."

Jericho nodded; his expression grim. "The academy has seen more than its fair share of darkness. You can feel it. Feel them."

"I must tell you guys some bad news. I found something," Macie confessed. She unzipped her backpack and pulled out a feather. "I didn't want this thing and I didn't put it in here. When I first found it, I threw it out the window but found it here again. Does that mean I'm next? Am I going to die too?" Macie was practically crying.

"No, Macie. They can't force you to take a gift," Cassidy assured her.

A sudden cold draft interrupted our conversation, causing our lights to flicker momentarily. Macie gasped and Jericho moved closer to her. He took the feather from her, but I don't know what he thought he was going to do with it. The temperature drop was palpable, our breaths visible in the chilling air.

This was a sign, a manifestation of a nearby supernatural presence.

"Burn it, Jericho! Light it up!" Midas barked at him. Jericho raised his eyebrows, unsure what to do. I agreed with Midas. Burning the cursed object would certainly demonstrate our intent. None of us wanted any of those hellish gifts.

I handed him a lighter and the feather went up in a few seconds. We watched the cinders fall to the floor.

The equipment began to register spikes in activity, lights flashed and audio recorders beeped indicating that they picked up indecipherable whispers.

So it begins.

I gripped my protection stone, muttering a silent prayer. The night was unfolding, and the presence of the Nalusa Falaya was becoming increasingly evident. Joshua's sarcastic voice broke the tension. "That certainly set the intention."

"We need to stay together," I cautioned the group. "Remember the teachings of the Choctaw. We must strike a balance; and ensure we do not give in to fear or despair. Macie, we will be alright."

Midas, looking determined, nodded in agreement. "That's right. Everyone, check your equipment and stay alert.
"
Every creak of the old wooden floor, the rustling of leaves outside the broken windows, sent chills down my spine. While the equipment continued to capture subtle anomalies, there wasn't any direct evidence, or confrontation, with the Nalusa Falaya. Yet.

Pausing in what seemed to be an old classroom, Cassidy set up a spirit box – a device that rapidly scans radio frequencies, allowing spirits to communicate using the white noise. As the static sound filled the room, everyone's attention was firmly fixed on the device, waiting for any sign of a message.

Suddenly, Macie's expression changed. She seemed distant; her gaze fixated on a corner of the room where the shadows seemed darker and denser.

"Jericho. Aaron," she whispered, her voice trembling, "I feel her... I feel Jocelyn."

Jericho moved closer, placing a protective hand on her shoulder, sensing the powerful connection she had to the spirit world. "Let her come through, but stay grounded, Macie."

The spirit box then crackled to life, with a faint, almost inaudible voice coming through. "Aaron? Why?"

The voice was unmistakably Jocelyn's. Memories of our last investigation, of the tragic night of her death, flooded back. Guilt, regret, and sorrow threatened to overwhelm me, but I had to stay focused.

"Jocelyn," I replied, my voice heavy with emotion, "we're here to help, to find out what happened to you. How did they pull you back? How did this happen?"

Another voice came through, this one deeper, more sinister. "Leave... now."

I exchanged a worried glance with Jericho. This wasn't just Jocelyn we were dealing with; something darker was at play. Taking a deep breath, I addressed the entity directly, leaning on my Choctaw teachings and ancestral knowledge.

"We are here with respect, seeking the truth. We will not be swayed by threats or fear," I spoke in my ancestral language.

The answer was a growl. An unmistakable growl. It was clear--
the Nalusa Falaya was making its presence known, and it was
not pleased that we were even considering fighting back.

Amid the chilling atmosphere, Midas's voice cut through,
bringing a semblance of grounding to the escalating situation.
"Remember, guys. We're here for Jocelyn." He directed a
searching look at me, the weight of our shared past evident in
his gaze. "Aaron, can you perform a ritual to clear the energy
in this room? We need a safe space. Sierra, will you help him?
We may as well start here."

I nodded, retrieving a small leather pouch from my bag. It
contained a mixture of sage, cedar, and sweetgrass—plants
traditionally used by my ancestors for cleansing and
protection. I also had a small abalone shell, which I used to
catch the ashes, and a feather to fan the smoke.

Sierra stood next to me. The tiny blonde had her eyes closed
and was quietly praying in her way.

Lighting the bundle, I began the purification ritual, letting the
aromatic smoke waft through the room. The words of an
ancient chant passed down through generations of my tribe,
resonated deeply as I sang, calling upon my ancestors and the
spirits of the land for protection and guidance.

"Stand back, dark ones. Stand away from the light. Honor the
sacred smoke for this is now a sacred space."
As the smoke spiraled upward, a shift occurred. The stifling
heaviness began to lift, replaced by a sense of calm and clarity.
The room felt lighter, and the oppressive energy dissipated.

Midas gave me a nod of appreciation, the first real acknowledgment between us in a long time. "Thank you, Aaron," he said sincerely. "I'm sorry for the past... for Jocelyn." I met his gaze, understanding and forgiveness reflecting in my eyes. "We both lost her that night," I replied softly. "But we have a chance to make things right."

Suddenly, a thud echoed from a distant corridor, drawing our attention. Our brief moment of camaraderie was shattered, a stark reminder that the Leaf Academy was still filled with mysteries and spirits awaiting discovery.

The Nalusa Falaya may have retreated momentarily, but they weren't defeated. We had to stay vigilant. The night was far from over.

"I've seen Jocelyn," she whispered, her voice trembling. "Not just in my dreams, Aaron. She's here, trapped, and she's trying to warn us."

And just like that, I saw her. She was standing before me. I took a step back, and the floorboard beneath me creaked loudly. She didn't vanish. *Was that her?* Jocelyn's eyes met mine. There was recognition there, and for a moment, I saw a glimmer of the vibrant person she once was.
Then, the darkness of the Nalusa Falaya enveloped the hallway, swallowing the light and plunging everything into an abyss.

"No!" I shouted against the image. This was only an image, wasn't it?
The last thing I saw was Jocelyn's hand reaching for me.

Once again, I failed her.

Chapter Twelve--Sierra/Moriah

The dust settled around the grounds of the Leaf Academy, making the world seem still and hazy for a moment. It felt like time was suspended as we regrouped, our breathing syncing up in the eerie quiet that followed the confrontation.

"What the hell just happened?" Cassidy murmured, her voice echoing the shock painted across all our faces.

Jericho clenched his fists, his jaw set in a grim line. "Ollie's more powerful than we realized. The Nalusa Falaya has its claws deep in him."

Macie sat on a metal chair, her head in her hands, her shoulders shaking. The raw emotion of the scene was taking its toll on her. After all, she had an intimate connection to this place, a bond that was both her strength and her vulnerability.

I put an arm around her, trying to offer some semblance of comfort. "Hey," I whispered, "we're going to get through this. Together."

She nodded, tears streaking her face, but didn't say anything.

Midas paced back and forth, his gaze distant. I could tell he was replaying the event in his mind, searching for clues, insights, and any detail that could provide us an advantage.

"I shouldn't have underestimated him," he muttered, more to himself than to any of us.
Aaron, who had been surprisingly calm through it all, finally spoke up. "We need to act, and we need to act fast."

"Agreed," Jericho chimed in. "But we need to approach the situation strategy, not just brute force. It's that balance you were talking about. We push, and pull back." The air was thick with tension, but also determination. Despite the setback, our resolve was stronger than ever.

I felt a strange sensation at the back of my head. It was as if someone was trying to get my attention. I glanced around, but no one seemed to be looking my way. Then, it hit me—Moriah Mitchell. The sensation grew stronger, more insistent.

Closing my eyes, I focused on the sensation of connecting with the dead.
I let Moriah's spirit guide my senses. The world around me faded, replaced by a rush of images and sounds that painted a vivid tapestry of a time long past.

Yes, so long ago. So very long ago. But I cannot forget, you see. What I have done...what I did to McCandlish was wrong. I knew what he would do.

The academy transformed before my eyes. And through his eyes, I saw the place how it used to be.

Once daunting and dilapidated, it now stood grand and majestic, its walls freshly painted and windows glistening in the sunlight. I could hear the melodious laughter of students and the busy chatter that comes with the start of a new day. The rich aroma of old books and polished wood wafted through the corridors, giving the place an aura of warmth and familiarity.

How I used to love teaching! Being here with the students and the others. But everything changed.

But beneath this serene facade, I almost immediately sensed a deeper layer of unrest.
Whispers echoed in hushed tones, shadows danced mischievously out of the corner of his eyes, and there were moments when he felt an eerie sensation of being watched by unseen eyes. Yes, unseen eyes that glow in the dark.

Yes, at the heart of this vision stood Moriah Mitchell.

I could see him clearly in all his regal demeanor—tall, dressed in distinguished robes befitting the headmaster of such an esteemed institution. He only wore the ceremonial garb during special occasions, but he felt worthy of them. He had worked so hard and so diligently. Yes, he belonged here.

Yet, the weight of some terrible knowledge bore down on him. His sharp eyes, usually so full of command and confidence, were clouded with unease.

As Moriah Mitchell, I felt the paper under my hands. Then I looked up and I was watching him. I was now detached from Mitchell, but still with him. I preferred watching from a distance.

Moriah Mitchell was in his office, papers scattered around, some filled with diagrams and symbols I couldn't understand. The room was dimly lit, the only source of light being a single candle that flickered erratically. He was shuffling around his desk, looking for something. But what? Moriah's hands trembled as he drew something on a piece of parchment—a map of the academy with a distinct mark at its very center.

Suddenly, he looked up, his gaze piercing through time and space to meet mine.

He can see me!

The connection was electrifying. It felt as if he was right there with me, trying to convey a message of paramount importance.

"They let them in. Before my time but I could have done more," he whispered urgently, his voice tinged with desperation. The room around him started to darken, shadows creeping up the walls, inching closer and closer.

"Who? Who let them in? Do you mean Ollie? Is that who they let in?"

His face began to fade before my eyes. "They let them in. Stop them. Free them, free me. Please."

Then shadows grew from the floor and grabbed at him. Moriah Mitchell screamed in horror as they enveloped him, the desk, and the entire room. I wanted to scream, too, but all I could do was cry.

The haunting vision started to dissolve, pulling me back to reality, and leaving me gasping for breath and clutching my chest, overwhelmed by the sheer intensity of the experience.

"Sierra? Sierra, are you okay?" Cassidy's concerned voice broke through my stupor.

Joshua was there beside me too. I blinked, looking around at the faces staring back at me, filled with worry.

"I... I saw the shadows. Moriah showed me...he confessed that someone let them in but I got the feeling it wasn't him. He knew about it, after the fact."

Cassidy exchanged a glance with Midas. "What did he show you?"

I recounted the vision, detailing everything I remembered. "A drawing on his desk. He was showing it to me. An eye inside a symbol. Probably more than that, but I am not the artist."

Midas' eyes darkened as he processed the information. "They let them in," he murmured. "That's what he said?"

"Yes," I confessed.
"Whoever let them in, the portal in the downstairs room has to be where it happened. That must be how they got in. They whoever they were, had to have opened a door, whether deliberately or accidentally. That's what we've been missing."

It felt like we had been handed the last piece of a jigsaw puzzle. But this wasn't just any puzzle—it held the fate of Jocelyn, and possibly many more terrified spirits.
We had our next lead, our next mission. The stakes had never been higher, and time was running out.

Cassidy leaned in, her eyes narrowing with a mix of concern and curiosity. "The portal, if it's real and not just metaphorical, it's the key. It's what's tying Jocelyn here, it's what's giving the Nalusa Falaya strength."

Jericho nodded, his usually jovial face stern. "And if it was opened, it can be closed. We need to find out how."

Midas looked around, his gaze settling on each one of us as if measuring our resolve. "We've dealt with entities before, but this... this is different. If we're going to do this, it's going to take all of us. Every ounce of strength and wit."

Macie wiped away a tear and straightened her back, determination shining in her eyes. "Let's do this. For Jocelyn. For all the souls trapped here."

Just as the group was soaking in Macie's words, the unmistakable sound of soft footsteps echoed down the nearby hallway.

Cassidy's eyes widened. "Anyone got a recorder running? I swear that sounded like a child." Everyone turned in unison, straining their ears to discern any additional sounds.
Midas raised a finger to his lips, signaling everyone to remain silent. "They're listening," he whispered, his eyes darting around the room. The atmosphere grew tense as the reality of the situation settled in.

Aaron's eyes narrowed. "They always listen. This place is alive."

Cassidy took a deep breath. "Every move, every plan, we must assume they know." The footsteps returned and faded, leaving behind an oppressive silence. But our group's resolve had only strengthened.

Aaron stepped forward, laying his journal in the center of the circle. "We'll need to combine our knowledge. Sierra, your connection with Moriah might be our biggest advantage. And this," he pointed to the journal, "contains everything my ancestors knew about the Nalusa Falaya."

The night was deepening, the moon hanging high, casting long, eerie shadows on the grounds of the Leaf Academy. But there was a new energy in our group, a collective determination that was palpable.

A chilling gust of wind swept through the hallway, despite the trees outside being still. I could see them quite well from my vantage point. The shadows around the tree seemed to lengthen and twist, taking on shapes that defied logic. The air grew colder, the kind of cold that seeps into your bones.

"Joshua? Do you see that?" I was standing close to my husband hoping and praying that I wasn't the only one.

"Uh, yeah. Shadows. Tall, menacing shadows. Where's RYDER, Chris? Is she charged yet?"

"Yeah, it should be. Hold on." Chris rumbled through cases and retrieved the headset.

"I thought this only worked on living people. You find attachments with it. Right?" Midas asked curiously as he reached for the headset. Chris surrendered it and helped him adjust the strap. We were all staring out the broken window now. The shadows were real and getting more real by the second.

"I have a theory," Chris whispered. "RYDER might detect attachments connected to other things too, like trees."

Joshua flipped open the monitor to see what Midas was seeing. "Interesting. Light green flecks, like orbs. Nothing else."

As we studied the shadowscape, a hauntingly familiar melody began to play, coming from the direction of the auditorium. It was a melancholic tune like an old lullaby, played on a broken piano. The notes were discordant, and twisted, turning a once comforting sound into a spine-chilling dirge.

Midas whispered like a freight train. "They are headed this way. Moving together, in waves. I can't count how many." He tugged at RYDER and handed her back to Chris. Joshua saved the footage and closed the monitor.

"Hell! Incoming! What do we do?"
From the corner of her eye, I spotted movement at one of the academy's upper windows.
It was the silhouette of a girl in a tattered dress, clutching a worn-out teddy bear. She swayed to the rhythm of the eerie lullaby, her movements jerky and unnatural. Then, in a fleeting second, she vanished, replaced by a series of handprints that appeared and streaked down the glass, as if someone inside was trying to escape.

"She's not real! There were no girls here!" I closed my eyes and turned my back on the activity. "They are playing games with us. They want us to gather in that auditorium. We can't do that! Stay out of the auditorium, y'all!"

The ground beneath us trembled subtly, causing a few pieces of loose flooring to shift. Whispered voices, too low to discern any words, seemed to come from the very earth, growing in volume until they became an unintelligible chorus.

Midas, taking a defensive stance, spoke through gritted teeth, "They're putting on a show for us."

Aaron took a step forward, his gaze fixed on the academy's entrance. "It's a warning. They know we're onto something."

A series of lights started to flicker inside the academy, casting an otherworldly glow over the building. Then, just as suddenly as it had begun, everything went silent. The lullaby stopped, the whispers died down, and darkness reclaimed the academy.

Cassidy grabbed my hand. "Come on, guys. It's time to go face the portal. Grab whatever you need and run. Run like hell. This isn't going to be pretty." As she said that, a barrage of black shadows, hooded with torn black gowns undulated toward us. On occasion, a bone-white hand or skull appeared only to be hidden again in the mess of darkness.
Without further argument, I did as she directed and ran as fast as my tiny feet would carry me. At least one of us had her thinking cap on. And that sure as heck wasn't me.

"Joshua, leave it! Grab RYDER and come on!" I shouted at my husband who dawdled behind. I was relieved to see Chris tug at his sleeve which appeared to break whatever hold they had on him.

We all ran fast and furious to the statue in the courtyard. That was the only way to access the secret meeting room.

God help us if the shadows were there too.

Chapter Thirteen—Cassidy

The dim light of the room welcomed us as we rushed in, desperately shutting the door behind us. "Holy crap!" I swore under my breath. I wasn't great at swearing, but in situations like these, I was tempted to let it fly. Joshua and Chris did enough cussing for all of us.

The echoing sounds of our heavy breaths reverberated in the space as if the room itself was alive and breathing with us. For a fleeting moment, I could hear the faint cries and mournful wails of the spirits above us but thankfully, they halted at the threshold of the stairs, as if some unseen barrier prevented them from descending further.

A wave of relief washed over me, even if it might only be temporary. Midas squeezed my hand and I squeezed his back.

I could feel the weight of the room's history pressing down on me, the air thick with memories of the past. "Let's get some lights on," Midas suggested as everyone dug out flashlights, cell phones, and whatever else they had close by.

Without wasting a moment, I pulled out my sketchbook and began to sketch the room in all its intricate detail. The process would normally be therapeutic for me, allowing my mind to drown out the chaos. Not so this time. Desperation and fear fueled my sketch.
While I sketched, Aaron and Sierra, having a keen sense of the supernatural, began their search for the portal. It didn't take long to discern a possible location. Sierra, eyes widening, pointed towards the center of the room.

"There it is, y'all. There is an indention—on the floor. See?" She squatted down and pointed her flashlight at the irregular spot.

"Yep, I see it," Aaron whispered, a note of awe in his voice. He touched the stonework and Midas checked it out too. "Right beneath our feet."

"I've got an idea," Joshua said with some excitement. "Let's use RYDER. Maybe she'll help us see something spectral. Chris, you manage the monitor."

The headset illuminated the area, and to my complete surprise, revealed faint but unmistakable ancient symbols, which danced and shimmered as RYDER's technology deciphered them.

I could hardly believe it. "Hold on a second. I thought RYDER only saw spirits attached or near people. How is this possible?"

"These symbols..." Joshua murmured, tracing them with his fingers, "They have some sort of spiritual essence. Some sort of spectral stamp. This is definitely where the portal is located. These markings... they're like the ones I saw in Aaron's journal. Right, Aaron?"

Aaron's handsome face hovered near the screen that Chris was tapping on. "Yes. Exactly. Our people did not have a specific written language, but we did use symbols and specific markings to share information and even warn other people. These markings are a sure warning."

As they pondered their discovery, I continued sketching. It was easy to integrate the symbols and their arrangements into my work. I felt so strange.

So connected to the past. So connected to the spirits here. Everything felt so tangible, so real.

For a moment I did not feel fear and that worried me. I should be afraid, I thought absently as I drew an ominous figure.

As I looked down at the drawing I had just made, a shiver ran down my spine.

The figure on the paper was Ollie, but not the Ollie we knew. This entity mimicked his form, but the more I stared, the more the grotesque differences became apparent. Yes, Ollie had once been a boy. A boy like any other boy except he'd been targeted. Just like Midas was now being targeted.

I stared at the drawing again. Where Ollie's eyes once sparkled with mischief and life, these were dark, bottomless voids. They held no emotion, just an endless, haunting malevolence. The face was distorted.

Its body, though bearing semblance to a child's, was oddly stretched and seemed to be in a state of constant flux, like it was made of shifting shadows and mist. The fingers unnerved me the most—so much longer than they should be, ending in sharp, talon-like claws.

But it was the aura around the entity in my drawing that made my hands tremble.

Even as a mere sketch, the oppressive energy radiating from it was palpable. The very space around it on the paper seemed to be bending and warping, echoing the dark, chilling vibes it gave off.

I swallowed hard, trying to steady my hands. Despite the terror it evoked, I couldn't deny the strange pull of the drawing. It was as if I'd managed to capture not just its likeness but its very essence, the raw, overpowering evil that seeped from every line and shade I'd sketched.

"Midas, this is it," I handed him the sketchbook. Everyone rushed to see what I'd captured. Even Joshua and Chris shut down RYDER to examine the sketch.

"Good Lord," Sierra whispered. "I don't know how you managed to do it, Cassidy but you captured its essence. I mean captured it."

As our focus remained intently on the sketch, a subtle shift in the room's atmosphere caught my attention. It felt like a gathering storm. I looked up, as did everyone else, and my heart lurched. The ceiling above us was alive, but not with fixtures or designs. Shadows, countless numbers of them, writhed and intertwined, creating a dark canopy that seemed to be slowly descending upon us.

The light in the room began to dim, almost as if the shadows were swallowing the light whole. Chris, ever the quick thinker, focused his light on the ceiling; its beam piercing the growing darkness. Others followed suit, our combined beams illuminating the ceiling with an eerie, stark light. The shadows twisted and moved away. The light repelled them.

Suddenly, he was there. I hadn't heard his footsteps, or seen him arrive, but he was certainly here. Ollie stood there, at the far end of the room, eyes hollow but fixed intently on Midas. But behind him, barely visible yet impossible to ignore, was a larger, more menacing shadow. It towered over Ollie, its shape constantly shifting, its form eluding definition.

There was an undeniable presence about it – an ancient, malevolent energy that radiated pure malice.

Sierra, eyes wide, whispered to me, "This room, it's not just a room. It's... it's alive. Can you feel it? The pulsating energy?"

Macie, her face pale, nodded in agreement. "I can feel it too. It's like... like the very walls have a heartbeat." She moved closer to Jericho, who instinctively wrapped an arm around her, trying to offer some semblance of protection.

As the tension grew, Chris's voice broke the silence, tinged with a mix of astonishment and dread. "Guys, you need to see this." He beckoned us over, pointing to the RYDER monitor. On the screen, amidst the familiar green hues, was a sight that left us all stunned. "RYDER isn't even on!"
On the RYDER monitor, amidst the swirls of green and blue energy signals, the unmistakable outline of a portal glowed. But that wasn't the most chilling part.
A figure, distorted and writhing, was pressing against it, its form convulsing and pushing against the boundaries of the energetic doorway. The distorted silhouette was eerily human, but its movements were frantic, and desperate, as if trapped between two worlds.

Ollie growled at us, but he was alone now. The shadowy being had vanished. Where had it gone? Then it occurred to me that seeing that shadow had only been an illusion. It was still trapped behind the portal door. Somehow, someway, it had been trapped but the trap wasn't going to hold.

"We need to shut that RYDER down, now," Midas exclaimed, his usually calm demeanor replaced with urgency. "It's using it!"

Jericho nodded as he closed the monitor and struggled to remove the battery from RYDER. "Whatever's trying to come through... it's not going to be friendly."

Aaron, deep in thought, muttered, "These portals, they're doorways, and every door has a lock. This doorway should never have been opened in this location. The people here, the people who built the Leaf Academy, didn't believe in the Nalusa Falaya. They didn't believe yet they did believe in ghosts and spirits. Strange isn't it?" Aaron wiped his damp eyes with the backs of his hands. "My brothers and I, came here after Jocelyn died. We managed to lock the door, to shove them back into the darkness, but I knew it wouldn't keep. I had to try though, for Jocelyn. I am sorry, Macie."

Macie shook her head and put her hand on his shoulder. "It's nobody's fault. Nobody living. I thank you for what you tried to do, but we can't stop."

I quickly chimed in, "The symbols. The ones Joshua saw through RYDER. They're the key. Were they part of the ritual to activate or seal the portal, Aaron?"

"Yes, I can interpret them for you, but we don't have time for that. I have chalk in my bag. We need it to make the markings. Unfortunately, I left my bag upstairs."

As Aaron delivered the bad news, black feathers began to gently float down from the ceiling. At first, it was just a few, twirling gracefully to the floor. But soon, it was a cascade, darkening the room further and blanketing the floor.

Macie, her eyes widening in alarm, exclaimed, "This isn't just paranormal. It's a sign, a warning of sorts." Chris looked around nervously. Was he going to run? I sure as heck wanted to. I held on to Cassidy instead.

The atmosphere in the room grew denser. We all felt it - the impending sense of something monumental about to happen. Time was running out, and the answers we sought seemed just out of grasp. The portal's dormant state was becoming increasingly unstable.

Suddenly, the sharp, jarring sound of the hatch above the staircase being thrown open resonated through the room. The harsh echo bounced off the walls, amplifying the fear that was already palpable. We all turned to look upwards, dreading what we might see next. I can't say when, but the Ollie apparition had vanished. Whatever was coming was much worse.

Oh, so much worse.

Heavy, deliberate footsteps began to descend the staircase. Each step was a prolonged moment of dread, echoing through the chamber and making the hairs on the back of my neck stand on end. The rhythm was agonizingly slow, dragging out the terror.

A chilling wind accompanied the descent, and the flashlights went out one by one.
In the dimming glow, a familiar silhouette emerged, warped by the twisted light and shadow. Ollie. But this was not Ollie. This was something darker, more sinister.

The eyes were vacant, devoid of any humanity. I wasn't surprised. I didn't think this thing had ever been human. It contained a darkness that seemed to stretch into eternity.

It was tall, slender, and abnormally slow. Made of shadow, but I could see facial and hand features. A twisted smile curled the lips, revealing teeth that seemed unnaturally sharp. The facial skin was pale, almost translucent, with veins that appeared as dark tendrils beneath the surface.

Every feature, every detail screamed wrongness.

As he drew closer, the temperature plummeted even further. Each exhale now formed visible clouds of vapor in front of our faces. The cold was bone-deep, the kind of cold that chills the soul. It was a cold that spoke of graveyards and the space between stars.

Have I ever been so cold?

Midas, strong and ever the leader, suddenly staggered, his knees buckling beneath him. He crumpled to the floor, his hands clutching his head, his face twisted in agony. "He's in my head," he gasped, his voice filled with pain. "He's... everywhere."

Jericho reacted instantly. He moved towards Midas. As he placed his hand on Midas's head, the room was filled with a gentle, pulsating light. The contrast between the cold darkness and the healing warmth was stark. He did not speak aloud, but someone must have heard Jericho's prayer.

The pain in Midas's face began to recede; it was replaced by confusion and then clarity. With Jericho's aid, he slowly got to his feet. As he stood, there was a momentary blur, and then, in a blink, the entity was standing at the portal's location, looking determined, staring out of Ollie's soulless eyes.

The showdown had begun.

For a brief moment, Ollie's form wavered then began to shift and twist. The transformation was gruesome to witness—the bones snapped, the skin stretched, and the facial features contorted. I wanted to vomit.

In mere seconds, Ollie was gone. Instead, there stood Dom, Midas's young cousin who had tragically passed away years ago. I knew this because I'd seen his photograph. It was on my mantelpiece.

The sight of Dom hit Midas like a sledgehammer. His eyes widened, and his voice shook with a mix of rage and pain. "You dare take his form? Stop it, you bastard!"
Ollie, wearing Dom's innocent visage, simply smiled—a twisted, malevolent grin that looked all wrong on the face of a child. His voice, so eerily like Dom's, dripped with malevolence. "Does it hurt, Midas? Seeing me like this? You did this. You know you did."
"He's lying, Midas!"

Before he could react, Ollie's form blurred again, and suddenly I was staring at a mirror image of myself. Every detail, every nuance was replicated with terrifying accuracy. But the eyes— those weren't mine. They were cold, hollow, and void of any human emotion. And I was completely naked.

"Is this better?" Ollie's voice, now mimicking mine, was seductive, dripping with malevolence. He took a step closer, looking around the group with a cruel smirk. "I always wondered what it felt like, being Cassidy." The entity posed and smirked as it waved its fingers at Joshua. "You have to, haven't you?"

Joshua turned his face away as Sierra touched his arm. This thing was wreaking havoc.

Midas growled, taking a threatening step forward toward the entity, but Aaron intervened. "No, Midas. That's what he wants. You step on that portal, you are his."
Aaron's voice was deep and resonant, he began to chant in Choctaw. Each word was heavy, powerful, and demanding. It felt ancient, a command from times long past that still held authority.

The strange-looking entity's form began to waver again, but instead of reverting to his own, he maliciously shifted into Jocelyn. Her face, usually soft and kind, now bore the same cruel smirk as Ollie's. Turning to Aaron, she adopted a wounded tone, her eyes filled with fake tears.

"You don't love me anymore, Aaron? You want to banish me?" Her voice was sweet, but the words were daggers. The sheer audacity of Ollie's manipulation sent shivers down my spine. Every move was calculated to inflict maximum emotional pain, to destabilize us, to break us apart. We needed to regain control, and fast.
But how? The small hairs on the back of my neck stood up as a wave of cold air enveloped us. It felt like we were trapped inside a snow globe, with the world outside distorting and wavering.

The portal began to pulse, emitting a deep, resonant hum. Its edges grew jagged, like the maw of some massive beast, and tendrils of dark energy started to snake outwards. The walls around us began to bleed shadows, dark forms stretching and writhing as if they had a life of their own.

Was the portal breaking open?

I gripped Midas's hand tightly. Macie screamed as ghostly hands emerged from the floor, clutching at her ankles, trying to pull her down. Jericho swung wildly at the air, his hands passing through the apparitions, but doing no harm. Everywhere I looked, my team was under assault, the very room we stood in turning against us.

Above us, the ceiling seemed to dissolve, replaced by a swirling vortex of darkness. Black feathers began to rain down, each one turning into a shadowy wraith as it touched the floor. They circled us, their forms shifting and changing, taking on the appearance of our worst fears and memories.

Amid the chaos, Ollie, still wearing Jocelyn's face, laughed—a sound devoid of any humanity, echoing and warping as it bounced off the walls.

"You cannot stop us," he hissed, his voice layered, as if many were speaking at once.

"The portal will open, and we will come through. All of us. This world will be ours."

As the onslaught intensified, I felt a hand grasp mine, pulling me towards the center of the room. I looked up to see Aaron, his face determined, his eyes filled with purpose.

"We need to close the portal," he shouted over the din. "It's our only chance!" It was now or never. In the midst of the swirling, suffocating darkness, Aaron's voice rose above the chaos, clear and commanding. "Everyone! We need to unify our energies!"

He quickly started to lead us in an ancient chant. It was in Choctaw, the words melodic yet powerful. As he recited them, he urged us all to join in. The rhythm was steady, like the beat of a heart, and there was something intrinsically calming about it.

"Keep going," he yelled, "Focus on the words, let them be your anchor!" He picked up the chant again as did we all.
Sierra and Macie, hands tightly clasped, began to concentrate with closed eyes. It was almost visible, the energy we were summoning. It was a soft, gentle glow and it enveloped us all. Slowly, it expanded, forming a brighter, protective barrier.

Inside this bubble of light, the cold began to recede, the pressure lessened, and for the first time in what felt like hours, I could breathe without feeling like I was being crushed. Midas's face was wet with tears, but he was chanting too. We all were.
With each repetition of the chant, the room responded.

The writhing shadows recoiled, hissing and dissipating upon contact with our protective circle. The haunting wails of the wraiths grew fainter, their forms disintegrating like smoke caught in a breeze.

Midas, looking worn but resolute, continued to speak, adding his voice to ours. Each member of our team was now connected, both vocally and spiritually. The bond between us was tangible, our collective determination forming an unbreakable chain.

The portal, once frenetic with activity, began to calm, its wild pulsations slowing. The edges that had once looked jagged and menacing now started to smooth out, the dark tendrils retracting.

As the final word of the chant was spoken, there was a blinding flash of light, followed by an ear-splitting boom. And then, as suddenly as it had all begun, the room was still, the portal dormant once more, the shadows seemingly vanquished.

Gasping for breath, we all collapsed to the ground, drained but alive.

The floor beneath us vibrated, a low hum filling our ears, while the walls seemed to pulse with an energy all their own. It was as though the entire Leaf Academy was resonating with our intent.

But Ollie was still there.

Rather, the being that had taken his form, looked agitated.

His eyes, once brimming with malice, now held a hint of desperation. He began muttering words of his own, countering our chant.

The sounds he made were guttural, dark, and eerily discordant. It was clear that he wasn't going to let go of his hold on the portal without a fight. At one moment, the portal shone so brightly it was hard to look at, the next it dimmed to an almost imperceptible glimmer. It seemed to be reacting to the dueling energies, caught amid a power struggle it didn't ask for.

With each surge of power from Ollie, the temperature would drop precipitously, our breath visible in the chilling air. But as we picked up our chants again, and they grew louder, warmth would seep back, pushing back the cold.

It was exhausting, mentally and physically.

I could see the strain on everyone's faces, beads of sweat forming on their brows despite the cold. Macie's grip on Jericho's arm tightened, her face pale but determined. Sierra's voice wavered occasionally, but she soldiered on, her gaze fixed on the portal, willing it to obey.

The force in the room grew so strong that it became tangible. Papers fluttered, the old furniture creaked and groaned, and at one point, a gust of wind so powerful blew through the room that I had to shield my face.

It was Midas, summoning strength from some deep, inner reserve, who tipped the scales. Breaking from the chant for just a moment, he shouted, "Listen to me! You will not take any more from us! Ollie, if there's any part of you left, fight it!"

His voice boomed, echoing throughout the room, resonating with a power and conviction that I had never heard before. It was more than just words; it was a challenge, a declaration of war.

The figure that mirrored Ollie shuddered violently, the dark pits that were its eyes narrowing. An inhuman growl rumbled from its throat, filling the room with a sound so chilling it froze the blood in my veins.

For a brief, heart-stopping moment, everything stood still. The tension was a palpable force, pressing down on all of us. Then, as if answering Midas's call, a flicker of recognition—of humanity—passed over the entity's face.

But just as quickly, it vanished, replaced by a fury that seemed to ripple through the very air around us. The room grew colder, the oppressive darkness pressing in even more.

Midas, however, stood his ground, his gaze unwavering as he locked eyes with the entity. There was a determination there, a fire that even this malevolent force couldn't extinguish.

The team took up his cry, the combined force of our voices overpowering Ollie's dark incantations. With a final, concerted effort, the room was filled with a radiant light, and the oppressive energy was forced out, leaving behind a silence so profound it was deafening.

Gasping for breath, our team looked around. The portal was calm once more, its once wild energies tamed. Ollie, or the dark force that had been using his form, had vanished.

We had held our ground, but it was a reminder that the battle for the Leaf Academy was far from over.

Chapter Fourteen—Macie

The aftermath of our confrontation in the portal room was a swirling mix of emotions. Relief, exhaustion, and the creeping fear of the unknown were still ahead. I could feel the residual energy from the portal, like the low hum of electricity, prickling the back of my neck.

I suddenly worried about Sherman. When I got a chance, I'd have to go check on my good boy. Hopefully he was sleeping through all this paranormal craziness.
The room felt both foreign and familiar. The walls seemed to pulse with life, whispers from the past echoing in my ears.

"Is everyone alright?" I asked, my voice trembling. I felt a protective urge, especially toward Sierra, who had exposed herself to so much during the vision and chant.

"Just a bit shaken, but I'm good," Jericho replied, wrapping an arm around my shoulders for comfort. Everyone checked in and reported they were okay. It felt grounding, saying we were alright; it was a tether to the present.

Cassidy was inspecting the now dormant portal, her fingers grazing the ancient symbols.
"It's not over," she murmured, a hint of foreboding in her voice. "This was just a precursor. We've silenced it temporarily, but it's still very much active."

Panic welled up inside me, but before it could take hold, a faint, ghostly light illuminated the room. It wasn't coming from any external source but seemed to be radiating from the walls themselves. But it wasn't the ethereal glow that had my heart racing. The walls were no longer walls but transparent, shimmering barriers. And beyond them, a multitude of figures, faces twisted in agony and despair, their hands reaching out toward us, trapped.

"Do you see them?" Sierra whispered; her voice barely audible. I nodded, paralyzed by the sight. "Oh God. So many of them."

Midas clenched his fists. "Innocent souls. All the souls who've been trapped here over the years."

I wanted to believe that but what if it was a trap. "Are you sure? Could this be a trick?"
And then, the most horrifying realization hit. Among those faces, I recognized one. My sister. She was there among the former students, teachers, and goodness knows who else who had vanished without a trace during their time here. The weight of the academy's dark history bore down on me like never before.

"Jocelyn?" I cried as I walked toward the wall. Nobody stopped me. "I've been taking care of Sherman. I kept him, sister."

"I don't think she can hear you. This appears to be some sort of purgatory," Cassidy whispered, her eyes filled with tears. "She doesn't belong here. None of them do. And it's all centered around this portal."

The ghastly illumination from the walls intensified. That's when the murmurs started, soft and hesitant at first, growing into a cacophony of voices, all speaking at once. Desperate pleas, cries of anguish, and incoherent ramblings blended, creating a symphony of sorrow. I couldn't see Jocelyn anymore. Not fully. She was behind someone else, but she was there. I couldn't stop crying.

"Sister. I'm sorry I am sorry this happened to you.."

"We have to free her," Aaron declared, his face etched with determination.

"How? We don't even know how they got trapped in the first place," Jericho responded, trying to keep his voice steady.

"We'll have to open the portal, once and then close it forever," Cassidy asserted, "It's the epicenter of everything."

"We can't open it," Chris argued. But just as we began to discuss the path forward, another figure began to materialize. Not trapped behind the walls but forming right in front of the portal. A silhouette darker than the deepest shadows, its form constantly shifting, never settling.

A voice, dripping with malice, echoed through the room, *"You think you can stop what's been set in motion? This is only the beginning."*

I felt a chill, more profound than the cold air around us. The battle for the Leaf Academy had entered its most terrifying phase, and we were at the heart of it.

The silhouette in front of the portal began to solidify, taking on a more defined shape. The shimmering barriers around us darkened, the trapped souls becoming mere silhouettes, their agonized cries growing distant.

The figure was older than Ollie, more weathered, with eyes that glowed a piercing blue. His clothes, tattered and torn, floated around him, giving him an otherworldly appearance.

He looked at us with a mix of amusement and disdain. *"You think your feeble attempts will change anything?"* he sneered. The room seemed to close in on us as he spoke, the walls pulsating to his words.

Jericho, trying to maintain some semblance of control, took a step forward. "We're here to help Jocelyn, to close this portal, and to free those trapped here. Step aside, Ollie."

A cold, cruel laugh escaped Ollie's lips. *"Ollie? How he amuses me. Do you think I am the mastermind here? I am but a servant, a vessel. The true power lies beyond this portal, and you have no idea what you're dealing with. Go ahead. Open it."*

Cassidy tried to reason with him. "Ollie, we know about the Nalusa Falaya, the shadow beings. We know the academy was built on a sacred site. Tell us what you know, and help us make this right. You're in there somewhere, Ollie. I know you were only a boy when they took you, but you can help us."

Ollie's gaze drifted to Cassidy, a glint of recognition in his eyes. But it was quickly replaced by malice. *"You can't make it right. The damage is done. And soon, they will be free. You can't stop them. They're coming."*

The portal began to glow, casting an eerie light on Ollie's face. Shadows, darker and more menacing than before, began to emerge from the portal, swirling around Ollie, and enveloping him.
We braced ourselves, knowing that we were on the precipice of something monumental. The fight for the academy, for the souls trapped here, and perhaps even for the world, was about to begin in earnest.

The intensity in the room reached a fever pitch. With every passing second, the portal seemed to widen, drawing in the ambient energy, and casting an ever-deepening shadow. Every light source began to flicker and sputter, struggling against the overpowering darkness.

Midas, recovering from his earlier ordeal, yelled above the chaos, "We need to close this portal now, or we'll be overwhelmed!"

"I thought we had to open it!" I shouted at him. I couldn't hide my confusion. I suddenly started to believe no one knew what they were doing.

Jericho, gathering his strength, began to channel a bright, almost blinding light from his palms, aiming it directly at the portal. The light seemed to push against the darkness, creating a temporary barrier. "I can't hold them off forever!" he shouted.
In that dark, desperate moment, a glimmer of hope emerged.

Aaron stepped forward, the ancient chant he had taught us earlier resonating strongly from deep within his chest. "Join me!" he commanded. As we added our voices to his, the room seemed to vibrate with the combined energy of our intent.

It wasn't just a chant; it was our collective wail to protect, to save, and to overcome.
The portal's glow wavered, the sinister shadows recoiling. I could feel the tug of war, a literal battle of light against darkness. The figures behind the walls became more pronounced, their cries growing louder, pleading for release.

"We need to give it everything we've got! For Jocelyn!" I yelled; my voice filled with determination.

Sierra closed her eyes, murmuring under her breath. I could see the air shimmer around her, taking on a silver hue. *Strange. I've never seen auras before.* From her, a force emanated, joining our collective energies, and magnifying them.

Ollie, or whatever was left of him, screamed in defiance. "You cannot break what's been established for centuries!"

With each repetition, the pull of the portal weakened, the shadows shrinking back.
 It felt like an eternity, but the darkness was receding. The portal, once a vibrant beacon of malice, started to close, slowly but surely. With a final, determined push of our combined energies, it sealed shut, leaving only a faint outline on the floor.

The room was suddenly filled with a calm light, the walls returning to their solid state. The trapped souls were no longer visible, but their presence was still palpable, perhaps now resting or waiting for their ultimate release.

I collapsed, drained, my energy spent. The others looked equally exhausted. But at that moment, we also felt a shared sense of triumph, even if it was temporary.

"We did it," Cassidy whispered, her voice filled with awe. "Didn't we? Did we do it?"
But Midas, ever the realist, replied, "We've closed the door temporarily, but we still need to decide on how to proceed.

Should we open it? Is that going to set them free? Or should we lock it forever. I don't know."

The battle at the Leaf Academy was far from over, but we had taken a step towards victory. A step toward setting Jocelyn free.

Or so I hoped.

Chapter Fifteen – Jericho

The wind had a gentle chill as we stepped outside, a stark contrast to the stifling atmosphere of the portal room. The grounds of the Leaf Academy spread out before us, bathed in the silver glow of the moon. Here, amidst the whispering trees and rustling leaves, it was easier to think, to breathe.

We formed a circle, each of us lost in our thoughts, processing everything that had just transpired.

"I don't think we should open that portal," I began, my voice firm. "Whatever's behind it is more powerful, more malevolent than anything we've ever faced. It's not the same as opening and closing an actual door, Macie. It's not just about locking it, it's about ensuring it never gets opened again."

Macie nodded her head sadly. "I don't know what to think about any of it. I just want to help my sister."

I nodded, the weight of responsibility heavy on my shoulders. "There's a difference between facing our fears and recklessly dancing with the devil. Opening that portal might unleash something we can't control, something we can't fight. I can't help but think of Pandora's box."

To everyone's astonishment, it was Aaron who spoke up in agreement. "Jericho is right. My ancestors warned about the dangers of meddling with forces beyond our understanding. The portal isn't just a door; it's a bridge to a place we shouldn't tread. It's another dimension."

Cassidy sighed, brushing a strand of hair from her face. "But Jocelyn and all those other souls..."

"That's the thing," I interjected, "Jocelyn didn't pass through the portal. She died here, on these grounds. The others? They're victims of the academy's dark past. We can help them, not by opening doors to unknown realms, but by addressing the root of the evil. By banishing the Nalusa Falaya, aka the October People, once and for all."

Sierra leaned against a tree, thoughtful. "So, you're saying, we focus on moving the spirits on, to help them find peace. Jocelyn and the others. But after we defeat these shadows. That's the strategy."

I nodded, "Exactly. We cleanse the academy, purify it of the malevolent forces, and after help the trapped souls move on. We shouldn't do anything to open that portal."
Midas ran a hand through his hair, clearly conflicted. "Fine. It's risky, but at least it's a plan. One that doesn't involve jumping headfirst into the unknown."

Cassidy looked around at each of us, gauging our determination. "It's decided then. We focus on cleansing this place."

The wind picked up slightly, rustling the leaves in what almost sounded like a sigh of relief. The academy, with all its secrets and shadows, loomed in front of us. But with unity and purpose, we felt ready to face whatever came our way.

The path forward was crystal clear. I hugged Macie and kissed the top of her head.
"I worry about Sherman. I shouldn't have brought him." I walked over to a nearby window. I studied the SUV. "He's not

barking, nor is he tearing up the vehicle. He's asleep Macie. I think he's alright."

Macie breathed a sigh of relief.

With the Leaf Academy's towering silhouette ahead, each of us knew the roles we had to play in the impending ritual. As the shadows from the structure encroached upon us, we fortified ourselves, determined to drive away the darkness that had held sway for too long.

Sierra, reaching into her bag, produced a pouch filled with black salt. "This salt," she started, her voice solemn, "is powerful in warding off negative energy." She paused to demonstrate, sprinkling a pinch of the dark grains into her hand. "After each room is cleansed, I'll use this to seal the doorway, creating a barrier the October People can't penetrate."

Beside her, Aaron was preparing chalk for use in making Choctaw symbols. "The symbols I'll be using," he explained with reverence in his voice. "They represent protection and banishment. I'll mark each door frame after Sierra, ensuring the barrier is doubly fortified."

I took a deep breath, absorbed their words, and drew bundles of sage from my bag. Midas seemed to have gotten himself back in check. He was our leader again and I was glad to see it.

"No way are they going to lay down and let us do this. No one runs off alone. We do this together, we leave together."

I handed a bundle of white sage to Macie, and we both set the ends alight. The fragrant smoke began to curl upwards, filling the night with its cleansing aroma. "The sage will drive away any lingering negative energy, making way for Sierra and Aaron's protections," I said. "Is everyone ready?"

Macie answered with a hopeful smile, "I'm ready, Jericho."

With steadfast faces, everyone consented. This one was for all the marbles.

Starting from the topmost floor, our group proceeded with a single-minded purpose, moving from room to room. The academy's walls seemed to whisper secrets and long-forgotten memories, but as we advanced, the atmosphere became tense, charged with a defiant energy.

The first few rooms went smoothly, the sage's smoke and our determination driving away the shadowy vestiges that clung to the corners. However, as we delved deeper, we began to face resistance. At first, it was subtle; a sudden drop in temperature, a fleeting shadow darting away from the cleansing smoke, or an inexplicable gust of wind attempting to snuff out the burning sage.

In one particular room, as I waved the sage in the air, a chilling wail erupted, echoing through the room and making the hairs on the back of my neck stand on end. The room's windows rattled, and unseen forces seemed to push back against our efforts. I could feel the weight of dozens of unseen eyes on me, their anger palpable.
"We're not wanted here," Macie murmured, her voice shaky but her resolve firm. Holding her sage high, she recited a chant that seemed to calm the room momentarily, allowing Sierra to step in with her black salt.

But the further we went, the stronger the paranormal pushback became. There was a room where our torches and flashlights flickered, casting eerie, dancing shadows on the walls as if the spirits were trying to hide from the sage's light. Another room was stifling hot, the very walls seeming to sweat and resist our efforts.

In yet another chamber, as Aaron started drawing his protective symbols, an invisible hand smeared them, erasing his work faster than he could complete it. It took the combined efforts of Sierra and me, chanting in unison, to finally create a barrier strong enough to allow Aaron to finish.

As we made our way to one of the final rooms on the floor, an overwhelming sense of dread enveloped us. It was like walking into a wall of thick, icy fog. Every step became more burdensome, and the air was suffocatingly still. The room ahead looked no different from the others, but its door stood slightly ajar, revealing nothing but darkness beyond.

We approached cautiously, and as Cassidy pushed the door further open, an icy gust of wind swept out, extinguishing our torches, and plunging us into blackness.

Panic immediately set in, and we fumbled to relight our sources of illumination. When we did, the room revealed itself to be empty, save for a single figure standing in the center.

It was Ollie, or at least the entity that often took his form.

His silhouette flickered like an old television set with poor reception, and his eyes, usually so vacant, now blazed with an intense blue fire.

"You may cleanse every corner of this academy," he hissed, his voice echoing around us, "but you cannot banish me. I am in this place. I am its past, its present, and its future. LEAVE NOW!"

With a swift motion, he raised his hands, and the shadows in the room responded, creeping along the walls, the floor, and the ceiling, swirling and forming menacing shapes, figures that seemed to scream silently in anguish.

From the darkest corners of the room, the shadows began to elongate, stretching and snaking their way toward us. The atmosphere grew denser, each breath feeling like a weight upon our chests.

The room seemed to pulsate with malevolence, and before we could react, a particularly thick tendril of shadow wrapped itself around Macie's ankle. "No!" I screamed at the darkness.

"Jericho!" Her scream pierced the air as the shadowy coil tightened its grip and began dragging her backward, her fingers scraping the floor in a desperate attempt to resist. The room echoed with her cries, each shadow appearing to revel in her terror.

"Macie!" I shouted, my heart racing.
Without thinking, I lunged forward, my hand reaching out for her. With every ounce of strength and determination, I focused my energy, channeling the power I had harnessed over the years.

"In God's name, release her!" A brilliant, white light emanated from my palm, slicing through the dark tendril and releasing its grip on Macie.

She half collapsed on the floor, gasping for air, her face pale. I pulled her close, shielding her as the rest of the team rallied around us, forming a protective barrier.

Ollie's mocking laughter filled the room. "You can have her. I have Jocelyn," he sneered.

Sierra, ever the brave one, stepped forward, clutching her bag of black salt. "This is our academy now," she declared, her voice steady, "and you will no longer terrorize its halls."

Ollie laughed, a sound that was both eerie and filled with malice.
That hope was our driving force, our anchor in the storm.

It would have to be enough.

Chapter Sixteen—Aaron

The portal room, once a nexus of chaotic energies, was our battleground, our focal point in this war against the shadows. There was no getting away from that. I had to take a moment to gather my thoughts and reconnect with my higher power. To be honest, I didn't want to be here but for Jocelyn, I would endure hell itself.

Hopefully, that would not be a requirement today.

As we descended into the room, Chris and Joshua immediately began to assemble the RYDER headset. The room's atmosphere, thick with residual energy, seemed to shimmer under RYDER's augmented reality lens. The glowing interface projected onto the lenses, displaying swirls and streams of energies, making visible what was previously sensed or felt.

"We need to know exactly where to bolster our defenses," Chris remarked, adjusting the RYDER to get a clearer read on the room. "We know this will help. It proved that already."

"Yes, we also proved that the dark ones have the ability to use RYDER's battery so let's keep an eye on that," Midas added ruefully.

The screen showed us a dynamic representation of the room's energy flow. The portal stood out, a swirling vortex of intense activity, while other areas of the room pulsed with softer lights, indicative of residual energies and memories.

As Cassidy and Jericho began lighting candles at the points RYDER indicated as critical, I felt the atmosphere shift slightly, responding to the flames. The gentle light of the candles cast a warm, soothing glow, cutting through the room's oppressive feel.

Sierra approached next, clutching her pouch of black salt. Guided by the visual cues displayed by RYDER, she began to sprinkle her salt with precision, each granule sparkling momentarily as it landed.

I followed suit.

Drawing from my Choctaw heritage, I started etching protective symbols onto the door frames and walls. RYDER's overlay guided my hand, ensuring each sign was perfectly aligned with the room's energy flow.

A sense of purpose filled the room. The methodical process, each step guided and enhanced by RYDER, felt like weaving an intricate protective net.

We were claiming this space, pushing back against the shadowy invaders. The real confrontation was yet to come, but for now, we were laying the foundation, preparing ourselves for the challenge ahead.

With the room now fortified with our protections, I couldn't help but notice how the atmosphere inside had begun to shift. It was no longer as foreboding as it had been, though the energy around the portal remained dense and volatile.

Dare we hope to achieve what we'd come for?

I heard Chris swearing under his breath. The RYDER readings started to behave erratically. Numbers fluctuated, graphs peaked and troughed without rhythm, and the augmented reality visualization showed a pulsating turmoil around the portal.

"Watch out, guys," Chris warned, adjusting the RYDER's settings to stabilize the readings. It wasn't working. "Something's reacting to our setup."

Cassidy, standing closest to the portal, took a cautious step back, her eyes locked onto the swirling energies. "It feels like... resistance. As if the portal's trying to push back against our protections."

Jericho, flames dancing in his hands, nodded in agreement. "It's a response, alright. But whether it's a defensive mechanism or a challenge, that's hard to tell."

Macie, looking at the RYDER screen over Chris's shoulder, pointed to a series of symbols that began to emerge around the portal's edges. "What are those? They weren't there before."

"They look like some ancient script," Sierra mused, squinting to get a clearer view.

I recognized them immediately. "It's the language of my ancestors, but they are rarely used—or seen," I breathed, feeling a mix of pride and apprehension. "The portal is communicating. It's responding to us. The ancestors are with us." I let out a whoop and it echoed through the room. Macie smiled at my celebration. Even though it was short-lived, I did feel better.

Drawing a deep breath, I prepared myself to continue.

This was our chance to engage, to bridge the gap, and perhaps find some answers. But it was also a leap into the unknown, a step fraught with potential dangers. Either way, we couldn't back down now.

Taking my place in front of the portal, I began to speak, uttering words passed down through generations, addressing the very essence of the gateway in front of us. Normally these words wouldn't have been spoken in public, not in the presence of non-Choctaw, but I had permission to do so. Besides, these were my friends. We were all here because we loved Jocelyn and this terror needed to stop.

The portal's resonance grew louder, the humming vibrating the very floor beneath our feet. The room's ambient temperature started to drop rapidly, each exhale forming clouds of condensation in front of our faces.

The RYDER's screen displayed a vibrant dance of colors, representing the fluctuating energies around the portal. As I continued my dialogue with the ancient force, the shadows around the room grew more pronounced, their movements clearer and more agitated on the RYDER screen.

Chris looked up from the RYDER, his face a mask of concern. "The energy levels are off the charts. Aaron, whatever you're doing, it's causing a massive reaction." I didn't need the device to tell me that. I could feel it in my bones, in the electric charge that coursed through the air.

It was as if the portal, or the entity behind it, was waking up, recognizing a kindred spirit attempting to bridge the divide.

Yes, there was a spirit here. A spirit I knew. We all knew.

I took a moment to collect my thoughts, then resumed my chant, but this time, with more force, trying to impose my will upon the swirling maelstrom in front of me. The shadows seemed to react to my intent, their swirling forms taking on more discernible shapes, no longer just fleeting wraiths but entities with purpose and intent.

Behind me, I heard Sierra whispering words of encouragement, her voice filled with a calm determination.

Macie's grip tightened on Jericho's arm. As a unit, our combined strength grew, meeting the challenge presented by the portal head-on.

And then, through the cacophony of visual and auditory stimuli that the RYDER was capturing, a new sound emerged.

It was faint at first but grew steadily louder—a chorus of voices, ethereal and ancient, chanting in unison with me.

Through the RYDER's lens, I saw the shadows recede slightly, forming a semicircle around the portal. They appeared to be watching, waiting, as if assessing our intent.
We had made contact.

The next steps were critical, and we had to tread carefully. This wasn't just about opening or closing a door; it was about understanding the force behind it and finding a way to coexist.

I paused for a moment, my heart racing, taking in the energy that enveloped the room. Standing directly in front of the portal, I drew a deep breath and began addressing it in the ancient language of the Choctaw. The words flowed from my lips, each syllable imbued with years of tradition and respect.

As I spoke, Chris activated a feature on RYDER that translated my words into English, projecting them onto the screen.

The team followed along; their eyes fixed on the unfolding dialogue.

"Ancient spirits, guardians of the threshold, hear me. We come in peace, seeking understanding and harmony. Show us the way to mend the rift, to heal the wounds of time."

As the words filled the room, an unexpected calm descended upon us. The agitated energy from the portal seemed to ebb, replaced by a more contemplative force. The shadows that had earlier displayed aggression now appeared curious, their forms dancing and merging around the periphery of the room.

On the RYDER screen, faint images began to materialize, echoing my words.

Visions of serene landscapes, the sun setting over the Choctaw lands, and figures from the distant past. This was how it used to be here. Before the October People and before the builders of the school came and deliberately woke them up. It was as if the portal was showing us memories, fragments of its history.

The serenity was short-lived.
As the visions played out, a darker presence emerged on the screen. The entity was unknowable, its form shifting, never settling, its essence a vortex of darkness. Its voice, though not audible in the traditional sense, resonated within our minds.

Interloper, why do you seek to bridge our worlds? What do you hope to achieve?

I steadied myself, replying with clarity and conviction. "We seek to heal, to understand, to right the wrongs of the past. The bridge between our worlds has been tainted, causing suffering and anguish. We aim to restore balance here."

The entity seemed to ponder my words, its form constantly shifting, reflecting a turmoil of emotions. It was a tense standoff, one where the fate of the academy and possibly much more hung in the balance.

The room was thick with anticipation as RYDER's screen began to flicker.
Slowly, the portal displayed a procession of images, each more haunting and vibrant than the previous. Scenes that resonated with the ancient history of the Choctaw tribe appeared before us—there were joyful celebrations, gut-wrenching tragedies, and spiritual rituals, eventually culminating in moments of tranquility.

The very atmosphere of the room seemed to shift, becoming thick with voices. They were fleeting, ephemeral, reminiscent of a radio constantly searching for a signal. Their existence between the veils of our world and the next made them almost intangible, but they were there.

"Sierra set up the spirit box near the portal. Maybe we can enhance these voices," I instructed.

"On it," Sierra responded efficiently, positioning the device to catch any spectral communications.

However, before the spirit box could capture anything, a voice, resonating with clarity, enveloped us. It seemed to emanate from both the portal and the very air around us. "Macie..." the voice whispered. Our collective gaze was drawn to the RYDER screen, where a face we all recognized appeared – Jocelyn's.

Macie, her face pale and her eyes wide, took hesitant steps closer to the RYDER. "Jocelyn? Is that you?"

Jocelyn's voice, heartbreaking and ethereal, echoed from the spirit box. "Protect... you... the academy... it's not... safe..."

Macie's voice trembled, "Jocelyn, what are you saying? What do you mean?"

"The shadows... they're controlled... used as puppets... Don't trust... it's deceptive..."

The weight of Jocelyn's revelation hung heavy in the air as her image slowly dissipated from the RYDER screen. Her voice, imbued with an emotion I couldn't quite place, resounded once more, "Macie, don't leave. Please. Stay with me."

In the profound silence that followed, Macie, completely overwhelmed, stumbled and was caught in Jericho's supportive embrace.

Tears cascaded down her face, reflecting the pain of a sister's bond strained by the realms of the living and the dead.

I had never lost a sister, but I lost the woman I love. I wanted to cry too, but I had to keep it together. We were close to seeing this through. Somehow, the protections we used had kept the darkness at bay, it even allowed Jocelyn to speak to us, even though her message was broken and unclear.

That was something at least.

Chapter Seventeen—Macie

The chill that settled over the room after Jocelyn's warning was stifling. My heart was in turmoil, a blend of fear, hope, and a fierce determination to see this through. The very air felt electric, charged with anticipation.

If this was to be our final confrontation, I was ready. I would set her free or...no. I'm not even going to consider that anymore. Jericho needs me. I could never do what I planned to do. It would be wrong. I would literally be dead wrong.

I should have told someone what I had been thinking. I really should have, but I'd pulled through the depression and the grief. Or so I hoped.

It was at that moment that I knew I would never hide my struggles again. Not from the people I loved and I did love these people. Every single one of them. Especially Jericho. The only reason I'd pushed him away was because I didn't want him to know the truth about my thoughts. About my intentions. No more. I would never lie to him again.

With every step I took toward the portal, the energy seemed to shift. I felt brave and ready to face the devil himself for Jocelyn's eternal peace. One day I would see her again and we'd never be separated.

The RYDER screen, which had gone blank after Jocelyn's visage disappeared, flickered back to life.

The ominous shadows were clearer to see now, their movements more deliberate and synchronized. I couldn't be sure but it appeared that one of them, the tallest, was mockingly waving at me.

I felt an arm around me, Jericho's reassuring presence grounding me. "I'm here," he whispered, his voice strained with worry. "You won't face this alone." I smiled at him but my attention was locked on the screen. The shadows started to meld together, forming a colossal figure, a silhouette of pure darkness, the entity behind Ollie and all the torment.
"It's getting stronger," Cassidy warned, her voice full of authority.

The floor beneath us vibrated, the very walls of the academy moaning in distress. This entity, this force of malevolence, was no ordinary spirit. It was ancient and powerful, and now, it was aware of us. And it would love nothing more than to bury us under a pile of rubble.
Aaron stepped forward, brandishing a talisman he had kept hidden until now. "I hoped we wouldn't need this, but now..." he trailed off, watching the portal intently. He placed the lustrous black stone near the portal.

Suddenly, the RYDER gave a piercing alert, and the screen displayed readings off the charts. A cacophony of disembodied voices enveloped us—cries of pain, laughter, and whispers, all escalating into an overwhelming noise.

"God! What is that?" Sierra yelled over the frenzy. Why was she even asking? It was evil, the evil thing that lived here. Along with the sound came all the emotions. It was as if the portal was utilizing every trapped soul, every voice, every memory in a frenzied attempt to drown us in despair. I felt terror, hatred, sadness. I felt it all.

I could feel hands, cold and ethereal, trying to grab at me and pull me towards the portal.

"Jericho?" I asked, but I'd been snatched away yet again. How many times did this make?

In my peripheral vision, the shadows were materializing, becoming more corporeal, their forms dark and twisted. One, in particular, reached out for me, its fingers only inches from my face. A scream was lodged in my throat, terror rooting me to the spot.

"No! Leave her alone!" That's when Jericho acted.

In one swift motion, he summoned a burst of light, banishing the immediate shadows and freeing me from their grasp. But this was just the beginning because the room was alive with movement, shadows darting, swirling, attacking, and the very fabric of the academy seemed to be coming apart.

This was the most terrifying paranormal investigation I'd ever been a part of. Had we even needed equipment? This place was the epicenter of hell.

Sierra began to pray. "Guide us, oh Lord! Protect us from this evil!" Her voice, strong and unwavering, provided a beacon of hope amidst the chaos.

As the battle raged on, the portal pulsated, its light throbbing like a heartbeat. The true fight, the ultimate showdown, was approaching.

The room, which moments ago had been a battlefield of shadows and light, now bore witness to a standoff. At the heart of it all was the portal, now more volatile than ever, its energies swirling like a maelstrom.

With each passing second, the entity seemed to draw strength from the portal, its form becoming more pronounced and menacing. A shape reminiscent of a distorted human figure, but on a grander, more terrifying scale, stood poised to break through fully into our realm.

Chris shouted above the din, "The RYDER's picking up massive energy spikes! We need to shut this portal down now! I think this is becoming too dangerous, Midas!"

But it wouldn't be that simple. We needed to confront this entity, dispel it, and ensure the safety of the academy and the souls trapped within its walls.

Midas barked back, "We can't! Not yet. Jocelyn is still on the other side!"

Sierra, braving the forefront, tried to communicate with the entities blocking the portal.
"What do you want? Let them go!" Her voice wavered but she held her ground.

The entity's response, channeled through the spirit box, was chilling. "Bound... betrayed... freedom..." The voice was an amalgamation of many, fluctuating between tones of rage, sorrow, and desperation.

I felt a pull, a connection. "You were trapped here," I whispered, realization dawning. "But taking innocent souls, torturing them, that won't set you free. What you're doing isn't right!"

Aaron added, his voice resonating with ancient knowledge, "Nalusa Falaya! I, Aaron of the Choctaw speak to you! The cycle of pain and revenge will bind you further. We can help, but you need to let go of these souls. They don't belong here! They don't belong to you!"

For a moment, everything seemed to stand still. The swirling energies, the dancing shadows, the pulsating portal—all paused, as if the very fabric of time had stretched taut.

Then, in a voice that was at once soft yet filled with sorrow, the entity responded.

"Help... me..."

Was this a trap? Was this happening?

The words hung in the air; their implications were vast. The shadows seemed to retreat, the oppressive atmosphere lightening ever so slightly. We had a window, an opportunity to set things right. I could feel hope for the first time in forever.

With newfound determination, the team rallied together, ready for the final act, this would be the culmination of our journey at the Leaf Academy. We had one shot to free the trapped souls, appease the entity, and seal the portal.

Emerging from the darkest corner of the room, Ollie's familiar form took shape, his eyes gleaming with an unsettling mix of malice and desperation.

As he stepped forward, it was clear this wasn't the boyish spirit we'd encountered before but a version distorted and corrupted by the malevolent entity.

"Want to make a deal?" he drawled, his voice dripping with both menace and mockery.
We all exchanged uneasy glances, sensing the trap but unable to discern its true nature. Who the hell was he talking to? Midas took the lead.

"No. We're not making any deals. None of us. Let them go. You have no right to keep Jocelyn here. This is your only chance. If you refuse, it will be worse for you."

Ollie laughed at that threat. "One of you must stay. The rest of you can leave this place, unharmed, untouched," Ollie said, his eyes scanning each of our faces. "But in exchange, one must stay. A trade. A life for a life."

"No!" Midas shouted, his voice echoing throughout the room. "We're not playing by your rules anymore, Ollie. Or whoever the hell you are, devil! No one is staying. We're ending this, here and now!"

Ollie's grin widened, his now yellow teeth appearing unnaturally sharp. "Oh, are you? Are you ending this? Without even knowing the rules of the game?"

As tension filled the room, a sudden rush of energy swept through us, and for a moment, the oppressive darkness seemed to lift.

Then, through the RYDER's spirit box, Jocelyn's voice emerged, cutting through the darkness and Ollie's jeering laughter. "Don't listen to him. Ollie's true self is buried deep beneath that entity's influence. You need to reach him, remind him of who he was."

I clung to her words, my heart racing. "How, Jocelyn? How do we reach him?"

The spirit box crackled, and a series of images began to play out on the RYDER monitor.

Scenes from Ollie's past, moments of innocence, joy, and love. "Remind him of these memories, the true essence of his being," Jocelyn's voice implored. "It's the entity's vulnerability. Its grip on Ollie can be weakened. You can free him."

Armed with this newfound knowledge and driven by a surge of hope, we turned our focus back to Ollie, ready to challenge the dark force that had ensnared him and the academy.

We were not just fighting for our survival but for Ollie's lost soul and every trapped spirit within the academy's walls. The candles Cassidy and Jericho had lit earlier began to flicker wildly, despite there being no breeze. The walls themselves seemed to pulsate, exuding a palpable sense of malevolence.

Suddenly, the room plunged into a chilling darkness, save for the few candle flames that struggled to remain alight. Shadows began to form and solidify around us, their edges defined yet ever shifting, like a mirage.

Their whispers grew louder, a cacophony of voices echoing pain, anger, and sorrow.

In the center stood Ollie, or the dark reflection of him, surrounded by the most powerful of these shadow beings. They moved in tandem with him, reacting to his every gesture and mood.

It was clear they were all connected, part of a single, terrifying force. For the first time, I had genuine sympathy for the child Ollie had once been.

Yes, he had been a child. A boy. Just a little boy.

He had a mother and father. Dreams and hopes. He had heroes and aspirations. That is until he'd been tricked, probably by the simple act of accepting a feather. But was there anything left of him?

One by one, the shadows lunged at us, attempting to disorient and isolate us. Their touch was like an icy grip, sapping our warmth and strength. We all tried to counteract their advances with our protective tools, but it felt as though we were vastly outnumbered.

As Ollie began to chant in an ancient, indecipherable language, the floor beneath us started to tremble. Cracks appeared, revealing an eerie, bluish glow from below. It felt as though the very foundation of the academy was about to give way, to drag us into an abyss of unknown horrors.
Desperation clawed at my insides, but amid the chaos, the memory of Jocelyn's guidance and the knowledge she imparted shone like a beacon.

We needed to unify, to combine our strengths, to remind Ollie of his humanity and pull him from the grasp of the malevolent force.

Midas gripped my hand. Soon we were all holding hands. "You cannot break us. We're here for Jocelyn. You cannot hold her any longer! You can chant all you want. Our love, our unity, is stronger than you!"

Gathering our resolve, Aaron began to counter Ollie's chant. We all joined him.

Our combined voices rose above the din, carrying with them all the memories, hopes, and emotions we'd witnessed and felt. The battle between light and darkness, hope and despair, played out in a symphony of sound and energy, with the fate of the academy hanging in the balance.

Despite the overwhelming darkness and the seemingly insurmountable power of the shadows, a glimmer of hope began to emerge. It started as a small, almost imperceptible shift in the atmosphere. The cold, oppressive air started to warm slightly. The heavy, suffocating weight that pressed down on us began to lift.

Using RYDER, Chris amplified our collective energy, channeling it toward Ollie and the entity that held him. The augmented reality device displayed our progress, a visual representation of our fight against the overwhelming darkness. It showed bright connections between each of us, lines of energy weaving a protective web around the academy.

As our chants converged, a blinding light erupted from the center of our circle. It spread outwards, pushing back against the shadows, causing them to recoil and disintegrate upon contact. The room was filled with their agonized screams, each one fading into silence as the light overtook them.

Ollie, at the center of this maelstrom, appeared to be in intense pain.

I screamed at him. Not the entity but the little boy. "Ollie! Fight! This is your chance to be free! Fight, Ollie!" His body contorted in unnatural ways. I heard his bones snap like something I'd seen in a horror movie. He was struggling but he had not broken free yet.

He was moaning and screaming, his voice echoed with both his own and the dark entity's, locked in a battle for dominance.

As the light we'd created approached him, there was a moment of suspense—a silent plea in his eyes before he was enveloped, and then... silence.

The light receded, leaving the room in a soft glow. Ollie lay in the center, unconscious but breathing. The immediate threat was over, but the aftermath of the battle was all around us. The academy bore the scars of our confrontation, and the weight of the responsibility for what had transpired—and what was yet to come—settled heavily on our shoulders.

The dust settled, and the once vibrant energy of the room dulled to a calm stillness. The entire team, visibly exhausted, took a moment to gather themselves. Some sat on the floor, catching their breath; others stared at the now dormant portal, contemplating the events that had just transpired.

Macie slowly approached Ollie's motionless body, a mix of relief and sorrow evident in her eyes. "Is he...?" she began, her voice trailing off, not wanting to finish the thought.

Chris, using the RYDER device, checked Ollie's vitals.

"He's...he's a ghost," he confirmed. "He died a long time ago. Whatever happened to him, we can't change it but at least he's been freed."

Tears streamed down my face. I wasn't the only one crying. So was Midas only his tears were quiet.

"Ollie? Can you hear me?" Midas asked as he knelt a few feet away from the crumpled figure of Ollie, a long-dead boy.

Mesmerized, I watched the boy pick himself up and sit cross leg on the portal space. Yes, this child was a spirit, he lacked color and was mostly in black and white except for a bit of color in his cheeks and lips. His eyes were dark, but warm and full of fear.

He nodded his head to answer Midas. "It's time to go home, Ollie. Are you ready to go?"
Ollie rose to his feet. "I want my brother. Is he here? Has he gone home?" The child spoke with a soft accent. Irish, perhaps?

Sierra spoke as she stood next to Midas. "Yes, Ollie. Samuel has gone home. He says he's ready to play the game again. You know the one. The one you always play. Follow that beam of light. Step into the light and you'll be home."

As she spoke, a beam of light did appear at Ollie's feet. I wept even harder but was careful to keep quiet. No sense in terrifying the child further. He'd been locked in terror for longer than any of us had been alive.
"Really?" He slung his dark hair out of his eyes. "I can go?"

"Yes, you can go," Midas said with a smile. Without another word, Ollie stepped into the shaft of light and it immediately disappeared. Along with Ollie, dozens of orbs sailed up from the stone floor, other souls presumably all trapped by the October People, or as Aaron would call them, the Nalusa Falaya. All at once the orbs vanished up and out of the building.

Sierra, clutching her black salt, whispered a prayer of gratitude, her hands shaking slightly from the intensity of what we'd experienced, she began to sprinkle the salt on the portal. Aaron, meanwhile, carefully etched more of the chalk symbols near the portal, ensuring that nothing else could leave.

We'd done it. Somehow, with the help of the dead and the Light, we'd managed to push back the darkness and set the trapped souls free. It was an incredible feeling and yet I could not stop weeping.

Midas hugged Cassidy and whispered something in her ear. Everyone was hugging and thanking the heavens that we'd survived our time at the Leaf Academy.

The room was full of a new feeling. Not terror or an evil presence, but a collective sense of camaraderie. We'd done this together. Each of us no doubt was dead tired, even drained, but I experienced a renewed sense of purpose.

We had faced an unimaginable darkness and emerged victorious, but tomorrow was never promised.

I hadn't seen Jocelyn leave, but I knew she was gone. Gone to be with our family. Gone and free at least.

As Jericho held me, I pictured her smiling. I pictured her waving.

And that was enough.

Epilogue—Midas

The morning sun stretched its golden fingers across the grounds, its caress gentle, almost as if trying to heal the scars of the Leaf Academy.

Birds, which once hesitated to enter this space, now sang joyous tunes from the treetops. Everywhere I looked, there was life--flowers stretching up to the sky, and trees swaying with a newfound vigor.

I stood with the rest of the Gulf Coast Paranormal team at the edge of the grounds, taking in the beauty and peace that had settled over the place. A profound calm had replaced the previously palpable tension and dread. The air seemed lighter, purer.

Sierra, her eyes glistening with emotion, broke the silence. "Do you feel it? The tranquility? We did it, y'all."

I nodded, struggling to find the right words. "It's as if the very soul of this place has been healed."

Chris, always the skeptic, looked around, visibly softening. "It's hard to believe that this is the same academy where we faced so much darkness. I'm glad we'll never have to come back. Give me a residential case, any day of the week."

Cassidy took a deep breath, her eyes closed. "They're free," she whispered, the wind carrying her words. "Jocelyn, the countless other souls... they've found their peace."

Taking a moment to reflect on our journey, and the battles fought, both physically and emotionally, I felt a surge of pride for our team. We had faced one of our toughest challenges yet but standing here amidst the serene beauty of the Leaf Academy, it all felt worth it.

The peace wasn't just in the absence of shadows or the haunting cries.

It was in the very essence of the place – in every blade of grass, every fluttering leaf. The Leaf Academy had been reborn, its tormented past finally laid to rest. But that wouldn't change my mind. I bought this place for a purpose.

The deafening roar of the bulldozer's engine punctuated the still air as it powered up.
It felt strange to bring such a beastly machine to these serene grounds, but it was a necessary step in the healing process.

The old academy had been a locus of pain and suffering for far too long, and while we had managed to cleanse its spirit, the physical remnants needed to go.

Forever. Never to rise again.

As the bulldozer's massive blade made contact with the first wall, a cloud of dust arose, signaling the beginning of the end for the dilapidated structure. The walls, which had seen so much and housed countless dark secrets, crumbled under the force, giving way to a new era for these hallowed grounds.

Aaron, standing a safe distance away, watched with mixed emotions. I couldn't imagine what he must be feeling. This place, which had taken so much from his people, was being razed to the ground, yet the act wasn't about vengeance; it was about closure.

I prayed that he understood that.

The process would be long and methodical, the bulldozer would make its way through each section of the academy, reducing the once imposing structure to rubble.

Once it was done, Sierra wanted to return and salt the ground ensuring that the site would be protected from any lingering negative energies. I was totally on board with that.

"It's gone," Macie murmured, her eyes moist with tears, reflecting on the memories both harrowing and hopeful that the academy had given her. The Leaf Academy had claimed her sister, but Macie had helped to set her free.

I watched as another portion of the academy was cleared away. With its dismantling, I felt confident that the shadows that once roamed these grounds would never return.
The morning had dawned bright and clear, with a fresh wind signaling a new beginning. Today was the perfect day for this. The Leaf Academy would be no more, and in its place was a plot of land, rife with potential and history.

The bulldozed ground already looked like a scar on the landscape, a raw wound still healing. But there was one more thing to do. It was time to make this right. Put this land back in the hands of the people equipped to manage it.

Aaron had gathered members of his community to witness the handover of the land. This wasn't a transaction but rather a restorative act, a return of sacred grounds to those who held them dear.

The ceremony was simple yet profound. As the bulldozers did their work, I did mine.

Elders chanted in their native tongue, their voices melding harmoniously with the rustling of leaves and the chirping of birds. Their songs spoke of the land's ancient heritage, the spirits that roamed here, and the duty to protect and cherish it.

"The land has seen much pain," said Shining Ray, Aaron's uncle, his eyes deep and wise.

"But it's resilient, like our people. Today, it finds its way back to us. We will protect it."

Aaron nodded in agreement; his expression solemn. "Our fathers' land will once again be a place of silence and reverence."

Shining Ray placed a hand on Aaron's shoulder, offering a comforting squeeze. "It will be. With the spirits freed and the land cleansed, we'll ensure it remains a sanctuary, a testament to what was lost and what has been regained."

The gathering concluded with a shared meal, and members of the Gulf Coast Paranormal team and the Native American community came together in unity. The food, prepared using traditional recipes, was a bridge between the past and the present, reminding everyone present of the interconnectedness of all things.

As the day ended, the sun cast long shadows across the now-vacant plot. The land, once a place of horror and tragedy, had begun its journey toward healing and renewal. We stood staring at the land, still amazed at what occurred here.

"Good job, Big Brother." Sierra smiled at me, her fingers playing with the silver pendant around her neck. "We didn't just battle against malevolent spirits. We confronted the weight of history, the mistakes of the past, and our own personal demons. We will never forget Jocelyn. It's time you let her go too, Midas."

Macie, her eyes glistening with unshed tears, whispered, "Jocelyn's sacrifice, her love for you, for the team wasn't meant to bind you, Midas. It was an act of love. Don't let it become something else. Not again. True love never really dies."

I nodded in agreement and for the first time in as long as I could remember, I took a deep breath and felt the weight of her loss leave me. Cassidy studied me, her green eyes fastened on mine but she said nothing. Only smiled in agreement.

I came back the following day with Aaron. As the sun began its ascent, painting the sky in hues of orange and pink, we stood together on the cleared land. The breeze was gentle, carrying with it the earthy scent of the forest and the distant murmur of the river.

He closed his eyes for a moment, taking in the serenity, trying to connect one last time. "Thank you, Midas. Thank you for what you did. I know Jocelyn would have liked this too."

"I am sorry, Aaron. If there'd been a second, even a half second, I would have not given her the chance to do what she did. But I cannot say I am not grateful. Jocelyn gave her life for me, but not because she did not want to live on her own. She loved you, Aaron. Loved you with all her heart."

He turned away from me for a second, his dark hair fluttering around him. "I know. I still love her. I think I always will."

"She's at peace, and she'll always be with you, watching over."

He turned to me, eyes bright with unshed tears, but also a newfound clarity. "Jocelyn wouldn't want either of us to be chained to the past. She wants us to move forward, to help more people. Every sunrise, every sunset, I'll remember her. But I'll also remember to live."

I agreed with him and was grateful for the bond we shared, the shared pain, and now, the shared healing. "We will honor her best when we live our lives fully. Remembering her, cherishing the memories, but also making new ones."

"I've long forgiven you, Midas. This wasn't your fault. I hope you know that." He smiled a genuine smile that reached his eyes. "Let's keep going, Midas."

"Roger that. Let's do it."
We stood there for a few more moments, but I was ready to walk away from this place and never look back.

It was a new day, a new beginning.

We walked away from the rubble, leaving behind the shadows of the past, but carrying with us the lessons learned.

Our bonds were forged anew, but I made a silent vow. No one would ever have to give their life for me again.

The work would continue, but I'd learned a hard lesson at the Leaf Academy. Yes, the dead had been helped, but the cost had been too great.

I will never forget you, Jocelyn. I did not hear her answer me but I felt peace. Deep and healing peace.

Aaron and I headed back to the office.

The next case waited for us.

Sherman's Tale

A Short Story
By M. L. Bullock

Sherman had always been different from other dogs. From the moment he found himself wandering the streets, he felt an unspoken duty to find his home. He'd had one once, but that had been a long time ago. Maybe that's why he never fit in anywhere.

The last home he'd been ejected from had been a horrible place. Even the children were cruel and frequently forgot to feed him or take him for walks. He was only remembered when they needed someone to blame for breaking things or eating snacks that were off-limits.

Didn't they understand that he had to go make water? Didn't they understand he hungered and thirsted, just like they did? Sherman was a humble animal, but he knew he deserved better treatment.

Eventually, he was tied to a gnarled old tree in the backyard behind the dilapidated house and was quickly forgotten. He never barked, despite the gnawing hunger. He dreaded the beatings that would come if he barked too loud.

A few times a week, the man would toss leftovers into his unwashed bowl, but it was often rotten food. Ants and other insects were crawling all over the dish. Realizing he would never survive the Wilson family's care, he began working on the rope that held him prisoner. His stomach burned with hunger, his teeth were sharp and cutting.

Perfect for the task at hand.

He was careful to avoid chewing the rope whenever the kids were outside or when the man was working in his garage with his music blaring. Instead, he stayed quiet and tried to remain unseen, but it was virtually impossible. The boy liked throwing things at him and the girl poked him with sticks. Sherman knew if he fought back, he would suffer, so he did his best to escape their attention.

Eventually, they got bored with him, and for that, he was grateful. One afternoon, at last, he chewed the last of the rope and without thinking it through, took off running toward the gate.

Sherman's heart raced in his furry chest. Seeing no way out, he ran around the yard. There was no hiding from the family now.

The kids were yelling at him, calling him by a name that was not his. Sherman's heart pumped wildly in his furry chest as he did his best to avoid capture. He raced down the fence line looking for an exit but, in the end, it was useless. He spotted a weak piece of board, but before he could begin working on it, he felt the man's belt strike him.

He was again captured by the man who handled him roughly, picking the large dog up by the ruff of the neck. Instead of tying him back to the rope, he locked him in the garage and turned out the light. The man swore at Sherman and promised that he would return to punish him.

Swearing threats, the man and the children went inside to join the woman who no doubt had cooked the evening meal.

Sherman could smell the food. Hot dogs again. The man wouldn't like that. Not at all. That meant the man would be in a bad mood and would probably hurt the woman.

Sherman wanted to be gone before the man could take his anger out on him. Sherman would be forced to defend himself, but it wasn't in his nature to harm living humans.

But there were many dead humans here and even worse. Sherman knew the man could see them too. The man could see them because he made these ghosts.

There were mostly women but some men too, and somewhere, not far from the house, he could hear a child crying. Mostly at night, and it wasn't one of the two monster children inside the house. This was a dead child.

Sherman couldn't be sure who killed the child, but he was definitely dead.

Sherman didn't want to be a ghost, nor did he wish for the children, cruel as they were, to become ghosts either. He had to go for help. At the very least, he had to escape to save himself, for unlike people, when dogs die, they don't always get to come back.

Luckily for Sherman, or King, as this family liked to call him, he found a hole in the back fence, and once he was beaten and retied to the tree, he got to work on the chain. No more rope. He quickly realized he would never be able to chew through the chain. It was impossible.

What now? Would he die here? The smell of human decomposition was already too much for him to bear.

One dark night, when the moon was hidden by clouds, the ghost child appeared to him.

Sherman watched the little boy rise from the ground, but it didn't frighten him. He wanted to bark; it was the natural thing to do, but he couldn't bring himself to scare the already dead child.

The child squatted before him, his gray face sad, his eyes empty but not cruel. With a wave of his hand, the chain broke and Sherman found himself free. The boy smiled at him and waved his hand over his fur. He wanted to pet Sherman, but as he was dead and not strong at all, he didn't have the ability to move his fur. Sherman snorted a thank you and immediately ran to the back of the fence. He'd been eyeballing the potential weak spot for days.

It took work, but he managed to crack the board and crawl through it. It cut him, but he managed to wiggle free, and once he got free, he ran through the night. He ran until he could run no more. He was literally shaking with hunger and thirst.

When he stumbled upon Jocelyn's doorstep, it wasn't by chance; he was drawn there, compelled by an invisible force. One he barely understood, or then again, maybe he was just exhausted. He scratched on the door, but nobody came to see him.

The night was cold, and the moon hung low in the sky, casting eerie shadows across the street. Sherman had taken refuge under an abandoned car when he first saw Jocelyn Graves. Her aura was bright, a beacon in the darkness that had enveloped Sherman's life. He immediately liked her.

Jocelyn found him the next morning, shivering and alone. Her heart went out to the stray, and she quickly took him in. She named him Sherman, after her favorite Civil War general, finding the name fitting for a protector. Or at least that's what she believed. Sherman himself had been the one to inspire her to know his true name. It was easy to place thoughts in the minds of others, not complicated thoughts, just general feelings or sharing a name.

He loved Jocelyn instantly. She was petite but strong, tanned and had long blonde hair that she wore in dreads. Her spirit was kind and gentle. Sherman knew he had to protect her.

From that day on, Sherman was by the young woman's side, his loyalty unwavering. She confessed to him that she'd never had a pet before, not in a long time, and told him this was only a temporary arrangement, but he didn't believe that. Neither did she. He would make sure she saw the value in keeping him around.

Sherman and Jocelyn needed one another.

They spent days together, walking to the park, spending time watching television, although that wasn't really a pastime a dog generally enjoyed. Sherman listened as Jocelyn argued on the phone with Pete, a man she used to date.
From what Sherman heard, he'd bite Pete as soon as he saw him.

After one heated argument, Jocelyn threw her phone and sat on the floor and cried. Sherman nuzzled her, and she put her arm around him. She wept on him, but he didn't mind. It was nice to be needed.

A few more days went by, and Sherman began to notice things. Strange things. Spirits were coming in and out of the apartment, and they were coming for Jocelyn.

Some were benign, others were not. Sherman barked until she told him not to, but he wanted her to see the spirits. He knew she could see them if she'd only try. Humans were strange like that. Sometimes they hid their abilities, even from themselves.

Sherman could see them—the spirits that roamed the neighborhood. They were drawn to Jocelyn, some seeking help, others with darker intentions.

The boy, Ollie, was the worst of them.

His presence was malevolent, his intentions clear to Sherman from the start. Sherman would growl and bark, warning Jocelyn whenever Ollie was nearby. She didn't understand at first, but she soon learned to trust Sherman's instincts.

That's why he couldn't let her go to the Leaf Academy to investigate the place by herself. He needed to be with her. She was walking into a trap!

Jocelyn explained to Sherman that she'd only be gone a few days, but he didn't want to be left behind. He couldn't protect her from the boarding kennel. He kept barking until they finally relented and called Jocelyn to come back to get him. He had never been so happy to see any other human in his life.

"Okay, boy. I have no choice. You're coming with me; I'm assuming this is your first paranormal investigation. Listen to me and stay close, okay?"

One night, as the wind howled through the broken windows of the Leaf Academy, Sherman sensed a shift in the air.

Jocelyn was asleep, her breathing steady, but the room grew colder. The shadows lengthened, and Sherman saw Ollie standing at the foot of the bed, his eyes filled with hatred.

Without hesitation, Sherman sprang into action, barking furiously and baring his teeth.
The ghostly boy hesitated, then vanished into the night.
Jocelyn stirred, waking to find Sherman standing guard, his eyes fixed on the spot where Ollie had stood.

Jocelyn realized then that Sherman was no ordinary dog. He was her guardian, sent to protect her from the unseen dangers that lurked in the shadows of the Leaf Academy. As days turned into weeks, their bond grew stronger. Sherman could sense the growing danger, the escalating presence of the October People, and he knew that his role was more crucial than ever.

One fateful night, the full moon cast a silver glow over the Academy. Suddenly, the temperature dropped, and the lights flickered. Sherman stood up, his hackles raised, growling at the darkness.

Ollie appeared, his form more solid than ever, followed by the shadowy figures of the October People. The air was thick with their malevolent energy.

Sherman placed himself between Jocelyn and the spirits, barking fiercely. The shadows recoiled, but Ollie pressed forward, determined to break through Sherman's defense.

With a deep, guttural growl, Sherman lunged at Ollie, his teeth snapping at the ghostly form. Ollie screamed, a sound that echoed through the halls, and for a moment, his form wavered.

Sherman stood his ground, unrelenting, his eyes burning with the intensity of his protective instincts.

Jocelyn watched in awe as Sherman held the spirits at bay. The room filled with a bright light, pushing back the shadows and banishing Ollie and the October People into the void. Sherman, exhausted but triumphant, collapsed at Jocelyn's feet. She knelt beside him, tears streaming down her face, and whispered words of gratitude and love. He'd never done that before. He had no idea he could summon the light like that— maybe it wasn't him.

Oh, it must be Jocelyn! Did she know that she could summon the light?

From that day on, Sherman was not just a pet but a hero, a guardian who had saved her from the darkness. His presence was a constant reminder of the bond they shared and the power of loyalty. Sherman was determined to stay with her, so she would always be safe from the shadows that lingered in the corners of the Leaf Academy.

Because Sherman knew that Ollie wanted to keep Jocelyn. Keep her forever.

But Sherman wasn't going to let that happen. At least that was the plan.

Sherman had no idea how miserably he would fail.

Nobody beats the Leaf Academy, at least that's what the boy whispered to him.

Sherman whimpered in the darkness and cuddled closer to Jocelyn. He'd finally found a human to love. He would never let her go.

Not willingly.

Author's Note

Dear Readers,

Thank you for joining me on this eerie journey through the Haunted Chronicles of the Leaf Academy. Writing this collection has been an incredible experience, blending history, folklore, and my passion for the paranormal into a tapestry of haunting tales.

The Leaf Academy, a fictional place deeply rooted in the rich, ghostly traditions of the American South, serves as the perfect backdrop for exploring the thin veil between our world and the supernatural. From the chilling encounters with the October People to the courageous battles fought by our unlikely hero, Sherman, each story is crafted to send shivers down your spine while touching your heart.

As an author, I strive to create stories that not only entertain but also provoke thought about the unseen forces that may influence our lives. The paranormal, with its mysteries and shadows, offers a fascinating lens through which we can explore our fears, our hopes, and the enduring power of the human (and in Sherman's case, canine) spirit.

This collection is also a tribute to the resilience and loyalty found in the most unexpected places. Whether it's the bond between a stray dog and his new owner or the determination of a ghost seeking justice, these stories remind us that courage and kindness can shine even in the darkest of times.

I hope these tales have thrilled you, kept you up at night, and perhaps made you ponder the strange and wondrous world we live in. Thank you for allowing me to share my imagination with you, and I look forward to exploring more haunted paths together in the future.

Stay curious, stay brave, and never stop believing in the magic of a good ghost story.

With spooky regards,

M. L. Bullock

Made in the USA
Columbia, SC
11 August 2024

40026131R00235